Refiguring
ENGLISH
STUDIES

Refiguring English Studies provides a forum for scholarship on English Studies as a discipline, a profession, and a vocation. To that end, the series publishes historical work that considers the ways in which English Studies has constructed itself and its objects of study; investigations of the relationships among its constituent parts as conceived in both disciplinary and institutional terms; and examinations of the role the discipline has played or should play in the larger society and public policy. In addition, the series seeks to feature studies that, by their form or focus, challenge our notions about how the written "work" of English can or should be done and to feature writings that represent the professional lives of the discipline's members in both traditional and nontraditional settings. The series also includes scholarship that considers the discipline's possible futures or that draws upon work in other disciplines to shed light on developments in English Studies.

Volumes in the Series

D1219429

Class Politics: The Movement for the Students' Right to Their Own Language

STEPHEN PARKS

Temple University

National Council of Teachers of English
1111 W. Kenyon Road, Urbana, Illinois 61801-1096

Manuscript Editor: Karen Bojda
Production Editor: Rita D. Disroe
Prepress Services: Electronic Imaging
Cover Design: Carlton Bruett
Interior Design: Jenny Jensen Greenleaf

NCTE Stock Number: 06781-3050
ISSN 1073-9637

It is the policy of NCTE in its journals and other publications to provide a forum for the open discussion of ideas concerning the content and the teaching of English and the language arts. Publicity accorded to any particular point of view does not imply endorsement by the Executive Committee, the Board of Directors, or the membership at large, except in announcements of policy, where such endorsement is clearly specified.

Library of Congress Cataloging-in-Publication Data
Parks, Stephen, 1963–
        Class politics: the movement for the students' right to their own
        language / by Stephen Parks.
            p. cm.
        Includes bibliographical references and index.
        ISBN 0-8141-0678-1
        1. English language—Rhetoric—Study and teaching—Political
        aspects—United States. 2. Academic writing—Study and teaching
        (Higher)—Political aspects—United States. 3. Education, Higher—
        Political aspects—United States. 4. College students—United States
        —Political activity. 5. College students—United States—Language.
        6. Interdisciplinary approach in education. I. Title.
PE1405.U6 P3 1999
808'.042'071073—dc21
                                                            99-056418

to lori

CONTENTS

ACKNOWLEDGMENTS

In writing these acknowledgments, I need to begin with my family. Without Carole and Clinton Parks, Lois and Joseph Ryan, Chris and Mark Dusch, Greg and Dana Parks, Jessica, Greg, Keri, Kelsea, and Kevin, this book and my current career would not have occurred. Over two hundred pages of academic writing is small recompense for your labor and friendship, but thank-you.

I am also indebted to a working class ethic that valued success in college. Much of my graduate career was marked by short- and long-term "engagement" with the service economy. While I am not personally responsible for the "billions and billions sold," I certainly am not guiltless. I am grateful to all the managers, schedulers, and co-workers who, seeing the possibility of a different life and hoping I would not forget their actions, cut me slack, let me read at work, or covered for me. I am also grateful to Lori Shorr, Carol Kay, and Christine Ross for the political activism which produced affordable child care at the University of Pittsburgh; they made graduate school affordable for me and many other working-class student-parents. I hope that they will all see their values represented.

I have often said that without Gayatri Spivak coming to Pittsburgh, I never would have finished graduate school. She was my first true teacher. Without Jonathan Arac, I would not have wanted to finish graduate school. He was my first true colleague. As I moved into composition studies, David Bartholomae saw how my work could fit into the field. His support has always been a valued part of my graduate and professional career. I am also indebted to supportive friends and colleagues who helped out in countless ways during my time at Pittsburgh: Jim Seitz, Annette Seitz, Arjuna Parakrama, Lisa Schwartz, Sherry Cleary, Carolyn Ball, Nancy Glazener, Valerie Begley, John Groch, Johnny

Twyning, Mark Smith, Pia Basudev, David Sidore, Kate Nolan, Donna Dunbar-Odom, Annette Galluze, and Sandy Russo.

Temple University has also proved a wonderfully rich place to develop as a professional. Susan Wells, Eli Goldblatt, Dennis Lebofsky, Dan Tompkins, Lynda Hill, Evelyn Tribble, Dan O'Hara, Robert Caserio, Richard Shusterman, August Tarrier, and Vanessa Allen-Smith have provided unwavering and enthusiastic support. I have also been fortunate enough to encounter and learn from a set of talented graduate and undergraduate students: Rob Callahan, Shawn Christian, John Drake, Suzanne Henderson, Meera Nair, Brian Sammons, Alima Saffell, Mike Carter, Ribu John, Fred Barrett, and Robyn Wilcox. I am also grateful to Dean Carolyn Adams for allowing me to direct the Institute for the Study of Literature, Literacy, and Culture—a site where many of the pedagogical and political ideals in this book are being worked out. Finally, I would like to acknowledge my friends at Teachers for a Democratic Culture: Richard Ohmann, Donald Lazere, Paul Lauter, and Karyn Hollis. They have offered valuable insights on what it means for academics to organize politically.

The book itself would not have been possible without the active help of the National Council of Teachers of English (NCTE) and the Conference on College Composition and Communication (CCCC). Almost from my opening involvement with CCCC, I was fortunate enough to meet individuals such as Richard Lloyd-Jones. At my first CCCC conference, I sought him out to ask a quick question. That "quick" question turned into years of intellectual support and conversations. I am grateful as well to the many Students' Right to Their Own Language and New Left participants who have answered questions, supplied documents, and shared insights. The archival staff at NCTE has also been extremely helpful in hunting down "lost" documents. Steve North was responsible for the draft of these materials being seen by NCTE. Zarina Hock, Michael Greer, and Karen Bojda provided calm and insightful insights on how to pull all of these materials together into book form.

Finally, I want to express my love for Lori, Eliot, and Sadie. For the past eleven years, every day of my life has been happier and more fulfilling than I could ever have imagined. I don't suppose they will ever fully understand how much I have learned from them and their way of being. Kindness and spiritual calm are rare commodities. They have brought both to my life. I think of my life with them and feel blessed.

FOREWORD

RICHARD OHMANN
Professor Emeritus, Wesleyan University

Stephen Parks restores politics to the history of composition studies. As he says, scholars have located its formation as a discipline and a profession in the 1960s but have passed lightly over its connections with the social movements that made that decade a pivotal time in our history: civil rights and Black Power, New Left, antiwar, and women's liberation chief among them. Parks retells a story of great interest, which climaxed in the Conference on College Composition and Communication's 1974 approval of "The Students' Right to Their Own Language" and played out in professional skirmishes long after that date. Here was an organization staking out a new academic domain, amassing the dignity and authority that such a project seeks, yet endorsing a position on dialects and usage that might seem to undermine the standard professional claim to a special body of insider knowledge. Compare the earlier public and self-definition of "English" as guardian and arbiter of standard usage and grammar. ("Are you an English teacher? I'd better watch my grammar.") If every student's language is well formed and legitimate as is, what does the professionally trained instructor have to contribute? Yes, there were obvious and principled answers: invention, organization, style, and rhetoric's array of knowledge-based skills. Nonetheless, it strikes me as notable that in the moment of its early ascendancy, the profession's leaders (and many in its rank and file) relinquished a ground of authority the lay public had largely ceded: that writing instructors knew what was correct, in speech and writing, and could bring the grammar and usage of their clients (i.e., students) up to a recognized standard—curing incorrectness as physicians cured illness.

And the story Parks retells is anomalous in a still more obvious way, set against most other narratives of professionalization. The field of economics was typical. When it organized itself during the first wave of academic professionalism, the American Economic Association distanced itself from the great battles of the time (this was 1886, the year of Haymarket), offering to advance "human progress" through its research and other practices and help make peace in the "conflict between capital and labor" (Coats 1988, 358). The founders included partisans of both camps, but the ideal of neutrality prevailed. By 1900, most members of the new profession would have endorsed the view of Arthur T. Hadley of Yale, who in his presidential address held that economics must maintain a "dispassionate and critical attitude," that its "mission" was to be "representative and champion of the permanent interests of the whole community, in face of conflicting claims from representatives of temporary or partial ones" (Coats 1988, 371). Such language could serve as a touchstone for professional ideology in general. It might then at first seem normal that composition's most notable public statement, at the time of its professional consolidation, asserted the integrity and equality of all dialects and held that stigmatization of any dialect "amounts to an attempt of one social group to exert its dominance over another." But in historical context the universalist rhetoric clearly amounted to a defense of African Americans, other minorities, and working-class people, against white, middle- and upper-class domination. I think that's surprising.

But Parks nicely explains it, and much more. He weaves the story of the 1974 resolution together with that of composition studies as a professionalizing field and sets both against the larger history of 1960s movements, the liberal welfare state, and the Cold War. Working from the fertile hypothesis that "more than other disciplines, composition studies owes its current status to counterhegemonic struggles waged around access to higher education," he takes us through the Student Power, civil rights, Black Power, and New Left movements, both as they fought against and tried to extend the principles of the Great Society and as it sought to contain their challenges. He shows in satisfying archival detail that composition was by no means sealed off from these movements. Aside from the broad influence they exercised on university politics throughout the period, they were carried into academic and professional debates by activists trying to remake the university as part of an imagined egalitarian and democratic society. In particular, Parks explores the efforts of the New University Conference to radicalize the professions, and how its work in the CCCC intersected with work already underway by unaffiliated liberals and progressives in the organization. One result was "The Students' Right to Their Own Language." But Parks's analysis surrounds that particular struggle with a complex and enlightening study of how dissident and radical movements changed academic discourse and—within limits—gave the new profession a shape it would not otherwise have assumed. This is a very different history of composition from the kind that retraces internal contests among rhetorical schools, the evolution of the process movement, and so on, without much reference to racial conflict, Vietnam, and the breakup of postwar liberalism. Parks has made a fine contribution to the history of the field and to academic political history more generally, as well as providing a basis for thought about how and where we all might go from here.

Before I come back to that last subject, a few more reflections on the formation of composition studies. In the preprofessional phase of the field, up through the early 1960s, the CCCC's main journal (*College Composition and Communication*) admitted virtually no political discussion—not on anticommunism and the academic witch-hunts, free speech, the Cold War, nor the atomic bomb. But before the end of that decade, when the NUC first entered the lists at CCCC meetings, the journal was addressing a range of issues from the noisy arena of national politics: two-year colleges and egalitarian education, racial oppression, the question of dialect and power, campus uprisings, student power, the rhetoric of confrontation, and almost everything except for Vietnam itself. Furthermore, these political energies spilled over into discussion of teaching practices, classroom hierarchy, standards, grades, and even whether composition can be systematically taught at all. In short, the conventions of authority and dignity a profession would ordinarily call upon to set practitioner apart from client were all interrogated, and in the core venues of the discipline (see Ohmann, in press, for fuller discussion). *Class Politics* helps explain why. Because the field's "clients" included the broadest range of students newly coming into higher education, because many practitioners worked in community colleges and other non-elite institutions, and, I would add, because the CCCC was fighting its way "up" and "out" from a subordinate and derogated position within the parent field of English, much support existed there for populist leaders such as Ken Macrorie, Walker Gibson, and Wally Douglass, while new progressive leaders such as Liz McPherson and Greg Cowan emerged directly from the ranks of community college instructors—an institutional circumstance that set composition studies apart from almost every other academic discipline (e.g., computer science) that was professionalizing at this turbulent time.

As for the outcome of Parks's story so far: "The Students' Right to Their Own Language" remained for some years a field of contestation between egalitarians and more traditional professionalizers within the CCCC and NCTE—amended, never abandoned, yet for practical purposes relegated to the archive from which Parks has retrieved it. I am more cheerful than he about the consequences, over time, of this old battle. Although SRTOL never became the foundation on which official CCCC policy would be built or pedagogies developed, the class politics around it have made writing instruction very different from the policing of correctness that stood at its heart in 1960. And in the professional debates that partly constitute composition studies today, left and feminist concerns are respectable, even central, as witnessed by the prominence of scholars and activists such as the late James Berlin, Patricia Bizzell, John Trimbur, Ira Shor, and many others. This not to say that the CCCC is in the vanguard of social change, but to this observer it seems more engaged with questions of justice and equality than other such organizations, and not just at the level of theory. Yes, professional institutions swallow up and co-opt radical energies, but the institutions change as they do this. Hegemony is always to some degree unstable and open to challenge, as Parks well shows.

What encouragement and cautions are there in his study for those composition professionals who would like to work in the antiracist and democratic tradition of SRTOL now? I think he is right that such activists need an organization that spans the academic professions (a coalition of radical caucuses?), has an institutional home, and is capable of the growth and continuity that eluded the NUC. Certainly he is right that composition professionals would have to imagine and create alliances with people from their several communities, based in common interests and political outlooks. To say that, however, is to repeat what we have known and largely failed to achieve for thirty years. Does anything in the economic landscape make its achievement more likely now?

Parks conjectures, in his thoughtful concluding chapter, that universities may no longer be the "principal site of knowledge production." I think he identifies a deep change here. Yes, corporations are undertaking more and more in-house training for their employees and also subcontracting that work to other commercial providers of job-related education. They and their workers buy credentialing knowledge from for-profit institutions such as the 100-campus University of Phoenix and from burgeoning on-line providers. They are intervening more aggressively in the research and curricula of traditional universities through innumerable "partnerships." These universities themselves, in their efforts to make up for a long decline in public funding, are privatizing the business of knowledge in ways too numerous to mention here. And as is old but still painful news to likely readers of this book, universities rely ever more on an army of casual, low-paid, unbenefited teachers with very different work patterns from the "careers" that professionals seek. In this context, the academic professions are unwillingly surrendering their privileges, and the walls they built a hundred years ago to differentiate and defend themselves from workers with less intellectual capital are crumbling. The situation of doctors, lawyers, and other nonacademic professionals is similar (see, for instance, Krause 1996).

Perhaps the NUC's hope of persuading college teachers and graduate students to see themselves as embattled workers and citizens will make more urgent sense in the first decade of the new millennium than it did in 1970. We are already seeing alliances that would have seemed strange only a short while ago: graduate students with hotel and restaurant workers at Yale, teaching assistants with the United Auto Workers in California, academics with other intellectuals and trade unionists (Scholars,

Artists, and Writers for Social Justice), perhaps radicals across the disciplines (a project of Parks himself, through Teachers for a Democratic Culture). What about academics and corporate knowledge workers or freelancers? Academics and students? Or academics in the sort of community alliance Parks imagines? Time and political work will tell.

Finally, to return to the local terrain of "The Students' Right to Their Own Language": Gramsci once pointed out that when language becomes an explicit political issue, we can be sure we are in the presence of intense and shifting class conflict—to which one might add, for the United States, racial conflict. Parks traces this dynamic at work thirty years ago. Now, with battles over bilingual versus English-only education, phonics and whole language, political correctness in language about gender and race, high-stakes testing for high school students, usage and grammar tests used as disqualifiers for K–12 teachers, and—in a replay of SRTOL—"Ebonics," we can be sure that the analysis offered in this book remains pertinent.

References

Coats, A. W. 1988. "The Educational Revolution and the Professionalization of American Economics." In *Breaking the Academic Mold: Economists and American Higher Learning in the Nineteenth Century,* ed. W. J. Barber. Middletown, Conn.: Wesleyan University Press.

Krause, Elliott A. 1996. *Death of the Guilds: Professions, States, and the Advance of Capitalism, 1930 to the Present.* New Haven, Conn.: Yale University Press.

Ohmann, Richard. In press. "Professionalizing Politics." In *History, Reflection and Narrative: The Professionalization of Composition, 1963–1983,* ed. Mary Rosner, Beth Boehm, and Debra Journet. Stamford, Conn.: Ablex.

Rediscovering Class Politics

The inability of radical democratic inclusion politics to deal with inclusion retaining peripheralization is a key limitation, especially given that, in many liberal democratic societies, many subordinated groups have been "included" by being accorded certain formal rights like the right to vote. If inclusionary attempts often reaffirm "a hegemonic core to which the margins are added without any significant destabilization of that core" or continue to valorize the very center that is problematic to begin with, it is clear that the motivation to include needs questioning. The governing assumptions or conceptual logic guiding gestures to include must be interrogated in order to grapple with oppression in the form of appropriation, commodification, fetishization, and exoticization, to name a few.

AMALPAL K. DHALIWAL, *"Can the Subaltern Vote"*

In 1968 Professor Louis Kampf was arrested during the Modern Language Association (MLA) Convention for posting "Free Literature" signs in a hotel lobby. Later that year, in an effort to push a pro-leftist, anti–Vietnam War position, the New University Conference (NUC) disrupted the conventions of both the Conference on College Composition and Communication (CCCC) and the American History Association. Further actions were also planned for the American Association of Junior Colleges, the American Anthropology Association, and the American Psychological Association, among others. The meaning and import of these actions upon academia, however, has been greatly misrepresented. While these events have been discussed in scholarly works, they are too often portrayed as the excessive actions of a marginal collective. They are seen as exceptional episodes in which a discipline or a set of scholars "got out of hand."

Consequently, the literature does not set these events within a larger history of academic involvement in politics, nor are they set within frameworks that demonstrate how academics have historically attempted to create interdisciplinary and interorganizational movements for political change. Instead, these "moments" get recast as the type of academic and organizational behavior that *true professionalism* has rejected. Examined only within a particular discipline, a tradition of collective action by academics is fragmented and dispersed. In the process, scholarship created in the moment of political struggle has often been recast into "rhetorical schools." The activities of prominent activists of the time has been marginalized. Normative professional activity is reinstantiated. Arguments concerning social justice are forgotten. If a history of academic political work is to be written, then, a different type of framework is needed. A different set of materials and a different methodology are required.

Adding to the Archive

The search for such materials is not straightforward. While there have been many studies concerning the nature of social protest movements in the United States, the collapse of the United States liberal welfare state, and even the 1960s, few studies have attempted to articulate and document in a detailed manner the ways in which social protest movements have been an occasion for university-based academics to organize across disciplines to restructure not only their individual working environments, but, more generally, the institutions of higher education. That is, while there is much written on "the intellectual," there has been little scholarship focusing on actual academic political organizations.[1] Nor have the institutional and policy documents produced by these organizations and their impact on "mainstream" scholarship been an object of investigation. Thus, while current academic scholarship carries within it the trace of social protest movements, the effect of what it means for intellectuals to organize for collective action within a university context remains understudied, or rather, the studies that have been completed tend to focus on the nature of an individual's scholarship and not on the ways in which that scholarship was produced in conjunction with the goals of a political organization.[2]

This absence becomes even more acute if particular disciplines are examined. For instance, perhaps more than other disciplines, composition studies owes its current status to the counterhegemonic struggles waged around access to higher education. Without the efforts of the New Left, the Great Society, or Black Power, the reconceptualization of nontraditional students in the academy during the 1960s might not have occurred.[3] Mina Shaughnessy's *Error and Expectations* (1977) would not have had an existing market to formulate. David Bartholomae's "The Study of Error" (1980) would not have the same bureaucratic and institutional framework through which to be read.[4] An examination of extended histories of composition studies, however, demonstrates only a passing reference to these counterhegemonic struggles' simultaneous occurrence with the formation of composition as an "academic" discipline in the 1960s. For instance, Stephen North's *The Making of Knowledge in Composition* (1987) clearly envisions the 1960s as a founding moment for modern composition studies, yet, by breaking composition into different intellectual camps, he fails to mention key social movements of the time. Nor are any of the documents that emerged out of Black Power or the New Left brought in to evaluate the status of academic scholarship. James Berlin's *Rhetoric and Reality* (1987) is interesting in that it embeds composition scholarship within particular social time periods, yet it fails to concentrate on the role of the academic as political agent involved in building counterhegemonic organizations. As I later argue, scholars are too quickly shifted into rhetorical schools.

More recently, work has appeared that does attempt to situate the development of composition during the 1960s. Most notable of these efforts are Lester Faigley's *Fragments of Rationality* (1992) and Richard Marback's "Corbett's Hand" (1996). Both of these texts are interesting in that they attempt to draw a relationship between the social discourses of the time and the emergence of rhetorical paradigms in composition studies. In doing so, each invokes the activities of the NUC as a place where politics and scholarship met. Unfortunately, with the exception of the NUC resolutions, each work is devoid of the New Left documents that actively discuss the role of faculty in teaching and educating students. That is, by failing to integrate the variety of nonacademic scholarship then occurring, each of these histories fail to place composition, as a field, against the shifting political and social terrain of the time. More to the point, while these works might be said to account for the direct causal relationship between "the 60s" and "composition," they do not account for the ways in which a heterogeneous social terrain was reorganized (or disciplined) by an emerging professional class in composition in such a way as to exclude documents such as Jane Stembridge's "Notes about a Class Held by Stokely Carmichael" (1966) or the New University Conference's "Who(m) Does Standard English Serve? Who(m) Does Standard English Hurt?" (Knowles et al. 1969). Instead, what is emerging through these works is an understanding of the field in which certain journal articles, such as Murray's "Finding Your Own Voice: Teaching Composition in an Age of Dissent" (1969), gain seminal status. That is, as composition studies has increasingly defined itself as a discipline, I would argue that it has done so through the exclusion of historical materials that connect its formation with progressive organizations.

This failure to engage with the political and social materials of the time leaves unarticulated alternative formulations of the academic, the classroom, and the discipline that were then available. That is, to accurately present the social and political structures through which composition developed in the 1960s would mean to create a text in which NCTE minutes, CCCC position papers, Black Power speeches, NUC actions, individual scholarship, Vietnam protest literature, and classroom practice interacted.[5] It would mean to take as relevant the role of professors as political agents acting within and against disciplinary borders and organizations, yet the documents that would establish or reinvigorate composition's historical connection to the political remain unstudied.

Indeed, these documents are being thrown out.[6] Too often during the course of writing this book, I found academics who save student papers but throw out drafts of CCCC resolutions, committee correspondence, caucus newsletters, and protest literature. Somehow, the student paper is supposed to carry the weight of its time period, yet a student paper cannot be made to speak for the ways in which academics organized outside the classroom. I believe that in our discipline we need to focus more on the *seemingly* tangential caucuses and organizations that attempt to create *institutional* change. A combined focus on the institutional documents of professional organizations, coupled with the earlier-mentioned documents from leftist caucuses and organizations would allow a history to emerge that creates disciplinary space for politically organized academics to gain a voice.

The CCCC's 1974 "Students' Right to Their Own Language" (SRTOL) is my lever to produce a history highlighting the importance of collective action by academics. It will bring into the debate the newsletters, organizational documents, radical polemics, and caucus activism that marked the beginning of composition's expansion during the 1960s. These documents reveal that at the outset the SRTOL was an argument about forming broad-based alliances against class and racial oppression. It was not concerned with endorsing "a country proud of its diverse racial heritage," but with critiquing the corporate economy of the United States and its treatment of working-class citizens of all races and ethnicities. This progressive alliance, however, was quickly shunted aside by an expanding CCCC and replaced with a muted endorsement of Black English as a symbol of the United States' possibilities. In the following pages, then, I offer a countertruth through which to read the development of composition studies and its relationship to movements for social and economic justice.

In fact, I argue throughout this work that, as a field, composition studies too quickly appropriated African American struggles for social and economic justice into educational paradigms that reinforced hegemonic understandings of how race and class work in the United States. Or rather, a certain brand of white benevolence took on the image of "African American oppression" to validate its political legitimacy at the cost of an integrated examination of the dynamics of race and economics.[7] Bringing into the historical record the multiple versions and revisions of the SRTOL and placing them next to the work of radical caucuses can clarify the slow process by which arguments for economic and racial justice were altered to a form of American nationalism. As a corrective to finessing out such concerns within the homogenized terrain of "diversity," I would argue that attention to the economic aspects of discrimination based on race, gender, or sexual preference should become an integrated part of the CCCC's institutional focus. As an organization, that is, the CCCC should focus its efforts on analyzing the interrelationship among economic, racial, and gender structures and offering concrete strategies to engage composition scholars in working for broad-based social justice that goes beyond classroom and university practices.

I am convinced, however, that such a focus will not occur without caucuses and organizations devoted to studying the connections between the corporate economy, racism, sexism, heterosexism, classism, and writing instruction. I would argue that most efforts in the history of the CCCC calling for the organization to take up such a critique have originated through such caucuses as the Progressive Composition Caucus. But even the efforts of NUC-type organizations within the CCCC are limited without the simultaneous publication and dispersion of arguments designed to support broad-based coalitions for social justice. While caucus newsletters allow greater freedom for institutional analysis of our professional organizations, they are poor substitutes for commissioned studies by the CCCC or NCTE. They are poor substitutes for a shift in *College English* and *College Composition and Communication* to essays that publicize the activities of caucuses and the political work of academics.

Nevertheless, in the absence of such support, caucuses remain an important subtext in which arguments about social justice and writing instruction can occur. Thus, it is my hope that this book, by highlighting the valuable work of such organizations, will also reinvigorate debates concerning the need for radical professional organizations and caucuses designed to link the teaching of writing with larger political efforts to combat the corporate economy that so marks current U.S. culture. Such debates, I hope, will lead to discussion about how to make the activities of these organizations more widely known to the entire field. One of my aims in producing this history is thus both to expand the archive that historians use when writing the history of composition studies and, in doing so, to reinvigorate the calls for radical academic political organizations.

Coalition Politics

Rather than an aberration, the SRTOL is read in this text as a moment in the extended history of progressive academic activism. It is analyzed as an example of the possibilities and difficulties of progressive coalition politics. Indeed, as stated earlier, my argument is that the SRTOL began as an attempt by the NUC to align the standards of professional academics with goals of the 1960s student protest movements. Rejecting professional models aligned with the liberal welfare state, the NUC argued that academics should align themselves with activities that fight class, race, and gender oppression. In particular, the NUC was attempting to create an image of the student that would allow such activism to enter the university classroom. To produce such a possibility, the NUC aligned with other leftist political organizations. They also attempted to alter the institutional politics of professional organizations such as the CCCC. The SRTOL is the result of one such attempt.

This leftist coalition, however, was unable to sustain itself within the CCCC proper, for while the SRTOL was an important step forward for the CCCC, it is clearly not an example of a leftist, class-based analysis of language politics. Its "student" is not seen as facing class oppression (or rather, while language is seen to produce class stratification, the SRTOL is not arguing against the capitalist system that produces such oppression). Nor in its invocation of the United States' "diverse heritage" is the SRTOL particularly critical of the ethnic paradigm and its role in creating racial injustice. Faced with the challenge of the radical left, the institutional workings of the CCCC produced a moderate version of a student's rights. (As will be seen, however, even this moderate version became radical as the New Right redefined the goals of a progressive educator.)

Within the development of the SRTOL, then, the role of class in progressive politics necessarily emerges. At certain moments, class even takes on a primary role in an organization or an individual's politics. In studying the role of class analysis in forming certain coalitions, however, I do not want to conjure up hardcore economic models of history (although there are moments when organizations within these pages invoke such images). Nor by focusing on how class arguments worked in this time period do I wish to bring back class as a means to dilute the necessity of forming integrated progressive organizations dedicated to fighting racism, homophobia, or gender bias. Class oppression is not the foundation of all oppression, nor is success in battling such oppression a guarantee of freedom for all. Instead, I endorse a more inclusive definition of class politics. As Robin D. G. Kelley (1997) writes in "Identity Politics and Class Struggle,"

> So how might people build upon class solidarity without suppressing or ignoring differences? How can we build on differences—by which I mean different kinds of oppression as well as different identities—rather than in spite of them? One way to conceive of alliances across race and gender is as a set of "affiliations," of building unity by supporting and perhaps even participating in other peoples struggles for social justice. Basically, that old fashioned IWW slogan, "An injury to one is an injury to all." (93)

I do not want the study of how class politics were invoked in the formation of the SRTOL to be read as my endorsing a theoretical model that cannot account for the ways in which the historical struggle for economic equality occurs through the slow coalition building, discourse borrowing, and pragmatic field work of activists in many domains. At moments when my sympathies for the goals of the NUC are evident, I hope to be heard as saying that class-based activism must always be integrated with actions to fight other forms of discrimination as well. I hope it is self-evident that I believe such activism must be a part of a faculty's career outside the classroom.

In attempting to demonstrate how the SRTOL was animated by such sentiments at its origins, however, I must first work against previous attempts to place the SRTOL's progressive politics historically. Here I am not interested in responding to figures on the right, such as John Simons and others, who are interested only in mocking the attempts of socially progressive scholars to articulate the political impact of their work. Instead, I am more interested in the work of progressive scholars, such as James Berlin, who have participated in organizations such as the Progressive Composition Caucus or the Marxist Literary Group. These scholars can realistically be expected to have a sense of the diverse terrain upon which academic work in composition occurs. In fact, Berlin is a particularly interesting case, for at the same time that his work offers a nonstatist, progressive model of social change, it simultaneously weds that model to traditional visions of academic work. By investigating and expanding the implications of his model, a theoretical method can be established that demonstrates the importance of scholarship linked to collective efforts for social change.

In *Rhetoric and Reality* (1987), Berlin offers a taxonomy through which to read the history of composition studies. In particular, Berlin establishes three rhetorical categories: objective, subjective, and transactional. Each of these categories have been extensively discussed within composition studies. For my purposes, Berlin's invocation of epistemic rhetoric, a subcategory of transactional rhetoric, is most relevant:

> Epistemic rhetoric posits a transaction that involves all elements of the rhetorical situation: interlocutor, audience, material reality, and language. The most significant difference is that language enters into this transaction and is present in every instance of its manifestation. The reason for this is that interlocutor, audience, and material world are all regarded as verbal constructs. . . . In epistemic rhetoric there is never a division between experience and language, whether the experience involves the subject, the subject and other subjects, or the subject and the material world. . . . Rhetoric thus becomes implicated in all human behavior. All truths arise out of dialectic, out of the interaction of individuals within discourse communities. (16)

For students in the classroom, such a focus leads to a rhetorical examination of how such issues as class, race, and gender are embedded in all subject–audience relationships. As a possible example of such work, Berlin cites Richard Ohmann's "In Lieu of a New Rhetoric" (1964). In that essay, Ohmann argues that students should learn how self-expression occurs within the confines of a discourse community. In particular, Ohmann argues that students should focus on dialects as a tool to understand the power standard English supplies to its users. For Berlin (1987, 170), "the object, ultimately, is training for citizenship in a democracy: the student 'becomes a voting citizen of his world, rather than a bound vassal to an inherited ontology.'" In fact, given Ohmann's own involvement in organizations like the NUC, such a rhetoric could clearly initiate a study of how composition interacted with the social and political movements of the time. Berlin, however, did not take this route in *Rhetoric and Reality*.

In fact, I would argue that although Berlin endorses an epistemic rhetoric for students in the classroom, his own text can still be seen to inhabit a historical methodology that relies heavily on objectivist rhetoric. For despite Berlin's argument about the rhetorical mutability of the material world, his actual historical method is quite traditional. For instance, in "The Renaissance of Rhetoric, 1960–1975," the final chapters of *Rhetoric and Reality*, Berlin attempts to demonstrate how composition studies responded and interacted with the historical events of the time period. In this way, the text attempts to use the position of an epistemic rhetorician to demonstrate how a particular discourse community, composition studies, could construct itself as a discipline within the then current definitions of what constituted the social. Berlin begins by detailing the historical forces that shaped composition studies at that time:

> The most crucial events for the fate of writing instruction during the sixties and seventies were the intensification of the Cold War and the changes in economic, social, and political arrangements that resulted in a dramatic increase in the number of students attending college. The space race signaled by the launching of Sputnik in 1957 eventually led to federal funds being invested in the teaching of literature and composition for the first time in American history. This in turn brought

about a reintegration of the efforts of the NCTE and MLA after a separation of nearly fifty years. The product of this mutual effort was new activities to improve the teaching of writing in both high schools and college. The growth in the number of students attending college was as much an effect of the expansion of the corporate and state sectors of the economy as it was a result of the growing size of the student-age population. As colleges during the sixties became the training centers for the new specialists needed in business and government, their power, prestige, size, and numbers increased. And, as in the 1890's, with the appearance of the new university, the research ideal again proved to be the dominant influence in higher education. . . . While this development worked against writing courses because of their position in the undergraduate curriculum, it also encouraged the professionalization of composition teachers, an effort that had been underway since the formation of the CCCC in the fifties. The larger student population necessitated more writing teachers, and these teachers began to promote graduate training for their discipline. By 1975, graduate programs in rhetoric and composition were forming and rhetoric was becoming a respectable academic specialty. (120–121)

This historical accounting of the time period moves from the Cold War to state politics to the classroom. It moves from the corporate world to reforming the university to the NCTE and MLA. Each of these terms is written as if self-evident in their meaning, both to the reader and to the time period. In this sense, Berlin has posited an epistemic rhetoric that exists within preestablished boundaries of meaning. Rather than seeing the ways in which the terms were sites for conflicting interpretations, thus demonstrating the interconnection between rhetorical conduct, material practices, and political alliances, Berlin nestles the development of composition studies within an established set of categories that essentially block the ways in which the social terrain was constructed and dismantled by activist academics, progressive organizations, and political parties.

Given this framework, it is not surprising that Berlin also discusses academics within the traditional and narrow conception of the "academic professional." For instance, in Berlin's view, the New Rhetoric of the 1960s grew out of an attempt to redefine the study of writing away from usage and toward a rhetorical school that features how discourse works. Once Berlin has placed this scholarly movement within a limited social terrain, he then locates scholars along different professional axes: Macrorie and Ohmann are seen as important for their work as editors of *College Composition and Communication* and *College English;* Hans P. Guth is important for his argument against linguistics; Corbett, Tate, and Winterowd are important for their development of textbooks; Lloyd-Jones is important for "Research in Written Composition." These figures and their work thus are constituted not by the diverse and pluralistic social movements that were occurring at the time, but by the ways in which rhetoric developed in the field of composition studies, narrowly defined. Figures whose scholarship might have held very different interpretations or alliances during the 1960s are reduced to objective, transactional, and epistemic rhetoricians.

The constrictive nature of Berlin's text is most apparent in his discussion of the SRTOL. In Berlin's book, the discussion of this moment in CCCC history occurs almost as a footnote to the chapter concerning the 1960s and 1970s. After discussing the reaction of objectivist, subjective, and transactional rhetorics to the 1960s, Berlin pauses to discuss the role of linguistics:

> As was repeatedly noted in earlier chapters, linguistics research has also been crucial in reminding teachers of the social basis of language and of the class structure on which it is based. This effort, begun early in the century with the likes of Fred Newton Scott and two of his students, Sterling Andrus Leonard and Charles Fries, has been carried on more recently in the work of James Sledd, and bore conspicuous fruit in the CCCC's position statement entitled "Students' Right To Their Own Language" in 1974. (135–136)

By marking it as a product of linguistics, an activity outside Berlin's rhetorical schools, the SRTOL fails to gain disciplinary importance. Arguments and activities by composition activists concerning the role of class, race, and gender in progressive coalitions become completely covered over; the NUC's efforts in initiating the SRTOL are completely ignored. In fact, at this moment in the text, coalition politics becomes an issue that historians of composition locate outside the central concerns of composition studies. Such alliances are not an issue that appears to affect composition scholarship proper. Driven by a morphology of tripartite rhetoric, the SRTOL thus seems to become a minor, unaccountable contingency.

There is more at work, however, in Berlin's casting off of coalition politics. Earlier it was stated that having defined the relationship between the New Rhetoric and the Cold War, Berlin locates Larson, Corbett, Lloyd-Jones, Ohmann, and Macrorie in terms of their scholarly production, yet each of these figures also participated in the SRTOL's development, either through institutional or activist roles. New Left academic groups, such as the NUC, to which some of them belonged, also pushed the CCCC toward a new vision of scholarship and intellectual activity based on race, gender, and class politics. Each of these moments was also simultaneously responding to and renegotiating new social formations made possible by the counterhegemonic work of the antiwar and civil rights movements. Within Berlin's work, however, the diverse and nonunified social terrain in which arguments concerning the formation of a class-informed, progressive coalition occurred is simplified into a cause–effect dynamic; in such a world, coalition politics vanish from composition studies.

It is for this reason that Dhaliwal's work (quoted in the epigraph to this chapter) becomes an important filter through which to read Berlin's marginalization of the SRTOL. Dhaliwal argues that the inclusion of the margin through established criteria does not constitute an enabling structure for that margin. For Dhaliwal, to be a radical inclusion, the margin must reconstitute the very criteria to which it is introduced. In Berlin's work, the SRTOL can be read as a countermoment to the general story of composition studies. As such, it becomes the margin through which a center, defining itself through the production of academic-based work divorced from politics or political organizations, can establish its identity. Indeed, a traditional academic identity is established for composition studies that leaves activist politics outside the norm. The net result of Berlin's failure to fully represent the possibilities of an epistemic criticism, then, is that different discursive or counterhegemonic communities concerned with linking composition to broader social issues appear as having lacked access to, or currency within, the field's development.

Berlin's version of epistemic rhetoric thus fails to account for that middle zone where alliances and meanings are determined. For Berlin's epistemic rhetoric to act as a progressive tool in the history of composition studies, I argue, it needs to be reunderstood within the Marxist concept of hegemony. In *Hegemony and Socialist Practice,* Ernesto Laclau and Chantal Mouffe (1993) argue that the concept of hegemony grew out of a crisis between the strict statist logic inherent in some Marxist scholarship and the historical situation of the working class; that is, while theory argued that history would lead to the formation of the proletariat, history showed that this process failed to take effect. Hegemony was introduced to suture these two different realms; it became the middle zone of political struggle through which the working class came to represent itself. But now working-class dominance was but one possible political instantiation within the social sphere. Laclau and Mouffe write: "[I]n our view, in order to advance in the determination of social antagonisms, it is necessary to analyze the plurality of diverse and frequently contradictory positions and to discard the idea of a perfectly unified and homogenous agent, such as the 'working class.' The search for the 'true' working class and its limits is a false problem and as such lacks any theoretical and political relevance" (84).

The role of the Marxist scholar-activist now becomes the study and implementation of coalitions that allow progressive economic and social relations to attain political representation. If taken to initiate a historical project, a materially based epistemic rhetoric would entail an examination of the ways in which the current hegemonic social space was historically formed and worked to deny certain affiliations and identifications as legitimate. (Forces of classism or sexism, for instance, would be studied to see how they prevented communities from working on behalf of racial equality.) Such a history would detail the ways in which certain alliances were deemed illegitimate, examine the impact of the failure of organizations to align, and open up a space for alternative, progressive, collective action. In particular, it would examine the formation of key nodal points of activity, such as family values, and the system of practices and alliances organized around its creation and dispersal. This work would support the efforts of counterhegemonic organizations attempting to expand the set of possible alliances and push for broad-based social justice.

Within such a history, the work of academics and academic scholarship could not be examined simply for its immediate disciplinary relationship to existing ideas in the field. Instead, scholarship (and the activities of scholars) should be read for how it was part of a general social renegotiation of the political and economic status of marginalized groups. Such an emphasis might seem to produce misreadings. For instance, Ken Macrorie was not explicitly attempting to form a relationship to the Black Panthers in his book *Uptaught* (1970). Nor was Macrorie overtly stating a relationship between his work and Abbie Hoffman's Yippie movement. As a public document, however, his writing worked within rhetorical and political boundaries being constructed by such organizations. He must be read, then, in terms of how his work situated student writing, composition classrooms, and composition studies to these counterhegemonic organizations. Such a reading demonstrates not only the variety of possible counterhegemonic alliances available to composition scholars at that time, but also the ways in which the CCCC worked to distance itself from such alliances.

Indeed, for the purpose of this book, one nodal point for the political and pragmatic activity of organizations such as the CCCC, NCTE, and NUC was the black-dialect speaker. Each of these organizations articulated their arguments concerning race and social justice through a redefinition of this rhetorical figure. In particular, as the civil rights movement reframed the politics and policies defining the status of African Americans, the legitimacy and political power associated with this rearticulation was borrowed (or appropriated) by other organizations attempting to foster change in their fields of practice. As argued throughout this book, civil rights organizations such as the Southern Christian Leadership Conference (SCLC) and the Student Nonviolent Coordinating Committee (SNCC) succeeded in bringing African Americans into segments of the liberal welfare-state economy of post–World War II America. They did so by defining the black-dialect speaker as eager to participate in the post-WWII liberal welfare state. The struggle within composition studies to define its role in relationship to this speaker brought into play a different (yet linked) set of pedagogical, theoretical, professional, and disciplinary alliances. A study of the ways in which organizations such as the NCTE or CCCC struggled to position themselves as simultaneously supportive of the civil rights movement and against the more radical alternatives of the NUC and the Black Panther Party thus becomes an example of the general ways in which hegemonic relations are formed.

Such a focus on the struggles involved in positioning composition studies in relationship to the emerging liberal welfare state, I believe, represents a history informed by Berlin's epistemic rhetoric. It takes seriously the ways in which discourse communities interact and negotiate meanings through language. It examines how different organizations interacted with one another according to their own institutional perspectives, borrowing and reinterpreting key nodal points, that is, points that were shorthand for a set of socially determined practices. Furthermore, while existing within Berlin's theoretical model, this book also attempts to examine the historical moment before composition studies was able to slide its participants into academic categories. It attempts to highlight the alternative discursive and political communities in which scholars might have participated before becoming "process-movement advocates" or "new rhetoricians." Examining how composition studies defined itself as separate from organizations and political activities designed for progressive social change, I attempt to represent the moment before it was possible to have an academic career in composition studies. In effect, this work also attempts to highlight an alternative definition of an academic career.

The irony of writing such a history, however, is that it does not actually create that academic career. It does not fund hiring lines. It does not produce progressive organizations. One of the arguments of this book is that real change occurs through the building of coalitions and engagement with institutions. History can serve, however, to remind participants of alternative possibilities. That is, when certain ideals gain hegemonic status, history can remind us of their temporary and negotiated status. The momentary conjunction of interests cannot be mistaken for timeless truth. In 1999, when the National Association of Scholars

(NAS) is the preeminent political organization of conservative academics, perhaps there is a need to present a history (however partial) of how leftist academic activism was once a social force. Perhaps there is a need for such a reminder and such a history.

In saying this, however, the actions of the NUC or the politics of the SRTOL should not be solidified into a monument; it was not my intention to produce a touchstone of correctness or to create heroes to the "cause." In a culture of retro-chic, I am also not attempting to valorize the debates from the sixties; bell-bottom politics was not my intention. In fact, if there is a moral to this book, it is the problems that occur when a political alliance is naturalized into an objective truth. Victories, assumed permanent, are soon squandered. Indeed, more than anything, this work is a cautionary tale of what happens when academics fail to organize collectively as political agents or fail to remember the tentative nature of their successes. In the absence of collective action, that is, organizations like the NAS set the national agenda. Indeed, if the SRTOL were to become a politically effective vehicle for progressive politics today, it would have to become part of a coalition that includes nonacademic workers, labor, and other socially progressive movements. Within such a coalition, the role of academics would have to be announced and supported. Indeed, a decision would have to be made by CCCC and composition teachers as to whether the SRTOL can even serve such progressive purposes. Perhaps a new statement is needed.

My hope, however, is that a history of the SRTOL can serve as a tool in the general effort to establish an effective progressive response to current conservative politics, for the realities that mark the lives of the oppressed can gain political relevancy only through alliances committed to transforming the social terrain; that is, an informed student paper does not by necessity lead to political change. The future must be defined by collective action. Perhaps this history can remind us of that fact.

The Organization of This Book

In the first half of this book, I begin by examining how the term *student* organized the activities of organizations such as Student

Nonviolent Coordinating Committee, Students for a Democratic Society, and the Black Panthers. In chapter 1, I examine how each of these organizations created an image of the student as a way to position itself in relationship to the Cold War liberal welfare state. A secondary narrative within the chapter is how New Left organizations invoked African American student images to legitimate their own practices. I argue that the NUC emerged within this dynamic of race, student, and Cold War politics. The NUC positioned itself as a supporter of the student left's call for social justice while simultaneously repeating the rhetorical strategy of invoking "African American" politics and imagery. At the close of the chapter, I discuss how the NUC organized itself to take its politics into the academy.

NUC members, however, were not the only academics shaped by debates concerning student politics. In chapter 2, I examine how the process movement interacts with concerns over the Cold War and student activism. In particular, I demonstrate how the process movement was used by leftist scholars. I argue that the ability of leftist scholars to inject progressive politics into the process movement enabled the NUC's politics to gain a foothold in CCCC politics. Throughout, I also demonstrate how each text discussed participates in the rhetorical strategy of invoking African American students and their dialects for political legitimacy. That is, at key rhetorical moments, these texts imagine the protection of a student's identity through the images of African Americans or Black English speakers.

My final examination of student politics considers how the definition of the Black English speaker was affected by the rise of Black Power. In chapter 3, the narrative moves from the political invocations of civil rights by Lyndon Johnson to the imposition of a Black Panther photograph onto an article by Geneva Smitherman. Within this narrative, I demonstrate that by rejecting the ethnic paradigm and the consequent liberal welfare-state politics, Black Power advocates positioned Black English as a symbol of anticolonial or socialist politics. That is, while chapter 1 focuses on the African American student protester as an image that "guaranteed" the political legitimacy of the United States, chapter 3 demonstrates how the beliefs of Black Power gave Black English an oppositional character. The chapter ends with a consideration of how language scholars, such as William Labov, Geneva Smitherman, and J. L. Dillard, positioned their work and classroom practice in relationship to this emerging image of Black English.

The second half of this book studies how the previously mentioned political, scholarly, and organizational work around student politics produced the SRTOL. Chapter 4 begins with the NUC's actions at the MLA Convention and moves to its appearance at the CCCC. Throughout, I examine how the CCCC and NUC debated the role of the academic and the academic organization. I argue that while the NUC saw the SRTOL as an attempt to radicalize a professional organization, the CCCC used it to redefine its relationship to the NCTE. Within this debate, the inability of the NUC to control its initiatives within the CCCC led to the muting of much of the radical intent of the SRTOL.

Through the use of archival materials, the debate concerning the language that would constitute the SRTOL and the SRTOL language statement is discussed in chapter 5. Here the continued interweaving of New Left, Black Power, and NUC rhetoric is used to situate the CCCC's SRTOL in relationship to alternative views of language politics and scholarly activity then available. It is also at this moment that the moves by the CCCC to evade progressive politics are most pronounced, for here the rhetorical strategy of invoking African American dialects is embedded within a nationalist paradigm that effectively eliminates radical class and social politics. Such a paradigm effectively excludes the professional recognition of academic political caucuses in the SRTOL's formation, as well as the progressive agendas they represented. At this moment, then, the CCCC's SRTOL is seen as abandoning the social and economic politics from which it initially emerged.

The final chapter details the SRTOL's emergence as a historical document. Using the 1980s' Allen committee to illustrate, I argue that the CCCC failed to create an SRTOL statement that could articulate a social or political response to the emergence of the New Right. In fact, through the machinations produced by the existence of the Allen committee, the SRTOL became positioned as a document that had no effective use. Working from Louis Crew's response to the Allen committee and the actions of the Progressive Composition Caucus, I discuss the possible alternative politics that the SRTOL could have represented at that time. I conclude the book with a discussion of how a version of community-based critical pedagogy can produce a composition studies focused on issues of social justice and progressive politics.

1. The history of such organizations is an extended project of which this text is but one part.

2. An interesting exception to this assertion is Ellen Schrecker's *No Ivory Tower: McCarthyism and the Universities* (1986). Schrecker's narrative describes how academics' involvement with the Communist Party was scrutinized by McCarthyism.

3. Nor should the development of large state systems, such as in California, be ignored. In a different type of study the relationship between the development of large state systems and student activism would make a valuable contribution to the understanding of how *student* became a political category beginning in the late 1950s.

4. This is not to deny the historical role of rhetorical or remedial instruction in the university and college setting. In making these comments, I am referring to the modern situation of composition studies.

5. These documents would have to be supplemented with oral histories by participants and fellow travelers. Therefore, while this work primarily uses institutional documents, my hope is that it will soon be surrounded by the personal stories of participants such as Ernece Kelly, Vivian Davis, and Richard Lloyd-Jones.

6. It is in the interest of preserving documents and arguing for a different type of history that I cite at length institutional reports, minute meetings, and official letters.

7. This work does not directly discuss the formation of African American politics within composition. For such a discussion, see Keith Gilyard's "African American Contributions to Composition Studies" (1999).

Tracking the Student

Neal Resnikoff and his (NUC) associates virtually took over the equipment (two typewriters and a duplicating machine) in CCCC Headquarters and complained bitterly when the local chairman refused to open up the room on Friday night for additional "hot flashes." . . . [I]t would seem that the NUC will not be satisfied until some member of that group can dictate to NCTE and CCCC what its future aims and goals shall be.

WILLIAM DOSTER,
Local Chairman of the 1969 CCCC Convention

On another level, [OUTS] means doing the basic teaching to that growing mass of people who have minimal skills in reading and writing—skills necessary not only to college and job survival, but also in gaining critical mastery over their environment and engaging in political struggle. At the same time, the reverse is true: "We want education for our people that exposes the true nature of this decadent American society. We want education that teaches us our true history and our role in the present day society. We believe in an educational system that will give to our people a knowledge of self. If a man does not have knowledge of himself and his position in society and the world, then he has little chance to relate to anything else" (Point five of the Program of the Black Panther Party).

New University Conference, *Open Up the Schools*

The struggle between the Conference on College Composition and Communication (CCCC) and the New University Conference (NUC) concerning "students' right to their own language" occurred during a time of student protest, student activism, and student power. Although the CCCC–NUC struggle never reached the revolutionary fervor Doster intimates, this interaction highlighted the ways in which competing definitions of the "student" had begun to affect the actions of professional academics, for the CCCC and NUC did not so much affirm an existing student right as rearticulate existing professional standards in relationship to a new political situation. Any historical account of the Students' Right to Their Own Language resolution (SRTOL), then, must begin with an examination of how the term *student* came to organize the political and social agendas of the 1960s. It must begin with an accounting of activist organizations, such as the Student Nonviolent Coordinating Committee (SNCC), the Black Panther Party, and Students for a Democratic Society (SDS).

What will become immediately evident is that each of these organizations imagined student politics as a microcosm of national politics. For each, the status of the "student" was enmeshed within larger debates concerning the emerging liberal welfare state. For instance, witnessing how labor and racial politics were being brought within this paradigm, SDS questioned the possibility of a militant labor movement. Witnessing the same trend, the Black Panther Party worked to create a space for an economically and politically organized African American population. But each organization also worked in response to SNCC and the larger civil rights movement's successful redefinition of the liberal welfare state to include a new political identity for southern African Americans. For this reason, to examine the development of students' rights during the 1960s necessarily brings into play questions about the role of labor, liberalism, and Cold War politics in creating or diminishing the possibility of socially progressive politics.

The term *student* can also serve as an indicator for how minority identity came to serve as a legitimating trope for the left (and leftist academics) in public debate. For as the left framed its relationship to the civil rights movement, one result was a rhetorical strategy by white student activists to imagine their experiences as "other": black, Third World, or Latin American. (In fact, the preceding citation of the Black Panthers by the NUC highlights how minority identity was used to add legitimacy to white leftist organizations.) A history of this cross-referencing shows how a very intense and very short-lived segment of these protest movements sutured "student" into "other." This complex suturing remains even after student activism receded as a cultural force. In fact, this rendering of the student sets a conceptual framework for the profession-based movements, such as the NUC, that survive the student protests. In later chapters, the extent to which this strategy, when adopted by professional scholars, enabled the original concerns of the civil rights movement about race and class equity to become embedded within questions of language politics will be evident. It is through an examination of these competing definitions, then, that an accounting of the SRTOL in the 1960s must begin.

Cold War Democracy

One month before Resnikoff's encounter with the CCCC, the NUC published "The Student Rebellion" (1968b). For the NUC, this rebellion was the result of students, who, having "taken democratic ideas most seriously," confronted institutions which only *seemed* to support democratic ends. According to the NUC, the "student rebellion" represented

- ◆ the struggle by humanist and radical white youth to end the complicity of the university with war and imperialism, with racism and domestic suppression of black and other minorities, with bureaucratic values and corporate interests.

- ◆ the struggle by black students for full cultural recognition and autonomy on white campuses, for an end to paternalistic control at black colleges, and for full community control at community colleges.

- ◆ the struggle by large groups of students for full citizenship in the university as a just end in itself, for recognition of their adult status, and for a curriculum which is useful to their search for personal meaning and social relevance rather than one which is oriented toward the needs of the corporation and the state for trained manpower. (NUC 1968b)

In support of the students' goals, the Interim Committee of the NUC drafted several resolutions demanding that "[t]he class biases of university governing boards must be eliminated," "[u]niversities should be free of militarist and corporate domination," and "[u]niversities must end policies which support 'institutional racism.'"[1] In doing so, the NUC imagined itself to be working cooperatively with the student rebellion's call for greater democratic participation.

Within this framework, NUC activists felt that the CCCC had a vision of democracy which de facto endorsed a Cold War liberal welfare-state paradigm. Indeed, such a characterization would not be totally inaccurate. The National Council of Teachers of English (NCTE) initiated the CCCC in 1948 as a two-day conference for college writing teachers. Within three years, the success of this conference would earn it a permanent place within the NCTE. During its first ten years of existence, the CCCC consistently focused on how to improve the institutional status of its members. In its journal, there were calls for accreditation standards, new graduate programs, increased pay, and reduced workloads. Pedagogical debates focused on the difficulty of teaching writing, the importance of linguistics, how to structure a writing assignment, and the role of literature. There is no discussion, however, of the social terrain upon which this professionalization and teaching occurred; World War II, the atom bomb, the Korean War, Sputnik, and the civil rights movement are not mentioned.

Not until 1958 is the CCCC positioned in relationship to events occurring in the post-WWII United States. Even then, it is the NCTE speaking on its behalf. In *The National Interest and the Teaching of English* (NITE), the NCTE links instruction in English and composition to the United States' growing economic and political power. Using such linkages to argue for increased support from the federal government, NITE (1958) stated:

The goal of total literacy has practically been reached, and it is no accident that the achievement of literacy has resulted in valuable economic, cultural, and political by-products: the most productive economy in the world, leadership in the sciences and arts, and an increasing extension of democratic rights and responsibilities to most of our citizens. (23)

Composition, then, was positioned as a soldier in the Cold War effort to rebuild the United States. Its mission linked to the extension of "democratic rights." Its students were the hope for the future of the United States. That is, initiated during the outset of the Cold War, the NCTE's CCCC was imagined as the organization which not only would enable composition teachers to gain increased status in the postwar United States, but would also prepare students to participate in the battle for democracy.

This image of the student is directly in line with the student protester emerging from the early civil rights movement, for much of the activity by early civil rights organizations was designed to integrate African Americans into the new social and political economy of the post-WWII United States. Unlike the prewar economy, which was marked by a proprietor-dominated middle class, this economy would be marked by the formation of a new middle class ensconced within large multinational corporations, a portion of whose positions benefited from labor union contracts.[2] Coupled with sympathetic federal policies toward home ownership, this dynamic ensured a labor pool that had both the need and the income to purchase newly marketed consumer goods.[3] As Mike Davis (1986) writes, "the advance of the intensive regime of accumulation . . . signified not only the integration of the auto-house-electrical appliance complex as the mainspring of the economic growth, but also the vast social-spatial transformation that resulted from it. Between 1950 and 1960, suburbs grew *forty* times faster than central city areas, while automobile registrations increased by 22 million" (emphasis in original, 191). The suburbs emerged.

The expanding economy, however, was not benefiting all citizens equally. Members of the white working class were not brought into this emerging dynamic, and southern African American citizens were systematically excluded from engaging in the wage benefits of the consumer economy. In *Class, Race, and the Civil Rights Movement* (1987), Jack Bloom argues that through political maneuvering by "aristocratic land owners," southern

African American laborers were placed in a caste relationship to the rest of the U.S. economy. Unlike other laborers who, within the confines of a labor legislation, could market their skills, African Americans were denied access to the types of jobs which the economy and mass higher-education programs were creating (18–57 passim). Instead, they were left to depend either on the black community itself to support indigenous businesses or on the benevolence of white business owners for work.

To eliminate such discrimination, the early civil rights movement combined local action with calls for national intervention. As is well known, its rhetoric was often informed by Christian ethics and U.S. nationalism.[4] For the purposes of this chapter, however, the early civil rights movement's relationship to labor and existing economic structures seems primary. It is within this dynamic that an element of the civil rights movement's relationship to Cold War politics can be articulated. An initial strategy of the civil rights movement was to align its struggle with the goals of labor unions. In his book on the Montgomery bus strike, *Stride Toward Freedom* (1958), Martin Luther King Jr. argued:

> Not logic, but a hollow social distinction had separated the races. The economically depressed white accepts his poverty by telling himself that, if in no other respect, at least socially, he is above the Negro. For this empty pride in racial might he has paid the crushing price of insecurity, hunger, ignorance, and hopelessness for himself and his children.
>
> Strong ties must be made between those whites and Negroes who have problems in common. White and Negro workers have mutual aspirations for a fairer share of the products of industries and farms. Both seek job security, old-age security, health and welfare protection. The organized labor movement, which has contributed so much to the economic security and well-being of millions, must concentrate its powerful forces on bringing economic emancipation to white and Negro by organizing them in social equality. (166)

Indeed, Congress on Racial Equality (CORE) Director James Farmer also drew analogies between labor and the civil rights movement:

> In the thirties, labor was on the streets; labor was accused of violating property rights. Today Civil Rights forces are in the streets and we are accused of violating property rights. . . .
>
> The very same people who are anti–Civil Rights are the folks who are pushing for the so-called right to work laws. This natural alliance [between labor and the Civil Rights movement] should not be broken. (Levy 1994, 9)

Unions, however, were not entirely willing to share their economic rewards with the newly imagined "Negro laborer." During the 1958 Montgomery bus strike, the only union locals that participated were the Brotherhood of Sleeping Car Porters, several small United Auto Workers (UAW) locals and the United Packinghouse Workers' District 65 and New York Local 1199. Many southern unions actively opposed the strike. According to Manning Marable's *Race, Reform, and Rebellion* (1984, 55), "the all-white Bus Drivers Union and the Montgomery Building Trades Council took part in the vigilante attacks against Civil Rights leaders. Southern locals refused to process grievances of black members." As detailed by Marable, this moment was indicative of deeper conflicts in the relationship. For instance, he chronicles how in the early 1950s southern labor union chapters allowed Citizen Councils to use their local labor halls. In 1957, when AFL-CIO unions were invited to participate in Martin Luther King's "Prayer Pilgrimage for Freedom," "most refused or simply ignored the event" (Marable 1984, 55). Indeed, according to Marable, AFL-CIO President George Meany failed to expel racist unions or to take a strong stand against such policies.

In maintaining this public alliance with the labor movement, despite the reluctance of southern local chapters to fight racism, figures such as King and Farmer simultaneously created a distance between themselves and radical leftist labor activists. In fact, during the McCarthy era, labor unions had participated in leftist persecution. They had banned communists from their organizations and had driven individual chapters to expel known activists. (This would be an important fact in the development of SDS.) For instance, at the 1949 CIO convention, the fifty thousand–member United Electrical, Radio, and Machine Workers

Union was expelled "for being dominated by leftists" (Marable 1984, 20). A movement from 1951 to 1956 to establish a black progressive presence in labor unions, the National Negro Labor Council, came under attack from not only unions but the House Un-American Activities Committee as well. The civil rights movement, also suffering from media-driven accusations of being "red," actively distanced themselves from such forces and offered no sustained critique of labor union actions. Consequently, the early civil rights movement clearly framed itself within the hegemonic, anticommunist, Cold War, pro–liberal welfare-state politics of the United States.

The initial formulation of an African American student movement is firmly within this hegemonic formulation. When SNCC was founded, its purpose was to coordinate the student sit-ins then occurring throughout the South. As with the mainstream civil rights movement, however, these protesters embedded an implicit backing for liberal capitalism within a validation of larger cultural or institutional settings to gain political support.[5] They also located themselves firmly against the state and federal policies that blocked their participation in the emerging liberal welfare state. As with the larger civil rights movement, to solidify their alignment with these forces, SNCC resisted any aid from socialists or radicals. For instance, at the SNCC conference in Atlanta, Bayard Rustin's identification with social democracy led to his invitation being withdrawn. According to Marable (1984, 68), "it was only in mid-1961, that SNCC accepted a grant of $5000 from the progressive Southern Conference Educational fund."

This alignment by SNCC is not surprising given that, among the initial sit-in protesters, students from upper- or middle-class families far outnumbered rural or poor families, with wealthy colleges producing more activists than rural or poor colleges (Matthews and Protho 1969). Bloom (1987) argues that only as the movement tactics expanded into the community did the lower classes enter. He states, "the movement began under the leadership of a younger, better-educated, more militant, but still middle-class stratum" (172). Citing Debbie Louis, Marable (1984, 68–69) argues, "their perspective was toward ending segregation. Their involvement from the very beginning was based on a decision that this equality was important enough to suffer heavily for." The students, she states, "were motivated by a determination to secure the means for their own economic and social mobility, which in the circumstances clearly necessitated a direct assault on the tradition and law which limited them absolutely." SNCC's actions in particular were based upon the government interceding to ensure that federal rights would not be violated; in this sense, they were arguing for the right to participate in the economic and political paradigm being created for white-collar and labor union workers.

As is well known, the political coalition formed around this conception of an African American identity ultimately succeeded in shifting the political and economic power in the South. In fact, Bloom (1987) argues that the success of the civil rights movement lay in part in its ability to align its goals with emerging corporate and small-business concerns in the South, for such a move alienated the landed interests who had traditionally controlled southern politics. This enabled the city and small-business classes to finally assume full political and economic control, ending segregation as bad business practice. As Bloom writes, "In the end, the black movement was responsible for the transfer of political power from the rural and small-town cliques to the business and middle classes within cities. That was the historic accomplishment necessary to gain equal legal rights for blacks" (2). Thus, the civil rights movement in its earliest victories represented the integration of the southern economy into a national economy. To this extent, through economic boycotts and voting rights petitions, the civil rights students aided in the continuing emergence of a new U.S. economy.

The opening years of the CCCC's formation (1948 to 1960) thus saw the national consolidation of the liberal welfare-state paradigm. This consolidation occurred in an environment which linked civil rights student activism with the goals of the CCCC's writing student. That is, although speaking from different positions, the NCTE, CCCC, and SNCC appeared to be united about the political role of the United States and its economic future; further, each organization wanted its members to be full participants in that future. This alliance of student politics, liberal welfare-state policies, and the CCCC's professional development, however, proved to be momentary. As "student politics" moved outward from the South, the "student" became linked with urban needs, white student movements, presidential politics, and northern middle-class anxieties. These issues shifted the social terrain upon which the CCCC was founded and altered the image of the "student" who came into the writing classroom. A new definition of student activism emerged.

From Cold War Warriors to Black Panthers

By 1964, SNCC's African American student protester represented a powerful tool to critique caste relationships in the South at the same time as it reinstantiated the goals of the U.S. Cold War society. But the coalition of social, political, and economic forces which enabled this protester to be powerful soon began to fracture. As SNCC attempted to expand its role nationwide, competing political and economic interests emerged between former allies. For example, the role of white student activists became contentious. In 1964, SNCC, along with the Southern Christian Leadership Conference (SCLC), CORE, and NAACP, organized the Council of Federated Organizations (COFO) and sponsored the Freedom Summer. In many ways, Freedom Summer represented the outcome of the strategy of bringing African Americans into the liberal welfare state. Labor unions, white student activists, and liberals were brought together to aid the civil rights agenda, yet this experience left many SNCC participants unsure whether white union and white student involvement could have a positive effect on their organization. In "The Student Non-Violent Coordinating Committee: Rise and Fall of a Redemptive Organization" (1983), Emily Stoper argues that SNCC discovered that white members often had the effect of driving out African Americans, who felt uncomfortable making "anti-white statements" in front of them (125). Further, through their involvement, white student activists had gained leadership positions. Since SNCC had always been dominated by a small cadre of dedicated African American members, it was unprepared for the massive influx of a biracial constituency and the resulting loss of power by African Americans. The organic relationship between SNCC and its community appeared to be fractured by the participation of middle- to upper-class white students.

Attempts by white students to build upon Freedom Summer and to generate an organic relationship with African American protesters also met with mixed results. For instance, the 1964 Free Speech Movement (FSM) at Berkeley occurred in part as a response to the administration's refusal to allow CORE into the political life of the university. In "The Free Speech Movement and Civil Rights" (1965), Jack Weinberg, president of the CORE Berkeley chapter, directly tied the initial limits placed on student activism to the disruptive effect CORE activists were having on the local economy. After CORE student activists at Berkeley protested local businesses whose southern chains practiced segregation, Weinberg argues,

> Attempts were made by civil authorities and the power interests to contain the movement; harassing trials, biased news reporting, job intimidation, etc. But the attempts were unsuccessful, the movement grew, became more sophisticated, and began exploring other fronts on which it could attack the power structure. Throughout the summer, Berkeley Campus CORE maintained a hectic level of continuous and effective activity. The Ad Hoc Committee To End Discrimination planned and began executing a project against the Oakland Tribune. Since those who wished to contain the Civil Rights movement found no effective vehicles in the community, they began pressuring the university. Because a majority of participants were students, they maintained that the university was responsible. After initially resisting the pressure, the university finally succumbed, and promulgated restrictive regulations with the intent of undercutting the base of student support for the Civil Rights movement. The reactions to these regulations should have been predictable: immediate protest and a demand for their repeal. (184)

As a result of these regulations, Berkeley students began to position themselves as in a similar social situation to southern African Americans. FSM leader Mario Savio (1965, 6) argued that, due to the FSM movement, "The political consciousness of the Berkeley community has been quickened by this fight. The Berkeley students now demand what hopefully the rest of an oppressed white middle-class will some day demand: freedom for all Americans, not just Negroes." This imagery was supplemented by the actions of the students who used civil disobedience methods learned in the South: sit-ins, protests, and student strikes. An understanding quickly developed that represented the Berkeley student as facing oppression similar to African Americans. According to Savio (1965, 1), "what oppresses the American Negro community is merely an exaggerated, grotesque version of what oppresses the rest of the country—and this is eminently true of the middle-class, despite its affluence."

Such a conjunction, however, ignored the different economic and political realities of the white middle class and southern African Americans. For within the terms Savio sets out, it cannot rationally be said that the oppression of the middle class is equivalent to the oppression of the "American Negro." As indicated at the outset of this chapter, the southern African American population was politically and economically disenfranchised. The middle class was "oppressed" in the sense that an interweaving of corporate, national, and anticommunist interests had produced a limited national debate. The middle class, however, could also be said to be gaining the most economic benefit from this conjuncture of interests. That is, the FSM's attempt to create an alliance between "Negroes," white students, and the middle class ultimately failed because of its inability to bridge the different economic and political divides among the concerned constituencies.

In fact, beyond the role of white student activists, SNCC began to recognize how the interests of its political allies were at odds with African American empowerment. Even the support of the Democratic Party and labor unions began to carry too high a cost. For instance, in response to the monopoly that conservative "Dixiecrats" had over southern politics, SNCC sponsored the Mississippi Freedom Democratic Party (MFDP). In separate elections, the African American population of Mississippi elected representatives to attend the 1964 Democratic Convention. The MFDP's challenge was initially supported by Joseph Rauh, UAW general council, as well as by other UAW-influenced groups, such as Michigan's Democratic Party. To demonstrate its support of labor, the MFDP's platform proclaimed "the need for laws 'guaranteeing labor unions the right to organize freely'" (Levy 1994,

29). At the convention, however, the Democratic Party refused to sit the MFDP in place of the "properly" elected southern representatives. A compromise which would have given the party an honorary seat was supported by both liberal and union leaders. Seeing the compromise as an abandonment of their efforts, MFDP turned it down. The effect of this experience was to leave SNCC very suspicious of the commitment of white liberal elements of the Democratic Party to political and social change (Levy 1994, 38).

The actions of Democratic Mayor Richard Daley of Chicago toward King's SCLC did not relieve this suspicion. During the previous years, SCLC had proven its ability to wage successful civil rights struggles in southern cities, such as Montgomery and Atlanta.[6] In 1965, SCLC had sponsored a march to the Alabama state capital to dramatize its voter registration drive, an effort that helped push the Voter Rights Act through Congress. In 1966, at the request of the Coordinating Council of Community Organizations, SCLC attempted both to integrate the public school system and to improve inner-city housing in Chicago. SCLC was unprepared, however, for the resistance by Chicago's white working-class communities to racial integration of their neighborhoods. This move northward created hostility among the white middle class, which had previously supported southern campaigns. Further, as SCLC member Ralph Abernathy wrote, unlike previous campaigns waged in the South, where SCLC was the uncontested site of black leadership, Mayor Daley "had *created* the current black power structure in order to serve the ends of his own political organization" (1989, 362–399 passim). African American leaders, such as Representative William Dawson, "could do nothing about Chicago's local segregated school system, but . . . [they could] make certain that [their] constituents received some slices of the municipal pie" (395). Consequently, while SCLC had popular support among the black population, Daley was able to front black representatives who could criticize SCLC's politics and political actions. The combination of these factors led to an unsuccessful SCLC campaign. Although SCLC extracted a series of promises from the Daley machine, there was widespread pessimism that they would be enacted.[7] Beyond further alienating SNCC from the Democratic Party, these events left SNCC distrustful of "accepted" African American community leaders.

For SNCC, each of these incidents highlighted how liberalism and labor were too firmly entrenched in the status quo to actively seek an improved status for African Americans. Structurally, it seemed, the effect of this liberal–labor coalition was to block certain types of improvements for African Americans.[8] While unions appeared to support reform in the South as a way to shift the balance of power for labor laws, they acted as if they could not expand black membership without alienating or damaging the economic status of their members. While liberals supported African American political rights, they could not go against southern conservatives without losing national political support for the Democrats. Consequently, it appeared that African Americans were unable to gain access to the growing U.S. economy except through increased federal legislation (such as civil rights laws) or federal interventions in the marketplace (such as anti-discrimination policies). Neither of these federal efforts was producing marked change in northern or urban African American populations. To break away from this coalition and to work for immediate change, SNCC began to reframe the African American experience away from Cold War nationalism and toward an alliance with Third World revolutionary struggles.

It was out of this context, then, that SNCC Chairperson Stokely Carmichael would begin to articulate a new economic and political strategy for African American activists.[9] In *Black Power: The Politics of Liberation in America* (1967), Carmichael argued that the early civil rights movement, with its acceptance of a labor–liberal welfare state alliance, had failed to produce effective political representation for African Americans. Using the metaphor of colonialism, Carmichael argues that black neighborhoods have been set up as internal colonies:

> The colonies were sources from which raw materials were taken and markets to which finished products were sold. . . . This same economic status has been perpetuated on the black community in this country. Exploiters come into the ghetto from outside, bleed it dry, and leave it economically dependent on the larger society. As with the missionaries, these exploiters frequently come as the "friend of the Negro," pretending to offer worthwhile goods and services, when their basic motiva-

tion is personal profit and their basic impact is the maintenance of racism. (17–18)

Carmichael argued that African Americans should take effective economic and political control of their neighborhoods through creating separate black political organizations. To combat the influence of white liberals, a central tenant of these organizations was that they be dominated by African American leaders and an African American membership. The goal of such organizations would be to support the economic integrity of African American communities by supporting community businesses. Black Power thus effectively argued against the biracial politics earlier funded by labor or liberal organizations. (In fact, one of the effects of this shift away from a labor–liberal alliance was to dramatically reduce the funds which SNCC had to run programs.[10]) A memorandum published by SNCC stated, "Black Power recognizes—it must recognize—the ethnic basis of American politics as well as the power-oriented nature of American politics. Black Power therefore calls for black people to consolidate behind their own, so that they can bargain from a position of strength."[11] Black Power organizing, then, would ensure that African American–dominated organizations were in place to combat the social and economic deprivation U.S. policies and economy were perpetuating.

Carmichael's vision of Black Power affected how African American students organized politically. The most famous student organization to embed itself within this vision is the Black Panther Party for Self-Defense. To call the Black Panthers a student organization is not, perhaps, the usual way in which the organization is discussed, yet Bobby Seale traces the development of the Panthers from discussions concerning African American history at Meriot College and student efforts to change the college's curriculum. He argues that it was from a student discussion group's reading of Frantz Fanon that the impetus for a student political organization developed. (The founders of the Panthers were influenced by Frantz Fanon's view that riots could produce change; the Watts riots occurred just prior to their formation.) That is, as with SNCC, primary elements of the Black Panther Party attempted to represent themselves as college students.[12] Further, each member of the Black Panthers was expected to "become a student" within the organization, completing both a reading list and educational workshops.[13] In fact, the Panthers understood many of their initial activities as educating the community on how to defend itself.

Their initial community-education efforts were focused on demonstrating the community's power to organize against police brutality. As William Van Deburg argues in *New Day in Babylon* (1992), the Black Panthers believed that the white police

> served the same function within the black community as foreign troops occupying conquered territory. It was their duty to keep the peace and protect the way of life of those in power. More specifically, they were to keep "the peace for the Bank of America and General Motors" by maintaining black oppression. This was called "keeping niggers in check"—making sure that blacks were intimidated, locked in mortal fear, and paralyzed in their bid for freedom. Under this system, security was the byword. Justice was secondary. (159)

Nevertheless, Van Deburg overemphasizes the guns and fails to discuss the ways in which the guns and police-brutality campaign were a strategic symbol to declare independence. Throughout their efforts, the Panthers always handed out their ten-point program featuring issues of community control to spectators of their activities. To further these beliefs, the Black Panthers also set up African American community programs: free breakfasts for children, free shoes and clothing, legal assistance, medical care, and screening for sickle cell anemia.[14]

This image of the student protester is markedly different from the one SNCC had developed earlier. Whereas SNCC had previously focused on southern African Americans, the Black Panther Party coordinated their initial efforts on the urban African American underclass. Also, the southern student strategy was initially embedded within a hegemonic coalition in support of the liberal–labor welfare state. The Black Panther Party organized around the repudiation of that coalition.[15] As had Carmichael, the Black Panthers argued against the corporate and welfare structure of the United States.[16] Finally, whereas SNCC acted as a cadre organization, the diverse and multiple local incarnations of the Black Panther Party worked against a strong central ruling organization. Indeed, there were chapters that did not originate from college campuses. (Nor was every Black Panther chapter as politically pure as Seale describes in his book.) For our purposes, however, it is important to notice that it is the Panthers' self-representation as a new type of student–community organization that enabled their access to New Left student groups; that is, the Black Panthers offered a different articulation of what it meant to be a student activist. By 1966, then, the original SNCC student had been replaced by a more militant student, a student who sought examples from Africa and the Third World, not from white liberal or labor leaders. It was this student that the NUC would invoke in its *Open Up the Schools* (OUTS) document (1972). The terrain upon which the CCCC was founded was obviously beginning to shift.

The Student Rebellion

While the NUC would align itself with the Black Panthers, it would also benefit from the white student left's critique of the modern university. The NUC's concern with how corporations and the military distorted the university, for instance, had as its immediate predecessor the student strike at Columbia University. Its call for the elimination of grades was foreshadowed by Carl Davidson's "A Student Syndicalist Movement" (1966). To this point, however, white student politics have been discussed primarily for how they failed to enunciate effective alliances with African American protest movements, yet the debate within the white student left was pivotal to how university academics would organize politically. Approaching the question of student activism from the position of white student protest allows another image of the student to emerge; here the student is cast as a lever to reform the university and ultimately society as well.

In 1960, at approximately the same time as NITE and the Montgomery bus boycott, C. Wright Mills published "Letter to the New Left." It argued that the "old" left had mistakenly taken up the argument about the "end of ideology." This view claimed that, "in the West, there are no more real issues or even problems of great seriousness. The mixed economy plus the welfare state plus prosperity—that is the formula. U.S. capitalism will continue to be workable; the welfare state will continue along the road to ever greater justice" (19). (This argument criticizes many of the moves actually made by the NCTE's NITE document.) Within such a rubric, the classic Marxist view of agency, where the working class would lead the revolution against the capitalist state, was displaced by a belief in reformist institutions:

> So far as the *historic agency of change* is concerned, the end-of-ideology stands upon the identification of such agencies with going institutions; perhaps upon their piecemeal reform, but never upon the search for agencies that might be used or that might themselves make for a structural change of society. The problem of agency is never posed as a problem to solve, as our problem. Instead there is talk of the need to be pragmatic, flexible, open. Surely all this has already been adequately dealt with: such a view makes sense politically only if the blind drift of human affairs is in general beneficent. (Mills 1960, 20)

In fact, this was precisely the viewpoint of the hegemonic coalition that labor and Democrats had constructed; it was also the relationship that the original actors in the civil rights movement (and NITE) had attempted to penetrate. For Mills, however, such a world view would be "laughed at out loud" in Latin America, Africa, Asia, and the Soviet Bloc. Instead of endorsing the end of ideology, Mills argued that a New Left needed to begin a process of analyzing the structures and policies of progressive institutions. Once such a process was undertaken, many of the institutions that were previously held to be supportive of working-class rights would be found lacking. Organized labor, for instance, could no longer claim to serve the unique interests of the working class. In "The Structure of Power in American Society" (n.d.), Mills argued that in the 1930s

> it often seemed that labor would become an insurgent power independent of corporation and state. . . . Instead of economic and political struggles, it had become deeply entangled in administrative routines with both corporations and the state. . . .

In so far as it fights at all, it fights over a share of the goods of a single way of life and not over that way of life itself. The typical labor leader in the U.S.A. today is better understood as an adaptive creature of the main business drift than as an independent actor in a truly national context. (33)

In speaking of the "single way of life," Mills attaches the goals of organized labor in representing the working class to the emerging image of the American as a homeowner with a set of major appliances. To this extent, Mills argues that labor leaders were not concerned that workers become powerful players in corporate decision making, but rather that Ralph Kramden become as great a consumer of goods as Ward Cleaver. Consequently, Mills argues that the idea of the working class as the primary agent of change was "a legacy from Victorian Marxism that is now quite unrealistic" (22). Mills does not, however, give up the search for a uniquely qualified agent of change. Instead, Mills suggests that "the cultural apparatus, the intelligentsia," in particular the "young intelligentsia," might fill in the void (22). To make his case, he points to the role of student protests in Turkey, South Korea, and Japan.[17] In each of these countries, the student protests were presented as successful (or beginning to represent successful) attempts at overthrowing United States–backed governments.

It appears, however, that white student activists in the United States were less than impressed with the radical possibility of their fellow students. In "From Protest to Radicalism," SDS President Al Haber (1983, 41) argued that while "we have taken the initiative from the adult spokesmen and leadership," many of the "student leaders" cannot rightfully be called students: "[M]any are graduate students no longer in school at all. They have participated in radical or liberal activities throughout their college careers and are not strangers to firmly established liberal-left associations" (42). When undergraduate students did become involved, Haber argued, they tended to push off actions because "they [did not] want to make anyone unhappy" (43). Further, unlike the student protests of the South, which operated in the context of their community, Haber argued that the failure of northern student sit-ins to look beyond [their] own moral position is symptomatic of a protest, in contrast to a radical, movement. The movement rarely goes beyond the store front. Attention to community relations—to say nothing of student relations—is minimal. If we provide the initiative and manpower, our appeal is none-the-less to the community, and yet we make little effort to bring massive community involvement in the movement. (47)

Consequently, while students protested for disarmament, they "say nothing of what to do with the manpower, resources, industrial plant, and capital equipment that is tied up in the military machine" (47). Certainly, the Berkeley Free Speech Movement would demonstrate the logic of Haber's argument. What had originated as an off-campus protest issue soon became an issue of free speech on campus. For the brief period of several months, large numbers of students were actively involved in the protest. The level of involvement dwindled, however, once the particular campus issue and campus rules were concluded. After that, the majority of the student population was no longer involved. Consequently, while endorsing the immediate effects of nonviolent protest, Haber argued that an organization was needed which would structure the disparate white sit-in movements into a coherent organizational movement, a movement with ties to the community—a SNCC for white leftist students. Haber imagined SDS as such an organization.

To achieve this, SDS needed to situate the white student activist in a new relationship to labor, left, and Cold War politics. These attempts were complicated, however, by the original institutional situation of SDS. As a student organization within the League of Industrial Democracy (LID), SDS could not go against LID's harsh anticommunist line.[18] Nor, given the support of labor unions for their efforts, could they afford to condemn labor completely; the first SDS president, Al Haber, was hired only through a $10,000 grant from UAW (Levy 1994, 14). In response, SDS attempted to steer a middle course between the Cold War condemnation of communism and an investment in the working class as instruments of change. At the same time, the potential agency of students in social change also had to be explicated.

Initially, SDS attempted to praise the militancy of workers and criticize the actions of labor unions. In *The Port Huron State-*

ment, SDS charged that the labor movement had left behind a tradition of struggling for increased worker participation. (This argument would later be taken up by Carl Davidson's "A Student Syndicalist Movement" [1966], discussed later.) As cited by James Miller (1987, 112), the draft argued: "The general absence of union democracy finalizes worker apathy. Labor had grown 'too rich and sluggish' to act as a leading agency of social change; that change had to be taken over by radicals in the university." (The irony of the document being written by university radicals at a UAW labor camp was not lost on the participants.) The final draft of the statement maintained this harsh antilabor stance, while maintaining a general support for the possibilities of the rank and file to be progressive in their efforts. This line was also apparent in other documents written by SDS leaders. Al Haber wrote "Students and Labor," a "pamphlet that argued that unions suffered from poor reputations on college campuses and called on SDS to educate students on the history and importance of labor unions" (Levy 1994, 12). Simultaneously, Haber urged progressives within the labor movement to assert themselves.

Ultimately, as had SNCC with the early civil rights movement, SDS was unable to contain their emerging definition of student activism within this coalition; by 1964, they had left LID permanently. LID was unwilling to countenance SDS's acceptance of communist members; nor was LID willing to support SDS's "political protests." SDS also left behind labor unions as a principal agent of progressive activism. They did not, however, leave behind the general question of agency. Instead, as hinted at earlier, SDS found a new principal site of activism in the university. According to SDS, the university served a vital function. *The Port Huron Statement* had argued:

> First, the University is located in a permanent position of social influence. Its educational function makes it indispensable and automatically makes it a crucial institution in the formation of social attitudes. Second, in an unbelievably complicated world, it is the central institution for organizing, evaluating, and transmitting knowledge. Third, the extent to which academic resources presently are used to buttress immoral social practice is revealed first, by the extent to which defense contracts make the universities engineers of the arms race. Too,

the use of modern social science as a manipulative tool reveals itself in the "human relations" consultants to the modern corporations, who introduce trivial jobs to give laborers feelings of "participation" or "belonging," while actually deluding them in order to further exploit their labor. And, of course, the use of motivational research is already infamous as a manipulative aspect of American politics. But these social uses of the university's power on the men and storehouses of knowledge, this makes the university functionally tied to society in new ways, revealing new potentialities, new levers for change. Fourth, the university is the only mainstream institution that is open to participation by individuals of nearly any viewpoint . . . . [T]hese together make the university a potential base and agency in a movement of social change. (J. Miller 1987, 373)

In making this argument, SDS aligned itself with Mills's belief in the "young intelligentsia." It also produced the image of the university possessing a central place within the social and political order. In fact, *The Port Huron Statement* argued from this premise that from the nation's "schools and colleges [a] militant left might awaken its allies and by beginning the process toward peace, civil rights and labor struggles reinsert theory and idealism where too often reign confusion and political barter" (Miller 1987, 374). More important, it is the students' actions of protesting and highlighting the need for social equity that will undermine corporate and governmental interests.

To demonstrate the extent to which a common bond could exist between students, African Americans, and the working class, SDS created the Economic Research and Action Program (ERAP). This program was made possible from seed money of $5,000 provided by the UAW, who later provided another $2,500 (Levy 1994, 14). (Notably, the ideological split with labor unions did not include a complete break with unions.) The principal emphasis of ERAP was to convince university students to go into working class and predominantly black neighborhoods and set up worker–student neighborhood organizations.[19] The two most successful projects were the Newark and Cleveland projects. Unlike some other ERAP projects, the Cleveland project benefited from labor help; the AFL-CIO provided office space, ditto machines, and some income. With this support, the Cleveland project was able to organize various activities, such as a tenants' union, an unemployment council, and a recreation group. As Levy (1994, 33) writes, "The welfare mothers association, CUFAW (Citizens United for Adequate Welfare) was the most impressive of these. It planned a demonstration in which welfare mothers would demand a full set of clothes, school supplies for each child at the beginning of the year. . . . In February 1965, CUFAW mothers attended a 'Community People's Conference,' co-sponsored by SDS, where poor people's organizations from all over the country discussed their grassroots efforts." The Newark project gained a national presence through its success in creating tenant organizations and organizing rent strikes. Other ERAP projects successfully organized residents to lobby the local government for improved safety, street lights, stop signs, and expanded police control.[20]

Unlike the Black Panthers' move from the classroom to the community, however, ERAP failed to sustain itself on a national scale. In part, SDS greatly underestimated the effort necessary to gain the trust of a particular neighborhood's working-class youth. More to the point, the effort to organize working-class and African American concerns into demands for improved government services met with criticism. Such efforts smacked of reformism, a position SDS's *Port Huron Statement* explicitly rejected. That is, it was unclear to what extent the "student activism" was actually supporting the local Democratic–labor coalition through its organizing of the poor to demand more from the government. (In fact, even efforts to exploit Democratic–labor connections failed since local parties and chapters would not intervene to help. In several cases, unions actively blocked the work of ERAP projects [Levy 1994, 38].) Additionally, by this time, SDS was already displaying a lack of internal organizational control which would lead to its breakup. As a result, there was no central organized effort to keep the various ERAP projects in touch with one another. ERAP members often felt isolated and uninvolved with a larger project. By 1966, most of the ERAP projects had either failed or, through success, had incorporated themselves separately from SDS.[21]

With the end of ERAP, the Vietnam War and its impact on the university stepped into the void. In prior years, due to the image of SDS previously described, the National Council of SDS had attempted to steer clear from being perceived as only an antiwar organization. The original members of SDS, figures such as Hayden and Haber, stuck fast to their vision of SDS as an incorporative body involving the myriad of issues concerning the "student movement." By 1966, however, SDS's membership had been taken over by Prairie Power forces, activists whose principal experience of the New Left was as antiwar demonstrators. Originating in campuses such as Kent State, Penn State, and Oregon State, Prairie Power forced SDS to take on the Vietnam War and its impact on education directly.

In fact, Prairie Power activists had shown that a principal financial provider of the universities' educational mission was the Department of Defense. During the 1950s, the Department of Defense and Atomic Energy Commission accounted for over 43 percent of federal research dollars available to universities and colleges. Initially, the majority of these funds went to private or Ivy League schools. With the advent of the Project Themis in 1967, research dollars began to be provided to public and state schools as well. Whereas the early schools were funded in order to develop international policy, the latter schools' principal research came from military weapons development. By 1968, with universities spending over $300 billion annually for research, over 70 percent of this money came from the federal government and over half the money from defense-related agencies (Heineman 1993, 14). As a consequence, student protest began to focus on the complicity of higher education with the "war machine."

In "A Student Syndicalist Movement: University Reform Revisited" (1966), future SDS Vice President Carl Davidson uses "Student Power" to name New Left attempts to articulate the importance of antiwar student activism and university reform in restructuring society. In particular, Davidson's article attempted both to recognize the importance of the antiwar protest and to connect that protest to larger social issues. He writes:

> But let us return to our original question. What is the connection between dorm rules and the war in Vietnam? Superficially, both are aspects of corporate liberalism—a dehumanized and oppressive system. But let us be more specific. Who are the dehumanizers and oppressors? In a word, our past, present,

and future alumni—the finished product of our knowledge factories.[22] (2)

Through Davidson's article, then, the role of the student activist
in university reform was reimagined as something other than a
focus on dormitory policy or the simple addition of a class or
two. This model, which increased benefits without increasing
"workplace" control, echoed the strategies of unions, who appeared to be fixated only on gaining higher wages for their workers
(11).[23] Instead, Davidson argued, the student movement should
place itself within the syndicalist tradition where "unions worked
for industrial democracy and workers control." That is, the student movement was being reimagined as taking control of the
"rules" of the university.

Within this paradigm, then, grades must be eliminated (since
they cause alienation among students toward their work), emphasis must be placed on participatory democracy in the classroom (students should demand a say in how a syllabus is
constructed for a class), and the requirements for degrees must
be revised (allowing for greater student input in their education).
By emphasizing participatory democracy, control would also be
decentralized, allowing for greater input by students in nonacademic areas of the university. Ultimately, such reforms would point
toward students having power over how the university ran its
business. Students might then be able to eliminate the university's
involvement in corporate America's support of the war. Therefore, Davidson (1966) argues that currently "[t]his system requires that we passively agree to be manipulated. [Our] vision is
one of active participation. And this is the demand that our administrators cannot meet without putting themselves out of a
job. That is exactly why we should be making it" (11).

As in *The Port Huron Statement,* the revolution would thus
occur by transforming the consciousness of students. Yet *The
Port Huron Statement* had been used by SDS to call upon students to enter working-class neighborhoods and organize citizens. Davidson (1966) argues that students should focus on
transforming and reforming the university so that it no longer
serves as a "handmaiden" to U.S. foreign policy or business interests. In fact, he argues that a properly educated student popu-

lation will refuse to participate in the existing political and economic system.

> [P]erhaps we can see the vital connections our factories have with the present conditions of corporate liberalism when we ask ourselves what would happen if: the military found itself without ROTC students; the CIA found itself without recruits; paternalistic welfare departments found themselves without social workers; or the Democratic Party found itself without young liberal apologists and campaign workers? In short, what would happen to a manipulative society if its means of creating *manipulable* people were done away with? We might then have a fighting chance to change that system. (emphasis in text, 2)

Student activists would now attempt to reorganize universities and their curricula so that graduates would be morally incapable of accepting the current practices and policies of the U.S. government and U.S. corporations. Previous conceptions of a class revolution had focused on the proletariat. Within Davidson's article, a revolution would occur by infiltrating corporations with individuals trained to refocus corporate activity for the benefit of citizens, not for profits. In this sense, students, whether by organizing for university or corporate reform, would be participating in the larger New Left movement for social justice.

Indeed, over the course of the next year, it appeared as if the concept of student syndicalism was fulfilling Davidson's expectations. During 1966–67, for instance, SDS would adopt a strict antiwar policy. This policy included organizing draft-resister unions, direct action against preinduction activities and during induction ceremonies, antidraft and antiwar education to inductees and their families, demonstrations at draft boards, encouraging opposition to the war by existing troops, and circulating petitions refusing conscription (Sale 1973, 271). (These stances further alienated SDS from organized labor, which had maintained a consistently prowar stance.) In the autumn of 1966, Yale students signed the first "We Won't Go" pledges. During the winter and summer of that year, demonstrations were held at Berkeley against Marine recruitment as well as Dow and the CIA. In April of 1967, antiwar marches in New York and San Diego attracted crowds of over 200,000 and 65,000 respectively. Thirty thousand students participated in Vietnam Summer. The April "Days of Resistance" would see fifty colleges and universities sponsoring "rallies, marches, teach-ins, and sit-ins, climaxing in a one-day 'student strike' on April 26th in which an estimated one million students took part. Even high school students had become militant."[24] Sixty percent of secondary school principals reported student protests during this time. An estimated two thousand demonstrations took place from November to May. Radical high school unions were formed in many of America's larger cities (Sale 1973, 517).

While the extent to which the preceding protests successfully integrated student protests with community concerns is unclear, certainly the 1968 Columbia "student takeover" represents one such moment. The strike had been precipitated by Mark Rudd, later of the Weathermen, when he led students into the president's office to protest the treatment of six SDS leaders. In the ensuing crisis, five buildings were taken over by several thousand students. After eight days, the police, invited by university officials, stormed the buildings and arrested the participants. In "Who Rules Columbia," written by the North American Congress on Latin America (NACLA) during the strike, it was argued that "[t]he student contention that the trustees represent illegitimate power is based upon a concept fundamental to democracy; that the authority of the rulers is legitimate only insofar as it represents the ruled" (Teodori 1969, 336). In a detailed document that demonstrates the outside interests which dominated Columbia University's board of trustees, the NACLA argued that the interests of the students were secondary to the corporate or foreign policy aims of its trustees. In particular, the NACLA demonstrated how Columbia trustees, such as William Burden, were involved in weapons production by both producing weapons at Lockheed Aircraft and working for the Institute for Defense Analysis. In discussing what was perceived as the immediate cause for the student protest, Columbia's attempt to build an expanded gymnasium in Harlem, the NACLA wrote:

> The gym represented institutional expansion, creation of a service area for empire-building trainees—a frozen negation of domestic, irrelevant populations. Colonialized community and

colonialized student needs fused; as an unbearable tension was reached, this new community moved to stop the work on the gym and seized the buildings symbolic of their training and rededicated them to new purposes, seized property and rededicated it to anti-poverty priorities. This action symbolized the need to stop the destructive direction the country was taking. (Teodori 1969, 342)

The NACLA thus represented the Columbia University "rebellion" as the potential fulfillment of Davidson's argument. Students, in concert with larger social concerns, had recast university policy, temporarily "taking over" and demonstrating the real social goals of a university education. During the student strike that followed the reclaiming of the buildings by the Columbia administration, university reforms were initiated, supported by a $40,000 Ford Foundation grant. These reforms echoed a developing strategy to ease campus unrest by setting up committees concerning student affairs, faculty senates, and so on, all designed to give the school's population a greater say in how the university was run (Sale 1973, 444). Most notably, the gymnasium was never constructed.

What is important about the Columbia protest is the rhetorical linkages generated by the activists between the university and the immediate local community. A way of speaking had been developed which allowed the students to reunderstand their immediate position in relation to the economic and political situation of the Harlem community. Here the primary tool to generate this relationship was not race, but economics. The student advocates were able to understand the university as part of a larger economic system that was both imperialistic abroad (Vietnam) and at home (Harlem). As Tom Hayden wrote:

The striking students were not holding onto a narrow conception of students as a privileged class asking for inclusion in the University as it now exists. . . . The Columbia students were instead taking an internationalist and revolutionary view of themselves in opposition to the imperialism of the very institutions in which they have been groomed and educated. . . . They want a new and independent university standing against the mainstream of American society, or they want no university at all.[25] (Sale 1973, 346)

Such a political viewpoint clearly created the possibility of the student activist being involved in African American liberation struggles, yet it did so through a conscious recognition of how the student's subject position would also have to be altered for effective change to occur. To some extent, the Columbia protest is similar to the FSM protest. Mario Savio had said concerning Berkeley, "what oppresses the American Negro community is merely an exaggerated, grotesque version of what oppresses the rest of the country—and this is eminently true of the middle-class, despite its affluence." The Columbia University protest had also argued a linkage between African Americans and student protesters: "Colonialized community and colonialized student needs fused." But unlike the FSM, the Columbia University incident positioned the middle class (and future middle-class participants) as oppressors as well. The economic and political substratum which perpetuated oppression internationally was announced, and the university's role in creating this substratum was articulated. Initial moves to block its continuance (both in the classroom and the community) were begun. A vision of the university as linked to its immediate community was initiated. Finally, these efforts were partially situated within a national organization designed to support and spread other such protests. Potentially, then, a powerful rhetorical image, linked with institutional and community structures, was taking hold.

Or so it seemed. Despite the massive student protests and the "successes," such as at Columbia, it is not at all clear whether the majority of students perceived themselves within an "internationalist and revolutionary" project. On the one hand, Hayden's viewpoint seems correct. According to Kirkpatrick Sale (1973), one cautious survey in the fall of 1968 found approximately 368,000 people enrolled in universities and colleges who considered themselves revolutionaries. Another survey in the fall of 1970 counted no fewer than 1,170,000 self-proclaimed revolutionaries. The extent to which students were actually thinking of themselves as revolutionary (and what that might have meant to them) is open to question, of course. Of those calling themselves revolutionaries, it can be imagined that more students fell into the "liberal reform" aspect of the "revolution" than into the "internationalist" categories that Hayden describes. This seems particularly true if the relationship between SDS chapters and individual campus populations are taken into account. Whereas SDS chapters, such as Columbia's, were effective in turning out students for campus events, it is unclear to what extent merely showing up indicated support of SDS's emerging doctrine of Student Power. Concerning Columbia student attitude toward SDS, James Simon Kunen (1970, 28) wrote that, although about five hundred students were willing to follow Mark Rudd, "they don't particularly like [Rudd] because he always refers to President Kirk as 'that shithead.'" In fact, Kunen's writing demonstrates that, whereas students might have been sympathetic to many of the critiques used by SDS, actual attendance at an event may have had more to do with it being "an event" than endorsement of a political decision. The rhetoric of revolution was also satirized by popular magazines such as *LIFE* ("Mutiny at a Great University" 1968).

> With the brashness of a victorious banana-republic revolutionary, the mustachioed undergraduate sat in the chair of the president of New York's Columbia University and puffed on an expropriated cigar. He and his cohorts—a vociferous band of 600 campus activists—had seized the command center of one of the world's greatest centers of learning. For six turbulent days, while the insurgents defied every peaceful effort to dislodge them, the university was effectively out of business. (36)

Further, in *Our Time Is Now* (Birmingham 1970), in which selections from high school underground newspapers are reprinted, a survey of these papers reflects that many of these protests seemed to focus more on issues surrounding lost-and-found policies than internationalist concerns. That is, students focused more on the immediate rule or regulation than its broader economic impact.

Ultimately, Student Power was unable to even coalesce the competing forces within SDS. In the past, SDS had functioned almost like a cadre organization, personal bonds and associations patching over ideological differences. By 1967 and 1968, SDS found itself unable to formulate a cohesive ideology to pull the diverse elements of the organization together. The massive increase in student membership, coupled with loose voting procedures, had allowed SDS to break into several factions. National meetings were dominated by power struggles between SDS founders, Prairie Power, ERAP forces, progressive labor, and the large, nonideological student community. In such an environment, the traditional politics of progressive labor, acting as a unified organization of its own, was able to assume a more active role in SDS. By packing meetings, demanding group unity on votes, and co-opting SDS participatory rhetoric, progressive labor was able to gain strength out of proportion to its support.

As a consequence, SDS only briefly flirted with the concept of student power. Working against Davidson's vision, progressive labor reasserted the primacy of the working class.[26] Unable to form productive relationships with the Black Power movement, unwilling to a great extent to take up the project of feminism, Prairie Power's Student Power was discredited in favor of an economic analysis that prioritized working-class alliances. During 1968, SDS therefore moved away from its "new" working-class emphasis and back toward a "traditional" working-class analysis. One national office staff member wrote:

> Students as students, in my opinion, are not necessary for a revolution. The only reason even to attempt a campus movement is that students are useful and universities have a large concentration of young people whose middle-class and bourgeoisie values are not irreversibly entrenched; otherwise they are not worth the trouble. . . . If a person in the U.S. in 1967 considers himself or herself a student, he or she negates the meaning of being a revolutionary. (Sale 1973, 565)

The arguments made on behalf of Student Power, however, did not go away. Instead, Student Power would become a means to organize university faculty.

The New University Conference

By 1967, arguments critiquing the Cold War university were clearly in place; NITE's image of the student had clearly been supplanted by a radical, anticorporate, antimilitaristic, student protest movement, and as Davidson had predicted, student activists were beginning to enter the professions. SDS, however, had done little to prepare for this precipitous moment. Writing in 1966, Greg Nesemeier argued, "SDS [has made] no provision for non-university, part-time university, and post-university people" (4). Nor, as SDS began in 1966 to focus its attention back upon the student and Student Power, would there be much emphasis on considering the long-term needs of the poststudent activist. In "Getting by with a Little Help from Our Friends" (1969), Haber writes about this dilemma:

> The response of the movement to the idea of profession, or craft or specialized skill, is too often to regard it as an opting for privatistic gain or fulfillment, and as an abandonment of radical commitment.
> There is little recognition that decent motives toward professions exist and that the attempt by radicals in professions to invent and act out modes of practice that are infused with radical purpose is both valid and valuable. (296)

As a consequence, the work of professionals (or future professionals) to ensure "control of the work situation," a central tenant of Davidson's syndicalist movement, was denigrated, even as SDS attempted to create such future professionals to reform the U.S. corporate world. Further, any hope of individuals being able to sustain themselves from the movement proper was at odds with reality. Haber (1969, 291) argued that "the movement has created too limited a range of jobs, using too limited a range of skills, and provided too limited a range of personal satisfaction and financial support." As a consequence, when the particular political crisis that precipitated student protests passed and student activists entered the working world, the movement would not have created a network that could sustain long-term radical activity. A more rational emphasis, Haber argued, would be for the movement to also focus its attention on those who were actually involved in long-range institutional change: professionals.

Given the absence of such an organization, Haber successfully lobbied a reluctant SDS to organize the Radical Education Project (REP). REP's stated objective was to formulate and present literature that would serve as core documents for an expanding SDS. Haber (1966, 2) argued that REP "should seek to make explicit the meaning of radical democracy for America: the institutions and conditions that must be changed and the nature of the institutions and conditions that need be created in their place as well as those aspects of contemporary life that are important to preserve and strengthen." In effect, however, Haber intended to use REP as a place in which post-SDS student syndicalists could interact with one another concerning attempts to reform U.S. capitalism from the inside. That is, REP defined its mission as providing the opportunity for "radicals and democrats not now centrally involved 'in' the movement to interact, to stimulate one another and to define for themselves an identity and program appropriate for their social location—whether in universities, in trade unions, in the arts, in professions, or whatever" (2).

As a consequence, in July 1967, REP sponsored a Radicals in the Professions Conference. Attended by 250 participants, this conference was convened around the topic: Is it possible to be radical within the academic professions, or are such careers contradictory with the movement? As Irwin Unger (1985, 252) discusses it, the conference proposed that professionals should use their assured financial status and access to information to support full-time activists. During the conference, Haber argued that professionals must develop a new sense of ethics dominated by a concern for how their institutional position could be used by the movement. Haber (1969, 303) argued:

> A radical cannot have an orientation toward professional "success." . . .
>
> A radical cannot see his loyalty as being to the profession or institution in which he works. Our loyalty is to our political comrades and to the political aims for which we are organizing. . . .
>
> Radicals cannot accept without reservation the code of ethics and responsibility of their professions. . . . This means, for example, that we should have no "ethical" scruples about providing "cover" to movement people; using politics as a criterion in giving recommendations, references, jobs; that we will make professional resources such as equipment, supplies, travel funds, expense accounts, available to movement people under the guise of professional expense; that we might not respect the confidential status of documents, meetings, or privileged information.

Within such a paradigm, the organizing of professionals, such as college and university professionals, would constitute radical work for the movement. That is, by ensuring safe haven for radicals and doing the slow work of institutional change, professionals could work from the other end to create a radical, participatory environment, one with long-lasting effects. According to the REP conference, what was needed was an organization to solidify these activities. REP, however, would not be that organization. It would fail to sustain itself as SDS suffered its complicated demise.

Nevertheless, the image of the radical professional articulated by REP would give birth to the New University Conference. In March of 1968, the official call for a university organization, defined along the lines of REP and aimed at young professionals, would take place. In a draft of its initial policy statement (NUC n.d., Policy Statement, Draft 2), the NUC stated, "The New University Conference consists mainly of people in universities who are somewhat older than the current undergraduate generation. Many of us have been active in the student movement, most of us are deeply involved in the movements on and off the campus which have come to be called the 'New Left.'"[27]

Further, as was stated at the outset of this chapter, the NUC would build itself in relationship to the student protest movement. Unlike the criticism coming out of SDS in 1967 over student protests and their lack of militant action, the NUC supported "the new student movement, for we believe it is the main hope of creating a movement for social change in America and within the Universities" (NUC 1968b).

It should be noted, however, that the NUC was highly aware of the limited nature of its effects. The NUC never argued that its role was a primary one in producing social change. Instead, it repeatedly stated that change within the academic institution is a marginal but important task. Furthermore, reflecting Haber's earlier concerns, the NUC positioned itself as becoming a constant progressive force, a trait which would survive the particular form of the movement and work against its "history [of] ad-hoc organizations":

If [we seem] to put the university at the center of social struggle, when in fact, universities involve only a small fraction of the population of the country, several factors are responsible. A narrow professionalism is *not* one of them. Perhaps the most important factor is the very nature of American political folk-ways. Our history shows that we, as a people, are given to such ad-hoc organizations for real social change: mass organizations are created on the spot when a job needs doing. . . . As a result of our national characteristic, in between times of crisis and action, no mass organization exists to which the searching intellectual can give his support and allegiance. The NUC alleviates the atomization and isolation that he suffers.[28] (Zirker 1968, 1, 3)

Throughout its existence, the NUC thus was confronted with the issue of what it meant to organize a broad spectrum of professors into one organization; how did such an organization and its members relate to the movement? How did the NUC relate to reform within particular academic disciplines? That is, if the NUC was organizing to restructure American society, why organize along disciplinary lines? Or if the NUC organized professionals to reform their disciplines, how was this activity related to the movement's broader anticapitalist trend? Here is where SRTOL advocates begin to emerge from the web of relationships detailed throughout this chapter. Neal Resnikoff would lead the NUC efforts within the CCCC, particularly in the formation of the SRTOL. He would also play a role in how the NUC would decide to interact with existing professional organizations. As chair of the NUC's National Office's Subcommittee on Professional Organizing, Resnikoff would write in his "Progress Report" (1969c) that the committee's purpose was "to report on the state of professional organizing and the relationship which NUC should develop and/or avoid with the various professional caucuses and organizations."

In his report, Resnikoff detailed how respondents were formulating an argument which would position the NUC against efforts that merely reform scholarship. As expressed by Richard Rothstein (quoted in Resnikoff 1969c, 3), such organizing efforts were open to

the danger [that] an independent [disciplinary] caucus . . . will allow people to resolve these issues in a false way; it will allow people to "cop-out" by defining a new kind of professionalism (the "radical" kind) whereas professionalism is exactly what serious radicals should be struggling against. . . . [A]n independent radical caucus suggests to its members that "socialist scholarship" is an adequate response. . . . [I]t is arrogant to deal with that tension by stating it is our job to do the socialist scholarship and someone else's job to do the socialist action. In fact, only those engaged in the action should be developing our theory (and vice-versa).

Instead, it was argued, the NUC should work to move academics away from a disciplinary identification and toward political action within universities. Here the emphasis would not be on producing a Marxist interpretation of *Jane Eyre*, but on using leftist strategies to reform the social and political behavior of universities as institutions. For the NUC, professional organizations serve the purpose of bringing together academics into one space; as such, they are potentially productive places to organize academics for broader political activity. According to Louis Kampf (1970, 3), "The purpose of organizing at professional meetings should be to bring people into the academic sector of the movement as a whole (NUC) and into the movement—such as it is—as a whole." (In this sense, Doster was correct about the NUC attempting to alter the very nature of the CCCC.) The totality of such viewpoints was echoed in a resolution formulated by Resnikoff (1969c) which stated,

Though professional caucuses that raise radical perspectives in their fields and engage in radical activities (rather than mere non-radical "professionalism" or academic reformism) are valuable, we recommend that NUC encourage more than professional activity and attempt to have the caucuses join NUC. Where caucuses (such as Union for Radical Political Economists) may have services that will benefit NUC (or vice versa), NUC should use (or give) these services, even though the caucus may not be "radical."

It is out of this political framework that the NUC ultimately arrived at the CCCC. Taking the position that the NUC would involve itself in disciplinary caucuses for the purpose of bringing professionals into the movement, the NUC arranged to attend, and recruit at, a series of academic meetings and organizations.

From the end of 1969 to the beginning of 1970, NUC efforts therefore would focus on making connections with academic organizations. In 1969, for instance, the NUC would coordinate a radical caucus drive at the American Historical Association's Christmas meeting. At this meeting, the NUC failed to elect Staughton Lynd president but emerged as a continuing presence at the organization. At the same time, the NUC had or was also forming caucuses within philosophy (via the American Philosophical Association), anthropology (via the American Anthropology Association's Radical Caucus), sociology (via the Sociology Liberation Movement), and psychology (via the Psychologists for a Democratic Society). Further, Resnikoff (1969c, 1–2) writes, "perhaps a dozen other caucuses have developed in academic fields, in the medical profession, among social workers, and, in the MLA, even among job seekers."

To aid in the spreading of the NUC stance at these conferences, in September 1969 the NUC established an internal education committee "equipped with Marxist-oriented pamphlets and reading lists for the membership." In fact, in summarizing the conclusions of his committee, Resnikoff (1969c, 1) states,

> NUC needs to make explicit its views on the role of the intellectual and academic in whatever kind of organization NUC decides to become after it has decided the questions of how a revolution can succeed in this country and who can make it. Basic ideological directions should help determine the form and content or organizing within the academic sector of this society, and more specifically, relations with professional caucuses and organizations.

The most significant publication of its goals was the Open Up the Schools (OUTS) program. The OUTS movement began in the NUC during 1969, the same year as "The Student Rebellion," but it was not finished until 1970. To a great extent, OUTS represented the fullest articulation of the NUC's attempts to turn the antiwar protests (and protests against U.S. corporate involvement in the war) into an action policy for universities and colleges. It is also the fullest representation of how the NUC would work to produce "a new, American form of socialism and to replace an educational and social system that is an instrument of class, sexual and racial oppression with one that belongs to the people" (NUC 1969a, preamble; see note 27). As its preamble stated:

> This program is an attempt to integrate a general analysis of the political economy of higher education with a specific plan of action for NUC. In order for NUC to do more than perform the necessary educational function of bringing the issues of the movement to campus, we must find concrete ways of turning our role as teachers into a force in the class struggle. . . . This program is primarily intended for public institutions, and junior colleges. (1)

As had Davidson's "Syndicalist" article (1966), OUTS argued that higher education now served the function of training future employees for corporate America. To oppose this function, OUTS argued that the curriculum of the schools should be opened to include the experience of different populations. Free child care should be adopted in universities and colleges to ensure that nontraditional students would have the ability to attend. Tracking should be eliminated since it perpetuated racial and class divisions. Finally, echoing Davidson, grades should be eliminated. As the NUC's *Open Up the Schools* (1972, 1) states:

> Aside from curriculum content, one of the most central modes of [the student's] oppression is through the grading system, which maintains the authority of the teacher over the student, and the competition of the students one against the other. Grades constitute an illegitimate form of control over students, compelling them to perform tasks that are meaningless, alienating and oppressive. They are part of the tracking system as well and contribute to determining the life chances of students, even to their chances to get killed in Vietnam, in the case of men. In addition, they necessitate a competitive learning situation, which reduces students' capacity for collective learning and collective struggle.

Basic skills, however, were not abandoned. Elimination of grades, tracking, and traditional curriculum did not mean abandoning standard English instruction. As quoted in the epigraph to this chapter, OUTS aligned itself with the Black Panthers, arguing for both "minimal skills in reading and writing" and "education that teaches us our true history and our role in the present day society." To understand the validity of such an imagined alliance between the Black Panthers and the NUC, particularly as it relates to issues of basic skills, it is first necessary to detail the development of Black English as a political category. This work is done in chapter 2. For now, it is enough to note that the emphasis on university reform is intended to expand the services available for nontraditional students to ensure that they receive basic literacy skills; the role of the radicalized professor or teacher was to create a basic skills program that would generate critical thought against the corporate structure of the United States.

The funding for the basic skills programs, OUTS suggested, should come from the profits of companies in the local area. OUTS argued that the role of the university in providing basic literacy and specialized training actually functions to eliminate the need of companies to train workers. If corporate training had to be provided, a significant amount of a company's profits would be eliminated. These profits should go to fund education. It was the goal of OUTS and the NUC's Educational Program, then, to use the profits corporations were currently generating to support activities in universities and colleges intended to alter the nature of corporate America. As with Davidson's syndicalist movement, OUTS intended to transform the corporate structure by altering the values and skills students would bring to the corporate business world: "OUTS is a perspective for building a radical movement in the higher education system which aims at destroying the important capitalist functions of that system and replacing them with activities which will serve the people and the movement" (NUC 1972, 5).

It is within this intellectual and organizational framework that Neal Resnikoff would participate in the 1968 MLA Convention and the 1969 CCCC Convention. It is out of these efforts to produce an American socialism that the original SRTOL would emerge. That is, having participated in the NUC's framing of the role of professional organizations, Resnikoff would test the possible impact of the NUC student at the CCCC. The test would be whether the NUC student, who was portrayed as webbed within a series of capitalist, class, and racial categories, could act as a lever to redefine professional behavior as something other than reformed scholarship. Or rather, the test would be whether the reforming of academic practice would occur within a broader attempt to create socially and economically progressive institutional alliances among academics, departments, universities, and communities.

Conclusion

In the preceding pages, I have examined the development of *student* as a political category. In doing so, I have argued that rather than simply being a term which exists within our classrooms, the student has also served as a tool for political activism. For instance, the NCTE's NITE (1958) figured a student who could argue for the importance of English instruction in a Cold War environment. SNCC formulated the student as a means to integrate southern African Americans within the emerging U.S. social and economic landscape. Davidson (1966) used the same term to push for a counterhegemonic university politics. In the NUC, the student became a name through which to argue for an American socialism. At each moment, it thus was argued that the student could not be divorced from a particular social and economic goal, that is, liberal welfare-state capitalism, socialism, and so on. The student could not be divorced from a world view. (As should be clear, then, my own interest in the SRTOL is to examine how it also articulated a social and economic vision.) None of these students, however, should be imagined as the victor. Instead, what will become clear is how the SRTOL and composition studies interact with the work of SNCC, the Black Panther Party, SDS, and NUC. That is, this chapter was not designed to lead to a conclusion, but to begin to build the web in which the SRTOL exists.

In this chapter, I also began an analysis of a recurrent rhetorical strategy. At key rhetorical moments, each of the white protest movements examined—the FSM, SDS's takeover of Columbia, and the NUC's *Open Up the Schools* document (1972)—finally validated its politics through an image of the African American protester. Each did so with varying degrees of success. In the following chapter, I delineate the ways in which such appropriation marked not only an invocation, but a rewriting of these movements. That is, having articulated the different ways in which the *student* and the *Black student protestor* were positioned as key terms through which to reform society, it is now possible to assess the utility of these projects (and the violence done to them) when the additional element of composition scholarship is taken into account. How did composition interact with the various attempts to form a new hegemonic ideal of the social? How did its professional organizations and disciplinary activists attempt to integrate (or distance) their activities from the projects of the New Left, Black Power, and faculty power? It is to that work which I now turn.

---

1. The full text of the resolutions read as follows:

> *The class biases of university governing boards must be eliminated.* Trustees must be chosen by the entire university community and subject to recall. Decisions by the boards affecting the life of surrounding communities must be subject to democratic decision by such committees.

> *Universities should be free of militarist and corporate domination.* Research which aids in the manufacture of weapons, which is undertaken to aid government intelligence operations, or which is designed to support the military suppression of rebellious peoples should, as a matter of policy, be ruled off campus. As a general rule, mission-oriented research for the Defense Department, intelligence agencies or weapons manufacturers should be impermissible. There must be a constant commitment to avoid university policy control by the state and other financial sources. Universities should make special efforts to foster research for which funds are normally not available, and which aids "insurgent" interests and radical criticism. Special efforts must be taken to see that the results of research are as available to oppositional groups as they are to established elites. Faculty and students who are engaged in critical research, or who seek to communicate their work through unorthodox media, or who lend their skills to oppressed people rather than established interest groups, need to be seen as crucial assets in an authentic university.

> *Universities must end policies which support "institutional racism."* Universities must see themselves as responsible for providing educational opportunity to all classes and ethnic groups. Universities should give highest priority to the education of black youth and the youth of other racial and ethnic minorities. They

should also make special efforts to recruit and educate working-class youth. . . . In all such matters, and especially with regard to the deployment of resources and the development of surrounding neighborhoods, urban universities must be fully responsible to the people whose lives they affect and in whose midst they exist. (NUC 1968a, 8–9)

2. It should be noted, however, that only a small percentage of the entire U.S. labor force was ever covered by union contracts. A focus on alliances between labor unions and activist organizations thus should not be seen as telling the whole story. Instead, a constant undertone to this study should be the situation of the nonorganized working class. Such an emphasis, particularly in the South, makes clear the extent to which laws designed to exclude black citizens from voting also had the effect of excluding large numbers of poor white citizens. In *Class, Race, and the Civil Rights Movement* (1987), Bloom makes clear that this dual exclusion was a specific purpose of the restrictive voting laws. In this sense, later analogies between black oppression and the oppression of students (detailed throughout this work) should be read as eliding one primary similarity between blacks and whites: the continued exploitation of black and white service and nonorganized workers.

3. In summarizing the effect of this economic coalition, Mike Davis (1986) writes:

In other words, the "historical" standard of labor-power, as Marx defined it, had, for large sections of the white working class, come to encompass both home-ownership and a college education for their children Moreover, until the crisis of the 1970's, higher education did provide effective entry into expanding white collar, technical and educational sectors of employment: an inter-generational job-upgrading dynamic that is as fundamental to the intensive regime of accumulation as the turnover of new car models or the sale of suburban lots. (192)

4. Following chapters detail the use of nationalism in King's texts. For a discussion of the simultaneous development of the *poor* and *working poor,* which also affected and enabled the creation of liberal policies, see Barbara Ehrenreich's *Fear of Falling* (1989). For a seminal text in this genre, see Michael Harrington's *The Other America* (1992).

5. For instance, SNCC endorsed the power of nonviolence within a Christian tradition and appealed to the conscience of opponents: "Non-violence, as it grows from the Judeo-Christian tradition, seeks a social order of justice permeated by love. Integration of human endeavor represents the first crucial step towards such a society." As reproduced in Massimo Teodori's *The New Left: A Documentary History* (1969), the full SNCC statement reads:

We affirm the philosophical or religious ideal of non-violence as the manner of our purpose, the presupposition of our belief, and the manner of our action.

Non-violence, as it grows from the Judeo-Christian tradition, seeks a social order of justice permeated by love. Integration of human endeavor represents the crucial step towards such a society.

Through nonviolence, courage displaces fear. Love transcends hate. Acceptance dissipates prejudice; hope ends despair. Faith reconciles doubt. Peace dominates war. Mutual regards cancel enmity. Justice for all over-throws injustice. The redemptive community supersedes immoral social systems.

By appealing to conscience and standing on the moral nature of human existence, nonviolence nurtures the atmosphere in which reconciliation and justice become actual possibilities.

Although each local group in this movement must diligently work out the clear meaning of this statement of purpose, each act or phase of our corporate effort must reflect a genuine spirit of love and good-will. (99–100)

6. For an early account of the early civil rights campaigns in Montgomery led by Martin Luther King Jr., see his *Stride Toward Freedom* (1958).

7. As cited by Ralph Abernathy in *And the Walls Come Tumbling Down* (1989), the original list of demands read as follows:

1. The enforcement of the open housing ordinance already on the book.
2. The amendment of the ordinance to include a provision that outlawed discrimination by owners as well as brokers.
3. An agreement by the Chicago Real Estate Board to drop their legal challenge to existing ordinances.
4. An agreement to end opposition to a state-wide open housing provision.
5. A demand that the Chicago Housing Authority stop building all public housing projects in slums.
6. A demand that the Public Aid Department stop discrimination practices.
7. A demand that the Public Aid Department stop discriminating in their lending practices.
8. A demand that local labor unions end all discriminatory practices.
9. A demand that those responsible for urban renewal in Chicago stop discriminating against black neighborhoods. (386)

8. In fact, as early as 1963, John Lewis, then president of SNCC, was appealing for a more meaningful "revolution" in the United States; he explicitly rejected the March on Washington's support of the proposed 1960 Civil Rights Act as inadequate. See John Lewis, "A Serious Revolution," in Teodori (1969, 100–102).

9. According to William Van Deburg in *New Day in Babylon: The Black Power Movement and American Culture, 1965–75* (1992, 31–32), Black Power originated on June 16, 1966:

On that date, in Greenwood, Mississippi, an assembly of civil rights workers and reporters heard Stokely Carmichael declare, "The only way we gonna stop them white men from whuppin' us is to take over. We been saying freedom for six years and we ain't got nothin'. What we gonna start saying now is Black Power!" The audience responded immediately. "Black Power!" they roared, some six hundred strong. Seizing the moment, Carmichael's associate Willie Ricks, jumped to the speakers platform. "What do you want?" he yelled. "Black Power!" the audience shouted in unison, "Black Power! Black Power! Black Power!"

10. Douglass McAdams, in *Political Process and the Development of Black Insurgency, 1930–1970* (1982), argues that the shift to Black Power by organizations such as SNCC or CORE affected the willingness of white liberals to fund their activities. As a consequence, at a time when Black Power was the dominant image of the civil rights movement, especially after the assassination of Martin Luther King Jr., it was the NAACP that attracted the most funding and, as a consequence, was able to further consolidate its organizational capacities.

11. See SNCC, "The Basis of Black Power," *New York Times,* August 5, 1966.

12. Bobby Seale, Lecture, African Studies Program, Temple University, March 19, 1996. For an extended discussion of this point, see Bobby Seale's *Seize the Time* (1991), which traces the emergence of the Black Panther Party from earlier efforts, such as the Soul Students Advisory Council.

13. It is important to note, however, that the Panthers as a party never took on the arguments of the African cultural movement. That is, in works such as *Seize the Time* (1991), Seale argues that Cultural Nationalists failed to work adequately with the community to change actual economic structures or to engage the urban underclass.

14. In "The Black Panther Party: Platform and Program," the details of their agenda are outlined. See Teodori (1969, 283).

15. When the Black Panthers did participate in traditional labor union alliances, it was often to support "radical" movements within unions, such as DRUM. For a statement on such alliances and the political stance of the Black Panthers, see Hewitt (1995).

16. See Teodori (1969) for "The Black Panther Party: Platform and Program." For writings that reflect the Black Panther social viewpoint, see G. Louis Heath's *Off the Pigs: The History and Literature of the Black Panther Party* (1976).

17. In his "Letter" (1960), Mills points to the following as examples of the "young intelligentsia":

In the spring and early summer of 1960—more of the returns from the American decision and default are coming in. In Turkey, after student riots, a military junta takes over the state, of late run by Communist Container Menderes. In South Korea, too, students and others knock over the corrupt American-puppet regime of Syngman Rhee. . . . On Okinawa—a U.S. military base—the people get their first chance since World War II ended to demonstrate against U.S. seizure of their island; and some students take that chance, snake-dancing and chanting angrily, to the visiting President: "Go home, go home,—take your missiles." . . . And even in our own pleasant Southland, Negro and white students are—but let us keep that quiet; it really is disgraceful. (22–23)

18. For a detailed history of SDS, as well as LID, see Kirkpatrick Sale's *SDS* (1973).

19. For an account of an ERAP project, see "Summer Report, Newark Community Union" (1966). Also see Richard Rothstein's "Evolution of the ERAP Organizers" (1969).

20. For a detailed history of ERAP, see Kirkpatrick Sale's *SDS* (1973). Experiences of ERAP organizers, as well as theoretical documents, can be found in Teodori's *The New Left: A Documentary History* (1969).

21. For a personal account of how ERAP influenced the internal politics of SDS, see Todd Gitlin's *The Sixties: Year of Hope, Days of Rage* (1987).

22. The phrase "knowledge factories" echoed Clark Kerr's (1963) argument that the most important industry in the future would be the "knowledge industry" and that "the university is at the center of the knowledge process."

23. Such criticism and advice, however, ignored the extent to which, during the late 1950s and early 1960s, organized labor was under attack by Bowlerism, a general corporate strategy to improve production by increasing technological investment and seeking a reduction in union shop-floor control. As detailed by Mike Davis, "This strategy by management included the freezing of wage increases and the elimination of small groups of workers to gain concessions not originally in the union contract." At the same time, corporations were attempting to speed up the production line and shift factories to the south. These moves had the effect of blunting the power of labor (Davis 1986, 123–126). In response, during 1959 and 1960, miners, meat cutters, and longshoremen waged long labor strikes and work stoppages. Companies such as GE responded by using management to keep plants open and initiating a campaign to break the strike. Finally, the unions had to go back to work, losing cost-of-living increase allowances (COLAs) and allowing incentive pay (a precondition to speeding up production lines). That is, the major unions in the United States were politically unable to maintain the very struggles SDS was advocating. Further, by participating in an argument which portrayed as unions out of touch with the needs of working people, SDS was unintentionally participating in the conservative formation of an antiunion stance.

24. Mark Kleiman (1966) writes:

The radicalization of high school students is a much more realistic goal. The key to radicalization is development of self-respect and confidence. We must do for the high school student, essentially what Malcolm did for the Negro people. We must help students develop a sense of identity, and a feeling that they can change the quality of their lives. Changes such as this may be most easily brought about in conflict situations. . . . Forcing an administration to back down on the question of long hair creates a community of people who sense the potentialities of united action and supports their realization of the fact they are indeed individuals.

25. For a similar account, see Steve Halliwell, "Columbia: An Explanation" (1969).

26. For an analysis of SDS as an organization susceptible to takeovers from minority groups, see "The End of SDS and the Emergence of Weatherman: Demise through Success," in *Social Movements of the Sixties and Seventies* (1983).

27. In its constitutional preamble (NUC 1969a), the NUC characterized itself as follows:

The New University Conference (NUC) is a national organization of radicals who work in, around, and in spite of institutions of higher education. Formed in a time of imperialist war and domestic repression, the NUC is part of the struggle for the liberation of all peoples. It must therefore oppose imperialism, racism, economic exploitation and male supremacy.

We believe that institutions derive legitimacy and have the right to exist only to the extent that they serve the people. We see campuses not as havens, but as the immediate, though not exclusive settings for most of our activities.

We join all those committed to struggle politically to create a new, American form of socialism and to replace an educational and social system that is an instrument of class, sexual and racial oppression with one that belongs to the people.

28. Concern for faculty "isolation" was not just a personal matter. As the history of McCarthyism had shown, politically oriented professors had been the target of politically motivated firings. Whereas the 1960s might have created a tentative public space for professors to be politically active within the walls of the academy, such political work could still result in firings and demotions. In organizing professionals, then, one of the aims of the NUC would be to protect faculty whose political activity and research put them at odds with the university. Certainly, in "A Student Syndicalist Movement" (Davidson 1966), professors had been represented as reluctant advocates of change. Even in earlier student protest organizations, such as the Berkeley FSM or SDS, professors had played important, yet reluctant, roles. For the NUC, part of their reluctance grew from the university system's political use of the tenure decision. The NUC argued that academic standards were being used to discriminate against the nontraditional scholar, whose antiwar activities were seen as nonacademic or even antiacademic behavior. In

particular, through its newsletter, the NUC attempted to highlight the ways in which tenure and academic standards were used against particular professors. In "Whence Cometh the Axe? An Editorial" (1969), the cases of Jessie Lemisch and Staughton Lynd are discussed. The following conclusion is drawn: "In neither of the above cases were academic credentials questioned. In both cases an administration, sensitive to the outside conservative forces which supplied the funds and the power, acted in keeping with its cosmic bureaucratic role—to keep the machine running smoothly." The NUC, however, was never able to successfully defend a professor's dismissal. Instead, it attempted to create an academic job network where members could be hired. This inability to protect "their own" limited the effectiveness of the organization.

CHAPTER 2

New Left Politics and the Process Movement

Huck and Jim stand out as the only characters who put human values first. One can argue that their superior humanity is ironically related to their disapproved language. The point is not to wax sentimental about noble ignorance. Instead it is to note that Jim and Huck with their "inferior" dialects are people somewhat outside the American system. They have not been as successfully socialized into its racist values as Tom Sawyer, a middle class character, has been. The slave and the son of the ne'er-do-well know that the society considers property rights sacred, but they have not really internalized the idea that slaves are property first and human beings second if at all. But Tom can, without compunction, treat Jim as an object at the end of the novel. After all that is what he is expected to do as an adult solid citizen with versed interests in a slave society. It should be no surprise that both his attitude and his dialect differs from Huck's.

MARY TYLER KNOWLES, BETTY RESNIKOFF, AND
JACQUELINE ROSS, *"Who(m) Does Standard English Serve?
Who(m) Does Standard English Hurt?"*

A couple of years ago I read the complete Life and Times of Frederick Douglass, *a man I had long admired. He told of being sent to a professional slave-breaker known for his ability to crush the spirit of young men grown too thoughtful and independent. Looking back on receiving the full treatment, Douglass said:*

My natural elasticity was crushed, my intellect languished; the disposition to read departed, the cheerful spark that lingered about my eye died out. . . .

> *An apt description of students sitting row after row be-*
> *fore the lecturer in American universities. Walk down*
> *the hall and look in the open doors.*
>
> KEN MACRORIE, *Uptaught*

It is a peculiar fact about the SRTOL that there seem to exist no documents which detail how its name came into existence. Even if such a document could be found, the process of finding the true origin would be difficult at best. Instead, it is more appropriate to examine how the larger social arguments concerning a student's rights and a student's language affected composition scholars' definition of a writing student, for as noted previously, discussions concerning student rights were growing primarily out of organizations such as SNCC or SDS, which were turning increasingly against the politics of the Cold War. For composition scholars, the question became, How did these new student politics interact with the goals of writing instruction? How did such politics fit into discussions over a student's language?

Elements within the process movement attempted to provide answers to these questions. Developing concurrently with the emergence of Student Power and Black Power, this movement and its participants also attempted to critique Cold War policies and their effects on education. Unlike the aforementioned organizations, however, process advocates did not directly confront the U.S. capitalist culture. Instead, process advocates focused on the protection of a student's language. At academic conferences, such as Dartmouth, and in academic works, such as Ken Macrorie's *Uptaught* (1970), arguments were made for increased attention to the knowledge and language that students brought into the classroom. Through such a gesture, it was hoped that the writing classroom could be liberated from the economic and military needs of the Cold War United States.

The activism of the 1960s, however, placed the process movement's concern for protecting a student's language into the realm of militant politics. As the decade proceeded, process advocates witnessed their rhetoric of individuality being appropriated into larger social arguments about race and class. In particular, NUC activists attempting to reform the CCCC found in the process rhetoric a conceptual tool to expand the goals of the writing classroom into the New Left political realm. Consequently, although process advocates were not necessarily linked to the New Left, as the 1960s drew to a close, certain elements of their rhetoric became permeated by and associated with the New Left and progressive social movements. To understand the ability of the NUC to gain initial acceptance in the CCCC, then, the politics of the process movement must first be examined.

Protecting Students' Language

As discussed in chapter 1, Cold War politics affected the development of the CCCC. It also affected the development of composition studies. The 1957 Soviet launching of the Sputnik satellite produced an expansion of federal funding for university research, educational reforms, and curricular restructuring on an unprecedented scale.[1] Funded under the National Defense Education Act of 1958 (NDEA), these moneys were used principally to support projects in the hard sciences, yet the lesson of Sputnik did not go unheeded in other circles. Organizations such as the NCTE realized they needed to imagine a new relationship to national politics and the economy if their initiatives were to be funded. As discussed in chapter 1, *The National Interest and the Teaching of English* (1958; NITE) was the NCTE's attempt to embed writing instruction in the Cold War liberal welfare state. In fact, NITE was credited with producing Project English, a project added in 1964 when the Cooperative Research Program was amended to include English composition (North 1987, 18).

Project English, however, was seen as a latecomer to curriculum reform. In "The Government and English Teaching: A Retrospective View" (1967), Albert Kitzhaber argued that Project English "was, in the first place, little more than a somewhat delayed reflex reaction to the stimulus provided by Russian scientific achievements. In this respect, it was like the New Science and the New Math, an outgrowth of the Cold War" (135).[2] Initially, Project English attempted to incorporate the recent insights of Jerome Bruner concerning curriculum reform. In *The Process of Education* (1960), Bruner had written:

> The scientists constructing curricula in physics and mathematics have been highly mindful of the problem of teaching the structure of their subjects, and it may be that their early successes have been due to this emphasis. (8)

As a consequence, Project English argued for an English curriculum that would focus on the student as a participant within the discipline of English—a discipline which NITE had argued was integral to the national economic and political interest. As Bruner himself noted, however, what constituted a discipline, particularly in its relationship to the social and political life in which the student would participate, was a contentious question.

> The construction of curricula proceeds in a world where changing social, cultural, and political conditions continually alter the surroundings and the goals of schools and their students. We are concerned with curricula designed for Americans, for their ways and their needs in a complex world. Americans are a changing people; their geographical mobility makes imperative some degree of uniformity among high schools and primary schools. Yet the diversity of American communities and of American life in general makes equally imperative some degree of variety in curricula. . . . [T]here are also requirements for productivity to be met; are we producing enough scholars, scientists, poets, lawmakers, to meet the demands of our times? Moreover, schools must also contribute to the social and emotional development of the child if they are to fulfill their function of education for life in a democratic community and for fruitful family life. (8–9)

In the particular case of English studies, the question became, What were the general goals of the teaching of literature and writing in the United States? How did these goals interact with the increasing variety of university and college student populations? How did the need for increased focus on "English" and "diversity" intersect with Bruner's warning about the need to also produce "scholars, scientists, poets, [and] lawmakers"? What was the relationship of English studies to the Cold War?

As discussed in chapter 1, in the years since Sputnik, university professors and students had begun a sea change in their attitude toward the Cold War. In 1958, NDEA science and mathematics projects occurred in the context of broad public and university support for scientific and weapons research. By the time English scholars met at the Dartmouth Conference in 1966, the civil rights movement, coupled with the quickly emerging antiwar movement, had put in place forces which would begin to question the status of the university. Indeed, as shown in chapter 1, the university's relationship to weapons production, multinational corporations, and the Vietnam War would lead to student strikes and street protests. By the beginning of the 1970s, these actions would result in black studies and women's studies programs. Writing some twenty years earlier, Bruner had imagined a discipline connected in general terms to the maintenance of the social and economic fabric. Many of these emerging forces, policies, programs, and courses, however, would act as a critique of higher education's previous relationship to the status quo.

The disciplinary structure imagined by Bruner to be self-evident, then, was in the process of being altered by the emerging politics of 1960s social movements. As a consequence, it became difficult to define not only a student's relationship to a discipline, but also the relationship between a student's prior knowledge and the goals of a university education. In 1969, the NUC would present resolutions asking the CCCC to recognize and support efforts which would create "working class courses for working class students, women's studies courses for women students, and black studies courses for black students" (NUC 1969b). As discussed in chapter 1, in presenting this resolution, the NUC was attempting to align academic disciplines, such as composition studies, against the Cold War policies which had precipitated such efforts as Project English. With its departure from Cold War sensibilities and its partial endorsement of emerging social forces, the Dartmouth Conference might be seen as the opening gesture toward such a possibility within composition studies proper.

Unlike earlier NDEA curricular efforts in science and mathematics, the Dartmouth Conference would not endorse a vision of English studies that overtly supported Cold War political and economic goals. Nor would it justify English in terms of its effects on the national economy, as had NITE. In fact, in *Uses of English* (1967), Herbert J. Muller attempted to speak on behalf of the conference against such a characterization of English:

> [Today, the] national interest is defined in much more insistently practical terms. The billions that the government is spending on education and research are going chiefly to science and technology, primarily for the sake of the cold war; Congress would never appropriate such sums to support research for its educational value or for the disinterested pursuit of truth. Similarly the main argument for the little support English is beginning to get is the practical importance of "communication skills." (174)

Yet in distancing himself from elements of Cold War politics, Muller is careful not to invoke the more radical image of the New Left or Black Power. Instead, he argues that English can provide an education in larger democratic values than currently possible within the Cold War framework.

> Hence the plainest need in education today is to maintain other values that were fostered by the democratic principle of equality—the right of every person to have a mind and a life of his own, and the value of realizing his individuality. As for the study of literature, it may promote national unity, but it is more clearly helpful in the development of personality and of respect for quality. (35)

Given the historical context of 1966, in which Black Power had questioned the ability of democratic politics to support social change for African Americans, it seems Muller is aligning Dartmouth with more moderate politics, such as those of the early civil rights movement, for as the early civil rights movement had, Muller is clearly invoking a traditional conception of democracy and its goals.

This connection becomes more evident when Muller's goals are translated into practice. For within the writing classroom, this call for equality is translated into a concern for the individual student's language. According to John Dixon's report on the Dartmouth Conference, *Growth Through English* (1966), the process movement would focus the writing classroom on the particular experience of the student:

> A teacher of English, one could well say, spends his time in his better hours discovering *through* his pupils. This is not hyperbole. It follows inevitably if we accept personal experience as the vital core of English work. Then "good" creative work can only be spontaneous, and the teacher works best when he works with opportunities as they arise. (48)

Such an emphasis pushed the teacher toward an acceptance of a student's language as the starting place for classroom practice.

> [O]ne starts in teaching from a respect for each pupil as he is, and that means for what expresses his identity, notably his language. (49)

> One of the most intimate possessions of a person is his dialect. . . . The identification of the child with his community and his relationship to it must be protected. (30–31)

The resulting writing process, then, would initially ignore issues of grammar and correctness to make the student's experience of primary importance:

> Whatever our attitude to the forms of language, spoken or written, we have to leave the way open for things of importance to be said—to retain the position of trust. (18)

From these texts, the picture emerges of a classroom in which equality is initially attained through a protection and recognition of a student's language. In this way, the Dartmouth Conference can also be seen as bringing in and legitimating a variety of dialects.

The Dartmouth Conference does not, however, discuss how recognizing differing dialects might produce differing political viewpoints in the classroom. For instance, neither Muller's nor Dixon's text addresses what the introduction of such dialects, such as Black English, would mean to the general process of teaching composition or English. For Black Power or NUC advocates, however, the recognition of the Black English dialects would have been less an issue of emotional well-being (protecting dialects as a means to protect a student's self-image) than of political rights. In the case of the Black Panthers, such political rights would have called for an economic restructuring of the United States. Dartmouth does not seem to invoke such economic democracy. Instead, the political difficulties in recognizing dialects is embedded within a traditional view of the possibilities of American democracy—possibilities defined to a great extent by the politics of the liberal welfare state.

As had other documents that are discussed throughout this book, Dixon (1966) attempts to state the possibility of social and linguistic harmony through the voice of an African American. In line with the goals of the early civil rights movement, he cites the following passage from Ralph Ellison:

> So, in a world of insecurity and status preoccupations [as Ralph Ellison argued], "one uses the language which helps to preserve one's life, which helps to make one feel at peace with the world, and which screens out the greatest amount of chaos." . . . But "if you can show me," he goes on, "how I can cling to that which is real in me, while teaching me the way into the larger society, then I will . . . drop my defenses and my hostility." (19)

Under such a vision, if the English teacher could show how entry into larger society would not mean the abandonment of personal and cultural histories, students would not, it seems, be hostile to standard English instruction. According to Muller (1967), the English teacher could thus help to "overcome divisions between kinds of human beings [and] the deplorable social effects of separating and classifying youngsters" (20). It appears, then, that Dartmouth Conference participants such as Muller and Dixon hoped for a public sphere which would respond to the legitimately voiced concerns of students.

Participants in the conference were not naive, however, in expecting the actions of a composition or English teacher to change the social and political climate of the United States. If democracy and equality were the goals, they were not facts. During this time, the African American public had witnessed the unwillingness of Chicago's white working class to accord even the most basic of housing rights to them. In fact, when Dixon (1966) later states the general social and linguistic principles that justify an acceptance of an individual's language, he notes:

> Whatever the dialect, learning to use a regional variety of standard spoken . . . involves wanting to be accepted by speakers already using it. Social segregation in more or less extreme forms exists . . . and while it does, the children and young people who suffer from it are unlikely to see adequate reasons for changing their dialect. (19)

To fulfill the goals of the writing classroom, then, teachers also needed to participate in reforming the public sphere. Dartmouth does not, however, provide a blueprint for such work.

Nor does Ken Macrorie's *Uptaught* (1970) provide such a plan, despite its invocation of national politics and African American struggles, for as had other documents, Macrorie cites the history of African Americans to legitimate his own political work. That is, African American struggles for social equality become equated with his struggle to enable an English student's quest for personal freedom. Throughout his text, Macrorie repeatedly invokes the metaphor of slavery. He refers to teachers and students as "overseers" and "slaves." As quoted in the epigraph to this chapter, Macrorie also equates the effects of English instruction to the slave-breaking techniques suffered by Frederick Douglass. Macrorie's proof for such assertions are that currently students write papers that are stilted, boring, and wordy. Their prose, he states, is not "English," but "Engfish."

In response to this situation, Macrorie (1970) argues that writing teachers need to turn to the students' own experience and language. Throughout his book, Macrorie cites campus politics, the draft, and the lack of input in university policies as issues that matter most to students. Shifting to the social politics of the students' lives, he argues, would produce literate and well-written student papers. Yet while the paper from which the principal term of his text is drawn is decidedly nonconformist it is also decidedly nonpolitical:

A student stopped me in the hall and said, *"Do you think I should submit this to* The Review? *I have this terrible instructor who says I can't write. Therefore I shouldn't teach English. He really grinds me."*

I looked at the first two lines;

He finks it humorous to act like the Grape God Almighty, only the stridents in his glass lisdyke him immersely.

and thought they seemed like overdone James Joyce. I said I had better take the paper home and give it several readings before reacting. But she pushed, and I read the next lines,

Day each that we tumble into the glass he sez to mee, "Eets too badly that you someday fright preach Engfish."

I wanted to hug that girl. She had been studying Joyce in another class and had used his tongue to indict all of us Engfish teachers. . . .This girl had given me a name for the bloated, pretentious language I saw everywhere around me . . . [a] dialect in which words are almost never "attached to things," as Emerson said they should be. (18)

In discussing his success at combating "Engfish," he argues: "[I] had broken through and the students were speaking in their own voices about things that counted for them" (21). Within such a rubric, the ability of students to write in "their own language" becomes the political equivalent of escaping from slavery (or in the case of Joycean rhetoric, British colonialism). The escape, however, seems to have few social implications or little future involvement in actual movement activities.[3] "Engfish" seems to be cut off from the actual political movements which are part of the students' experience.

Indeed, in evaluating the larger political purposes and influences of Macrorie's (1970) work, an interesting argument could be made that Macrorie's primary influence was not the Dartmouth Conference or Black Power, but the Yippie movement. Despite its rhetoric of social justice, the Yippie movement's emphasis on personal liberation also raised questions about its political efficacy. And, in fact, there are parallels in both argument and structure between Macrorie's text and Yippie texts, such as Abbie Hoffman's *Revolution for the Hell of It* (1968). For instance, like Macrorie, Hoffman compares the situation of white students to "slaves":

> Runaways are the backbone of the youth revolution. We are all runaways, age is irrelevant. A fifteen-year-old kid who takes off from the middle-class American life is an escaped slave crossing the Mason-Dixon line. They are hunted down by professional bounty hunters, fidgety relatives and the law, because it's against the law to leave home (translate: bondage) until you have finished your servitude. (74)

Such a political characterization performs two acts simultaneously. First, it trivializes the actual situation of slaves (as does Macrorie). Second, it attempts to turn the historical oppression by white landowners into a symbol of middle-class oppression, an attempt which in its own way is an act of violence. These gestures deny the actual political and economic causes for "runaways" or "Engfish" and, in doing so, dilute and transmogrify the actual import of the civil rights/Black Power movement. Therefore, although both Macrorie's and Hoffman's texts act as if they are radical gestures toward freedom, they fail to perform a self-critique of their own political writings. In this way, these texts might be seen as radically nonpolitical in their attempts to "liberate" students.

Given an absence of an overt political agenda to intercede in the public sphere and the use to which other political movements are put, the work of Macrorie (1970) and the process movement has come to be seen as reactionary.[4] Certainly, some of its practitioners directly argued against the social movements of the 1960s. In "Finding Your Own Voice: Teaching Composition in an Age of Dissent" (1969), Donald Murray commends the process movement for its ability to contain the student protests then occurring. Surveying the then-current political terrain, Murray finds it lacking in coherent content. To improve the situation, he argues that the attention to student language is the first step to producing informed public debate. Further, as had the Dartmouth Conference, Murray argues that once students see the ability of standard English to disseminate their concerns to a larger audience, students will not feel as much distress in learning an additional dialect.

To make his argument, however, Murray must misread the student movement's history. First, Murray (1969) ironically trumpets the success of Student Power at the very moment that at least one prominent student organization, SDS, was abandoning it as a central principle of their organization (see chapter 1). Second, in his essay, he never quotes or cites any of the written material being published by the underground student press or by leading student organizations or activists. Instead, he writes:

> Student Power is no longer an issue, it is a fact. The war is being won—or lost—depending on your viewpoint, and one of the major weapons in the war is rhetoric that is crude, vigorous, usually uninformed, frequently obscene, and often threatening. (118)

Murray's vision of the student movement appears to be based upon the second wave of the Free Speech Movement at Berkeley. As noted earlier, whereas the first wave of the Free Speech Movement was dominated by demands that students be accorded the right to political speech, the second wave, which began with a student displaying the word "FUCK," concerned the limits of offensive speech, yet it is this second wave which Murray (1969) discusses:

> The free speech movement may start with dirty words, but a cliché is a cliché, and if the audience is not shocked or frightened by short transitive verbs, then the student can go on to say what he has to say. (122)

Having ignored the actual political content of the first Free Speech Movement, and given the perceived lack of "legitimate" political discussion occurring, Murray (1969) argues that students need to learn what free speech and political speech actually imply. (Any sampling of the actual extended documents produced by the Free Speech Movement would have demonstrated a knowledge of legitimate political discussion by the participants.) In the spirit of Dartmouth, Murray proposes turning the classroom into a workshop on civic responsibility. He writes:

> Democracy is forged out of a responsible Babel, and the mature English teacher welcomes a diversity of contradictory voices, each student speaking of his own concerns in his own way. There is no single standard, no one way to think or write, and we must not give our students [such an impression]. . . . Each teacher should be a revolutionary, doubting, questioning, challenging, and above all, encouraging his students to be individuals. He creates a constructive chaos which will allow the students to achieve effective communication. (118)

Yet at that time within popular political discourse, *revolutionary* stood for a large social movement that critiqued the United States' policies and culture. Murray, however, does not appear to intend such a view of the writing teacher. That is, while no one sector of the U.S. populace could be said to dictate what *revolutionary* meant, given the nature of Murray's essay, he appears to be softening the meaning generated by New Left or Black Panther activity. Rather, his view is much more in line with the idea of *democracy* presented at the Dartmouth Conference.

For instance, in his 1972 essay "Teach Writing as Process Not Product" (in Murray 1982), Murray reiterates his commitment to a classroom dominated by the student's voice and the student's language:

> The student uses his own language. Too often, as writer and teacher Thomas Williams points out, we teach English to our students as if it were a foreign language. Actually, most of our students have learned a great deal of language before they come to us, and they are quite willing to exploit that language if they are allowed to embark on a serious search for their own truth. (16)

Murray (1969) argues, however, that once "educated," the student protester can be part of a national tradition where "teen-age pioneers, sea captains in their early twenties, and statesman in their early thirties" have all contributed to the prosperity of the United States (118). (Murray leaves unstated any historical inequity that might have marked this "prosperity." Nor does his history take into account the ways different sexes and races experienced this "national tradition.") That is, his texts work to contain student resistance, as represented in a dialect, through an invocation of a democratic heritage. Murray's final goal of a literate democratic population thus imagines the same end point to the work on a students' language that was endorsed by the Dartmouth Conference. Both endorse a common view of democracy. Neither imagines how such work refigures the teacher as a political being nor how writing instruction interacts with social forces, such as the New Left or Black Power. In this sense, certainly part of the process movement can be seen as reactionary in terms of leftist politics.

But there were also at this time process movement textbooks that attempted to connect a students' language to leftist social politics. It is this element of the process movement that most clearly has allegiances to the NUC. For example, Dick Friedrich and David Kuester's *It's Mine and I'll Write It That Way* (1972) attempted to represent what political language would look like in the classroom. Published in the year in which the SRTOL was passed, the book is dedicated to Elisabeth McPherson and Gregory Cowan, two principal activists for leftist politics and the SRTOL in the CCCC. Like Macrorie's *Uptaught* (1970), Friedrich and Kuester's text presents itself as a "non-textbook." The graphics in the book are bold, invoking "Yellow Submarine" animated borders. In its list of acknowledgments are Abbie Hoffman, Jerry Rubin, Che Guevera, and other New Left luminaries. While the book echoes a respect for, and use of, student language in the classroom, its message is overtly political. It states that "language is a common property, and it's up to students to redefine what it means." This emphasis is clear from the opening sentences of chapter 1:

> "Hi there." "How's it going?" "I love you." "What this country needs is courageous, imaginative, and responsible leadership." "We are engaged in a massive attempt to pacify this village." These look like words, don't they? We can look them up in the dictionary and find out what they mean. And when we use them we know that our listener will understand. So we use them and talk and write and live and die with our mouths and pens constantly moving. Using words. (7)

Within the text, students are asked to redefine key words in American society according to their interpretation, their language.

In recording a conversation held in class, Kuester writes:

> [A]ll I want to say is this: the flag is here to serve us. We are not here to serve it. We are not imprisoned by the past, or by someone else's definition of patriotism. We can adapt the symbol to a new reality.
>
> And we can do that with words like "love" and "justice" and "freedom" and "equality," too.
>
> We can change our definitions of these words. We are no more enslaved by the past than we are by the flag. In fact, we are less enslaved by it, because no one has yet passed laws saying you can't mutilate the language, or tear up things you've written, and start over. (15)

Certainly, within the confines of the text, Friedrich and Kuester ask students to call upon their own experiences and their own languages to redefine key terms in their lives. Unlike the Dartmouth Conference, however, the imagined students here are in touch with the social and political climate of the New Left. Consequently, the political dynamics of choosing a language are necessarily wrapped up in the rejection of other languages. According to the parameters of the text, then, choosing one's own language represents taking a stance on the political and social issues of the day.

It soon becomes evident, however, that this text suffers from many of the same uncritical appropriations of African American culture as Macrorie's (1970) or Hoffman's (1968) texts. As with Macrorie's text, Friedrich and Kuester attempt to justify this writing classroom through a romanticization of African Americans. That is, this invocation to students to "start over" becomes symbolized in the writing journey of an African American student named Vernon. Within the text, the reader learns that Vernon "was originally placed in a remedial English class because he couldn't spell." Prefiguring literary figures used by the SRTOL language statement (1968), Kuester writes, "Couldn't spell! I think I remember that Ernest Hemingway couldn't spell. And neither could F. Scott Fitzgerald. But we go right on placing people in writing courses on the basis of spelling" (124). What appears to make such moments different from Macrorie's text or the Dartmouth Conference is the extent to which when Vernon "chooses" his own language, as opposed to "doing the assignment," it is not the voice of the "founding fathers." Instead, it is the voice of the Black Power movement, with its critique of the international and economic goals of the United States, that appears:

> *The characters are the President, whose name is Fascism, the first Rap, whose name is War Hawk, the second Rap whose name is Right Wing. The third Rap is A-Political Major General Du Won, whose name is Down East. Lieut. Col. Ebow O. J., whose name is Uncle Sam Tom.*
>
> *The scene is somewhere on Wall Street. The President and his raps are having a meeting about the political situation in Nigeria. Rap Three is over at the bar mixing cocktails. Rap Two is on the phone trying to line him up a chick.*

PRES: Boys, I have been getting alot of pressure from the tire manufactures about this major Gen. Du Won down in Nigeria. He is beginning to ask them for the land back they stole from his people.

RAP 1: That's the way those uppity niggers are. I say let's burn them.

RAP 2: Mr. President, the CIA informed me last night concerning a Lieut. Colonel by the name of Ebow O. J.

PRES: Yes, I heard about him. He was schooled in the West. He is a good man. What is he doing now?

RAP 2: He has some followers and he wants to set up his own government in Southern Nigeria.

RAP1: I say let's burn them. That's the American way.

PRES: What is the CIA doing about it?

RAP 2: They're supplying him with guns and money.

RAP 1: Let's drop the A-bomb on them niggers and take the country. That's the way we did with the Japs. Oh, wasn't it a great day for the American people. I hear they are still finding arms and legs over there.

RAP 3: Oil, diamonds, uranium, copper, gold, iron, rubber. (He keeps repeating this over and over.) . . .

At this point, the President picks up the phone. . . .

PRES: Hello, O. J. This is the President of the USA. That's right, the President. I hear you want to set up a government. Well, we are going to help you. We will do it like this. You see, we can't get involved. So we will give the Red Cross some planes, weapons, money, and they will be your contact from now on . . . . Tell me, why do you want to set up your own government?

O. J: Well, you see, Mr. President, this major General Du Won is against the Ebows and the wealthy of the country. He says he wants a country where the workers are regarded according to their output and production, so that everybody will be able to get what he needs regardless of the difference in abilities to produce the goods of life, and when it's done like that the Ebows will not be able to rule. It also means, Mr. President, that we will have to start producing because we don't produce no goods. We just own the factories. The workers produce the goods.

PRES: Your mind works just like an American. You will make a good puppet. (108–110)

The analysis that Vernon offers, then, is broadly in line with the internationalist viewpoint articulated and endorsed by Black Power advocates such as the Black Panthers. If this representation is to be believed, there is a sense in which the student is able to articulate a subject position that both delineates a position of power and is not immediately co-optable into a rhetoric of democracy or equality à la Dartmouth.

Friedrich and Kuester (1972) are uncomfortable, however, with this voice being expressed in the standard. Indeed, a later representation of Vernon demonstrates the extent to which he is called to fit an image of Black Power politics. Despite Kuester's earlier statement that Vernon's misspellings are not important, *it is Vernon* who wants to learn about spelling and transition rules. In a moment that echoes Ellison, Vernon wishes to know the "technical rules" of English so that he can express himself in standard English. Even though Kuester argues with Vernon that Black English represents a perfectly legitimate dialect, Vernon insists on learning the "rules":

I pointed out that his use of "ask" for past tense in his journal tonight was dialect. "But the truth is that upper-class and middle-class white speech—'asked'—is just another dialect."

"I know that," he said, "But I want to know it. Then I can choose."

So I'm teaching it to him, and we will see how he uses it, if at all. (90–91)

According to Friedrich and Kuester's text, the idea of an "own language" comes to represent the reconfiguring of a composition classroom away from spelling or grammar rules. Within such a classroom, language and writing instruction becomes a means by which to politicize the student population into what might largely be represented as Black Power or New Left ideologies. A desire to learn the "standard" is seen as either politically suspect or a sign of a consciousness not fully enlightened.

This representation of Vernon, then, is not innocent. While the text seems to successfully negotiate the twin demands of writing instruction and the political realm, it does so by reducing the actual complexity of language choice. Instead, it perpetuates the image of the English teacher as liberator—informing students of what their politics should be. Within Friedrich and Kuester's text, then, the writing classroom becomes the cutting edge for activism *by teachers*. The English teacher becomes the active enabler of social change. For instance, when recounting a discussion between a fellow teacher and himself, Kuester writes:

"You know something happened last semester?" he said.
"What's that?"
"Four of my students got Afro's."
"Oh."
"And you know why?"
I thought about how "naturals" were becoming the most popular hairstyle for blacks, but I didn't say anything.
"It was a direct result of what they learned about language."
(79)

In this scenario, it was only after this teacher "taught" them about language, presumably the politics of their own language, that Black Power could arise on campuses. While Kuester distances himself slightly from the teacher's naïveté, it does seem that his argument is that a good teacher is in touch with progressive social movements. But Friedrich and Kuester's text does not lead to a discussion of the teacher's role outside the classroom. That is, unlike the NUC, Kuester does not then go on to imagine the role of the teacher in non-classroom-based social activism, an activism in which the Black Panthers recognized the need for standard English. As in Macrorie's *Uptaught* (1970), politics becomes personal liberation, not the dynamics of group organization toward a political goal. That is, Friedrich and Kuester's text tries to be political without having to actually engage in the complexities of the political terrain.

Composition studies—as represented by the Dartmouth Conference, Macrorie (1970), Murray (1969), and Friedrich and Kuester (1972)—was not, however, the only site where the social role of writing instruction was being reevaluated. As noted in the previous chapter, the NUC also critiqued the university's relationship to government-directed Cold War research. In place of military research, the NUC argued that the university should concentrate its energies on improving the social life of its surrounding community. Instead of weapons research, research should be done to improve the social standing of low-income citizens. That is, as is evident in *Open Up the Schools* (1972; OUTS),[5] the NUC believed that a fundamental goal of education was to eliminate the racist and class-based society of the United States. This goal was actually an expansion upon Davidson's "A Student Syndicalist Movement" (1966), which had also argued that it was the duty of academics to produce a new type of student who would reform government and business practices. Davidson, however, had not specified what form such an education would actually take within a particular classroom. Although the NUC endorsed the general principles invoked by Davidson, OUTS had not articulated what this would mean practically for a writing classroom. Nor had it taken a position on what the status of different dialects would be in the classroom.

The beginning of a classroom practice is articulated in 1969 with "Who(m) Does Standard English Serve? Who(m) Does Standard English Hurt?" by Mary Tyler Knowles, Betty Resnikoff, and Jacqueline Ross. These authors, like Macrorie and other process practitioners, focus on the student's language. For these authors, however, the use of the English classroom to eradicate dialect differences does more than stifle individual freedom. For them, the emphasis on Standard English alienates working-class and minority students from their own dialects and discourses. Through consistent red marking of particular dialect expressions under the guise of "correct English," students are taught to be embarrassed or distanced from their own community. These authors argued that requiring standard English from working-class and minority students "downgrades them as human beings. The message they receive is that their home communities are inferior groups of people from whom they should separate themselves as quickly as possible if they want to embrace the American Dream" (4).

The NUC's emphasis on different dialects in classrooms, then, was aimed at demonstrating that certain cultural beliefs are used by the upper classes to stop the formation of a solid multiracial working-class movement. Knowles et al. (1969) argue that if "everyone were encouraged to use his or her own dialect in all situations (not just in the home or on the streets as several linguists have advocated) and, if no one dialect were given more prestige than another, one of the ideological props for the myth of upper-class intellectual superiority would be removed" (5). This is in line with the later incarnations of the Black Panthers, whom the NUC invoked in its OUTS program. As discussed in chapter 3, the Black Panthers endorsed a position of socialist class struggle as the 1960s progressed. Consequently, the call for a multiracial working-class movement was in line with the call for a unified Black Power movement, although the strategies and constituency alignments were left unarticulated.

Perhaps with a stronger justification than Macrorie (1970) or Hoffman (1968) had, then, the NUC persisted in the invocation of African American struggles to legitimate its goals and activities. In fact, as cited in the epigraph to this chapter, Knowles et al. (1969) argue for the existence of a common struggle among African Americans and working-class individuals through *The Adventures of Huckleberry Finn* and its characters of Huck and Jim. It is the NUC's race- and class-based reading of literature, and implicitly of student writing, which separates the NUC from the mainstream of the process movement. Unlike the process movement's attempts to reinvigorate the classroom though the use of a student's language, the NUC used the issue of dialect difference to initiate a discussion about the political and social policies of the United States. Unlike the Dartmouth Conference, the NUC was forcing the composition instructor to take up a political struggle to enforce the "right to one's own language." While the NUC's work is most similar to Friedrich and Kuester's (1972) text, these similarities also break down when the NUC's class analysis is taken into account.

At that historical moment, however, the work of Macrorie (1970) and Friedrich and Kuester (1972) was read as participating within the same social and political milieu as the more radical NUC forces. Although it is an act of self-aggrandizement when Macrorie in *Uptaught* recounts an episode in which he is called a "student lover," the image of the student invoked is the "Marxist internationalist student" whom Tom Hayden (Sale 1973) saw emerging from the Columbia student strike. In fact, Macrorie was actually a member of the NUC. It might be argued that Macrorie's own work does not participate in the larger social arguments only because he chose not to push process education to its alternative possibilities. As is demonstrated in later chapters, the type of politics that the NUC mission required ultimately led to the NUC's distancing itself from the work of those like Macrorie. At this point, however, the ambiguity led to an opening in the CCCC.

Conclusion

The process movement's attempt to separate writing instruction from Cold War politics centered around protecting the "students' language." The variety of politics defining this protection, however, gave the process movement texts an ambiguous status. While it is certainly true to say that the majority of these texts do not actively push a political agenda, it is also true that during the late 1960s it may have appeared otherwise. Consequently, the NUC had positioned itself as a unique entity. While appropriating much of the process movement's rhetoric concerning a student's language, it had embedded such rhetoric within a plan and an organization designed to affect the public sphere. In this way, the NUC represented an integration of public activism and classroom practice.

In chapter 4, I return to the NUC's attempts to politically organize academics. I also address what it meant to take a reiterated version of the Black Panther education program into an organization such as the CCCC. Before this, however, it is necessary to briefly examine how the civil rights and Black Power movement also affected the ways in which language politics worked. That is, it is important to see how language politics were also a part of the civil rights and Black Power movement. Chapter 3 thus focuses on attempts to redefine "Negro English" spoken by "Negroes" into "Black English" spoken by "African Americans." Through this examination, the discussion of the NUC's and CCCC's appropriation of the black-dialect speaker into their particular projects gains greater historical accuracy.

---

1. For a discussion of how such funding affected composition, see Stephen North, *The Making of Knowledge in Composition: Portrait of an Emerging Field* (1987).

2. For a more detailed account of Project English, see "Project English" by the United States Department of Health, Education, and Welfare's Office of Education (1962).

3. For a particular example of this apolitical writing, see Malcolm Huey's paper on pp. 29–30 of Macrorie (1970).

4. See Berlin (1988).

5. OUTS is discussed in detail in chapter 1.

CHAPTER 3

Black Power/Black English

Black Power is Black Language.

GENEVA SMITHERMAN,
"Black Power Is Black Language"

Take the English language. There are cats who come here from Italy, from Germany, from Poland, from France— in two generations they speak English perfectly. We have never spoken English perfectly, never have we spoken English perfectly, never, never, never. And that is because our people consciously resisted a language that did not belong to us. Never did, never will, anyhow they try to run it down our throat we ain't gonna have it, we ain't gonna have it. You must understand that as a level of resistance. Anybody can speak that simple honky's language correctly. Anybody can do it. We have not done it because we have resisted, resisted.

STOKELY CARMICHAEL, *"A Declaration of War"*

In attempting to situate the SRTOL in terms of a broader tradition of social and political activism, it was first necessary to delineate the ways in which 1960s social movements redefined the student's and the academic's relationship to the liberal welfare state. It was in part due to limitations placed upon African American activists by an alliance with the liberal welfare state that the possibility and actuality of Black Power emerged. But if Black Power was to affect the writing classroom, the politics that it expressed had to first be appropriated by the disciplinary concerns of writing teachers. To some extent, the politics of Black Power had to become associated with academic work on Black

English. To understand the SRTOL's relationship to the 1960s, then, it is important to understand the competing images of Black English during the period in which Black Power originated. This will make it possible in later chapters to judge the extent to which the SRTOL's valuing of Black English also entailed a commitment to the economic and political beliefs of Black Power. That is, did the SRTOL's recognition of Black English entail liberal welfare-state programs or an economic critique of the state? Did Black English represent the possibility of U.S. pluralism or its decline?

Such work is not intended, however, to provide a complete definition of Black English as a linguistic construct or a complete history of the debates surrounding its conception. Indeed, to adequately bring together the narratives of Black English and Black Power during the 1960s would be a book in itself. My purpose is more limited. I want to explore how the term *Black English* developed within the previously analyzed social forces, particularly its interaction with the already existing rhetorical and political strategies of the liberal welfare state. Such work demonstrates how the image of the black-dialect speaker, as articulated by figures such as Baraka or Carmichael, was then appropriated and refigured by progressive language scholars to support their conceptions of a politically forward-looking pedagogy. Before these connections became possible, however, the political possibilities of Black English had to emerge.

We Shall Overcome . . . Black English

In the previous chapters, the early civil rights movement was discussed in relationship to labor and Cold War politics. Only a passing reference was made concerning its rhetorical position on the role of ethnicity in U.S. history. As noted in chapter 1, during the Cold War period, labor portrayed its actions within a traditionalist U.S. rhetoric, symbolized in their flag-waving attacks on war protesters and their deliberate distancing from socialist members. Embedded in such actions was a belief in the *ethnic paradigm*, a paradigm largely created in the early twentieth century around European immigration to the United States. Central to this paradigm was a nationalism based upon the idea that new immigrant communities should seek to gain only the political power necessary to ensure traditional economic and political rights, that is, the right to a job, to buy a house, and so on. The goal was to become American by gaining the same individual liberties guaranteed to current citizens. To this extent, labor unions saw themselves as defending the "American way of life."

Initially, the ethnic paradigm would appear to be a positive force for African Americans and Black English. Indeed, Omi and Winant (1994, 14–23 passim) argue that the ethnicity creed was developed in opposition to the biological and scientific theories of race that had been used to define the "white man" as the pre-eminent example of "mankind." Under such theories, differences in intelligence, temperament, and sexuality, for instance, were deemed to be racial in character. Within this biological model, Black English had been used as "proof" that African Americans were inferior. Writing in 1884, J. A. Harrison argued that the "Negro" is biologically incapable of learning the higher forms, or more articulated codes, of English. He writes, "The humor and naïveté of the Negro are features which must not be over-looked in gauging his intellectual caliber and timbre; much of his talk is baby talk . . . the slang which is an ingrained part of his being as deep-dyed as his skin" (233). This reliance on an image of African Americans as mentally incapable of learning standard English continued into the early 1900s. Discussing the Gullah dialect of African Americans in "Gullah: A Negro Patois" (1908), John Bennet argues that Gullah English is the result of "negro ignorance . . . the quite logical wreck of once tolerable English, obsolete in pronunciation, dialectical in its usage, yet the natural result of a savage and primitive people's endeavor to acquire for themselves the highly organized language of a very highly civilized race" (338).

The ethnicity paradigm was intended to shift the discussion of race toward social factors. Accordingly, the question each immigrant group would now answer concerned its ability to live up to the "common circumstances" faced by previous immigrant groups. Omi and Winant (1994) argue that these circumstances were characterized by the "bootstraps" model, through which differences between immigrant groups were erased in the popular imagination and the European experience used as the common model. For Omi and Winant, such a theory had a necessarily conservative bent:

> Everything is mediated through "norms" internal to the group. If Chicanos don't do well in school, this cannot, even hypothetically, be due to low quality education; it has instead to do with Chicano values. After all, Jews and Japanese Americans did well in inferior schools, so why can't other groups. . . . It is the European immigrant analogy applied to all without reservation. (21)

Implicit within this conservative strain of the ethnicity paradigm, then, was an endorsement of the capitalist system, for the test of "being American" became the ability of a group to succeed economically. Or rather, ethnicity was used to reaffirm broad ideological aspects of U.S. capitalism.

During the 1920s, the ethnic paradigm thus created the possibility of a shift within language studies from a biological to a cultural explanation of differences. As previously noted, however, it did so through a traditionally conceptualized image of the United States. Unfortunately, Black English was not recast as representing the culture from which slaves initially came, the diverse community and social structures on the African continent. Instead, Black English became the place where eighteenth-century English still existed, although imperfectly learned. In "The English of the Negro" (1924), George Krapp clearly states this position:

> The Negro speaks English of the same kind and, class for class, of the same degree, as the English of the most authentic descendants of the first settlers at Jamestown and Plymouth.
> The Negroes, indeed, in acquiring English have done their work so thoroughly that they have retained not a trace of any native African speech. Neither have they transferred anything of importance from their native tongues to the general language. A few words, such as *voodoo, hoodoo,* and *buckra,* may have come into English from some original African dialect, but most of the words commonly supposed to be of Negro origin, e.g. *tote, jazz,* and *mosey,* are really derived from ancient English or other European sources. The native African dialects have been completely lost. (190)

For Krapp, the issue becomes the extent to which Black English forms can be traced or shown to be examples of literary or scientific standard English. He writes: "Generalizations are always dangerous, but it is reasonably safe to say that not a single detail of Negro pronunciation or of Negro syntax can be proved to have any other than an English origin" (191).

In fact, language scholars went so far as to argue that even Negro spirituals could be seen as imitations of white culture. In "The White Man in the Woodpile: Some Influences on Negro Secular Folk-Songs" (1929), Newman White writes that while the "majority of floating stanzas [in Negro secular songs] . . . originated in the minds of anonymous Negro singers . . . [t]here is a surprisingly large element in these songs which had an origin from without . . . the Negro Race." White argues that almost every element of Negro spirituals has its antecedents in the minstrel shows of the time: "The sources of these originally extraneous snatches are (1) traditional songs of the white people, (2) the ante-bellum minstrel stage, (3) the coon-songs writers of the 1890's and 1900's, (4) the vaudeville stage and 'ballet' writer . . . and, (5) the professional 'blues' composer" (209). He uses this set of influences to claim that the black spirituals were actually "a fairly accurate mirror of several of the more important song-crazes with which the whole country has been blest" (209). In this instance, black spirituals become the "degraded" record of American fad-music history. Concerning the ability of African Americans to create such "improvisational" work songs, White credits the "racial tendency toward variation and improvisation." Yet, ultimately, the racial quality he ends up associating with blacks is their "forgetfulness": "[A]s in the case of all other similar borrowings, the 'Negro' forgot that they were not originally his own" (210–211). Taken in combination, these language scholars present Black English as either the historical remnant of an earlier white Anglo-Saxon English or the result of low-culture song crazes. Within the "bootstraps" model of the ethnic paradigm, African Americans' inability to learn the proper English becomes a symbol of their "intellectual indolence" and "laziness." The result is a Black English characterized as "baby talk" and a culture which is not up to the norms of "American society."

Despite these limitations, the ethnicity paradigm was still a powerful tool for civil rights activists, for in the southern United States, civil rights activists found an economic and political system which was still based upon racial distinctions. In this situation, the ethnicity paradigm's shifting away from biologically based categories was an important lever in their struggle. To be used successfully, however, activists had to reinvent the image of African Americans within that paradigm. They had to work against theories that described African Americans as "culturally deprived." In negotiating these demands, then, the rhetoric of the early civil rights movement attempted to embed the collective subjectivity of African Americans within the ethnicity paradigm's traditional conception of the United States while simultaneously representing African Americans as the epitome of U.S. ideals.

This strategy is clear in texts such as King's *Stride Toward Freedom* (1958). In that work, King begins by recognizing the debilitating effects of racial segregation on individuals and communities. He then argues that through Christian love and the tactics of nonviolence, the Negro protesters were able to regain their dignity and pride, safely joining the true fabric of American values. For instance, when speaking to the Montgomery bus protesters for the first time, King argued that the long history of abuse and mistreatment had justified the actions Negroes were taking against the bus company, actions which the local government had tried to argue were against the law. "With this groundwork for militant action," King continued,

> I moved on to words of caution. I urged the people not to force anybody to refrain from riding the buses. "Our method will be that of persuasion, not coercion. We will only say to the people, 'Let your conscience be your guide.'" Emphasizing Christian doctrine of love, "our actions must be guided by the deepest principles of our Christian faith. Love must be our regulating ideal. Once again we must hear the words of Jesus echoing across the centuries: 'Love your enemies, bless them that curse you, and pray for them that spitefully use you.' If we fail to do this our protest will end up as a meaningless drama on the stage of history, and its memory will be shrouded with the ugly garments of shame." (51)

The boycott, King argued, had the ability to transform the self-image of the participants:

> During the rush hours the sidewalks were crowded with labor-ers and domestic workers, many of them well past middle age, trudging patiently to their jobs and home again, sometimes as much as twelve miles. They knew why they walked, and the knowledge was evident in the way they carried themselves. And as I watched them I knew that there is nothing more majestic than the determined courage of individuals willing to suffer and sacrifice for their freedom and dignity. (44)

The actions of this now revitalized community are then represented as part of the historical struggle of the United States to fulfill its ideals. Speaking of the lessons learned in the Montgomery campaign, King wrote:

> Along with the Negro's changing image of himself has come an awakening moral consciousness on the part of millions of white Americans concerning segregation. Ever since the Declaration of Independence, America has manifested a schizophrenic personality on the question of race. She has been torn between selves—a self in which she proudly professed democracy and a self in which she has sadly practiced the antithesis of democracy. The reality of segregation, like slavery, has always had to confront the ideals of democracy and Christianity. Indeed segregation and discrimination are strange paradoxes in a nation founded on the principle that all men are created equal. (154)

Within the early civil rights movement, then, there was created an image of the Negro protester as involved in efforts to complete the mandate of the Declaration of Independence; every Negro participant became a "freedom rider" working to fulfill the historical goals of the United States. Moments of harassment and injustice were recast as signs of the United States' failure to reach its own ideals. As King stated about his conviction for breaking the "anti-boycott laws,"

> I knew that I was a convicted criminal, but I was proud of my crime. It was the crime of joining my people in a nonviolent protest against injustice. It was the crime of seeking to instill within my people a sense of dignity and self-respect. It was the

crime of desiring for my people the *unalienable rights of life, liberty, and the pursuit of happiness.* It was above all the crime of seeking to convince my people that non-cooperation with evil is just as much a moral duty as is cooperation with good. (122, emphasis added)

According to King's rhetorical strategy, the Negro had been altered into a symbol of humanity at its best. Omi and Winant (1994) state, "to Martin Luther King, Jr., blacks were, collectively, the moral, spiritual, and political leadership of American society. They represented not only their own centuries-long struggle for freedom, but the highest and noblest aspirations of white America as well" (100). Yet, as noted in chapter 1, King had overtly tied the situation of African Americans to the situation of labor unions, the democratic party, and white liberals. Within this alliance, invoking the U.S. Constitution and the Declaration of Independence represents not just the fulfillment of U.S. ideals, but their fulfillment within the liberal welfare state.

The meaning of a rhetorical or political construction, however, cannot be limited by a particular context or intention; a particular instantiation of a rhetorical image can be made to serve contradictory or hostile social forces. If early civil rights activists hoped to use the ethnicity paradigm to reinvigorate cultural assumptions about African Americans, this same strategy was used by liberal forces in such a way as to reaffirm historical attitudes toward African American culture. For instance, although Lyndon Johnson explicitly argued for the elimination of racial discrimination, he did so within a model that reproduced negative images of minority communities. In a speech before a joint session of Congress, Johnson (1980) stated:

All Americans must have the privilege of citizenship regardless of race. And they are going to have those privileges of citizenship regardless of race.

But I would like to caution you and remind you that to exercise those privileges takes much more than just legal rights. It requires a trained mind and a healthy body. It requires a decent home, and the chance to find a job, and the opportunity to escape from the clutches of poverty.

Of course, people cannot contribute to the Nation if they are never taught to read or write, if their bodies are stunted from hunger, if their sickness goes untended, if their life is spent in hopeless poverty just drawing a welfare check.

So we want to open the gates of opportunity. But we are also going to give all our people, black and white, the help that they need to walk through those gates. (71)

As had King, Johnson invokes an image of the United States that demands attention to social injustice. Like King, he uses the image of the African American to link the fact of citizenship to the legal, educational, and social rights that should mark the United States:

> The real hero of this struggle is the American Negro. His actions and protests, his courage to risk safety and even to risk his life, have awakened the conscience of this Nation. . . . He has called upon us to make good the promise of America. And who among us can say that we would have made the same progress were it not for his persistent bravery, and his faith in American democracy? (70)

In taking on the rhetorical framework of the civil rights movement (even stating "we shall overcome" within the speech), however, Johnson offers a much different image of the minority communities than King does. Johnson argued that within the cultural requirements implicit in the ethnicity paradigm, minority cultures needed guaranteed access to mainstream institutions to "catch up." After having invoked the common rights of all citizens, Johnson (1980) then goes on to invoke his experience as a school teacher. He states,

> My first job after college was as a teacher in . . . a small Mexican-American school. Few of them could speak English, and I couldn't speak much Spanish. My students were poor and they often came to class without breakfast, hungry. They knew even in their youth the pain of prejudice. . . . I often walked home late in the afternoon . . . wishing there was more that I could do. But all I knew was to teach them the little that I knew, hoping that it might help them against the hardships that lay ahead. (71)

In a telegram to the National Educational Association, directly after his "Let Us Continue" speech, Johnson (1964) argues that the reason students do not succeed in continuing on to college after high school is primarily due to "financial inability or improper environmental or family motivation" (14). He had earlier characterized the culture within which those students exist as one where an adult's "life is spent in hopeless poverty just drawing a welfare check." According to Johnson's definition of the culture of poverty, more is needed than just personal growth or access to institutions. A reformation (or reconstruction) of a culture devastated by official discrimination is required.

Ultimately, Johnson's rhetoric produced government-funded research in education and public welfare. As this money began to produce results, a reinscription of historical attitudes toward African American culture occurred. Among those studying the culture and language of African Americans, for instance, was Martin Deutsch, who, in addition to receiving funding from the National Institute of Mental Health, was also supported by the Office of Economic Opportunity (a Johnson creation) and the Office of Education. In fact, Deutsch's work is emblematic of scholarship that focused on the African American community as "culturally deprived." In "Social Disadvantage as Related to Intellective and Language Development" (1968), co-written with Martin Whiteman, he tells the following story:

> One of the writers often drives through East Harlem on his way to work. There is a school on 111th Street, and as he stopped for a light one morning he noticed two Negro children, about ten years old, having a bit of friendly horseplay before going to class. One was banging the other over the head playfully with a notebook. But the notebook slipped out of his hand and fell into a puddle of water. The two children stared at the notebook and then suddenly turned toward each other with gales of laughter and walked off toward school arm in arm and without the notebook. A policeman who had been standing nearby walked over to the puddle with some degree of disbelief.
>
> This event can be understood in terms of a discontinuity between school requirements and the child's prior preparation and experiences. The child from a disadvantaged environment may have missed some of the experiences necessary for developing verbal, conceptual, attention and learning skills requisite to school success. These skills play a vital role for the child

in his understanding of the language of the school and the
teacher, in his adapting to school routines, and in his mastery
of such a fundamental school subject as reading. In this absence of the development of these skills by the child, there is a
progressive alienation of teacher from child and child from
teacher. In the school, the child may suffer from feelings of
inferiority because he is failing; he withdraws or becomes hostile, finding gratification elsewhere, such as in his peer group.
Notebooks may be left in puddles while camaraderie develops.
(86–87)

Apparently, it never occurs to either the linguist or the police
officer that a soaked notebook would not be much good for
school. Instead, Deutsch uses this instance as an example of his
larger argument that the African American family, in part due to
its cultural and economic status, fails to provide the necessary
social skills for students entering public schools. In "Some Psychosocial Aspects of Learning in the Disadvantaged" (1967c, 33),
Deutsch writes, "School curricula and learning techniques usually imply an assumption that the child has had prior experience
in the complex learning area, where there are logical assumptions as to appropriate behavior and where success is rewarded
and failure is disapproved."

In fact, Deutsch (1967a, 48) describes the "lower-class" home
as a series of unconnected and distracting noises, where little language skill or discipline is learned:

While the environment is a noisy one, the noise is not, for the
most part, meaningful in relation to the child, and for him most
of it is background. In the crowded apartments, with all the
daily living stresses, there is a minimum of non-instructional
conversation directed toward the child. In actuality, the situation is ideal for the child to learn inattention. Furthermore, he
does not get practice from adults correcting his enunciation,
pronunciation, and grammar.

For Deutsch, this situation is unlike that of middle-class children, who are presented with the proper attitudes and language
learning environment:

The middle-class child is more likely to have been continuously
prodded intellectually by his parents and rewarded for correct

answers. . . . [T]he middle class child is likely to have experienced, in the behavior of adults in his environment, the essential ingredients implicit in the role of the teacher. (Deutsch 1967c, 33)

The failures of "lower-class" homes and their lack of parental role models, visual stimulation, and practice in proper speech, according to Deutsch, are amplified in the "Negro family." Rhetorically placing the African American family firmly within the tradition of slavery, as did Johnson, Deutsch (1967a) states that the "Negro family" is still recovering from its forced destruction by the hands of slave owners:

This recovery has been made doubly difficult by recurrent recessions which have been particularly harsh on the Negro male. The chronic instability has greatly influenced the Negro man's concept of himself and his general motivation to succeed in competitive areas of society. . . . All these circumstances have contributed to the instability of the Negro family, and particularly to the fact that it is most often broken by the absence of the father. As a result, the lower-class Negro child entering school often has had no experience with a "successful" male model or thereby with the corresponding psychological framework in which efforts can result in at least the possibility of achievement. Yet the value system of the school and of the learning process is predicated on the assumption that efforts will result in achievement. (Deutsch 1967a, 43)

Consequently, the African American home and its parents (or parent) are seen as inhospitable to its children. Representing the life of inner-city African American families, Deutsch (1967a, 44) states that in such a child's home,

there is a scarcity of objects of all types, but especially of books, toys, puzzles, pencils, and scribbling paper. . . . Though many parents will share in the larger value system of having high aspirations for their children, they are unaware of the operational steps required for the preparation of the child to use optimally the learning opportunities in the school.

Based upon such research, other scholars argued that the government must step in to ensure that African American children receive the right education early on. For instance, Carl Bereiter (1968) argues that disadvantaged African American children should learn a "stripped-down" version of English. At the root of such a program is the following assumption:

> To describe the basic language program briefly, it presumes nothing more of the child at the outset than that he be capable of making some attempt at imitating what is said to him. Only two basic-statement forms are taught, the first being the identity statement, "This is a _____," and "This is not a _____." Once this statement type is mastered (and mastery of the not-statement is a major challenge to many seriously deprived children), the remainder of the beginning language program is devoted to work with the statement form, "This_____ is _____," with its negative and plural variations, introducing several different kinds of concepts that are used in the predicates of these statements: polar sets (big-little, hot-cold, and so on); nonpolar sets, such as colors and prepositional phrases; and subclass nouns, as in "This animal is a tiger." (341)

Implicit in this pedagogy is a belief that the child comes to the institution without a basic language or set of language concepts. Echoing Krapp's (1924) argument that African Americans have no "modern culture," Bereiter seems to argue they are a blank slate onto which correct language can be written. Indeed, before actually starting their education, they must learn a "basic language." In the same article where Bereiter (1968) discusses the preceding justification, he gives the following sample sentence:

> Verbatim repetition:
> Teacher: This block is red. Say it.
> Children: This block is red. (342)

The mere phrase "Say it" demonstrates the power relationship in the room. Obviously, this pedagogy is decidedly based on a presumption that individuals must change in order to be accepted into the school system. More to the point, part of the necessary change is the acceptance of a model that directly assaults the home and heritage of the students it was intended to instruct.[1]

In fact, I would argue that by connecting African American culture, morals, and language to the "failure" to enter the U.S.

mainstream, Deutsch and Bereiter are both participating in the previously discussed historical trend within studies concerning Black English. For although both clearly reject a biological basis for Black English, Deutsch and Bereiter represent African American culture as a degraded culture. Deutsch finds the ghetto community to be disorganized sound, which increases "inattention." In Bereiter's attempts to focus on African American students' imitation skills, he echoes previous understandings of the skills the African American population brought to language acquisition: imitation and forgetfulness. Indeed, by beginning at the level of "baby talk," he reinvokes in the name of liberal benevolence images of African Americans that could be considered racist.

Ultimately, however, their work also represents the extent to which the civil rights movement's rhetoric could not be contained within its own terms; instead, latent or implicit elements were taken up by the larger society. In making their arguments, both Deutsch and Bereiter were to some extent merely demonstrating the cultural racism historically part of the ethnicity paradigm. Therefore, it is not ironic that the same book (*Social Class, Race, and Psychological Development* 1968) in which Deutsch and Bereiter argue that Negro children must be taught as if they had no prior language is dedicated to Martin Luther King Jr., and the acknowledgments offer the following citation from a speech King gave to the American Psychological Association in Washington D.C. in September 1967:

> And I assert at this time that once again we must reaffirm our belief in building a democratic society, in which blacks and whites can live together as brothers, where we will all come to see that integration is not a problem, but an opportunity to participate in the beauty of diversity.

Within their paradigm, a "belief in building a democratic society" becomes a shibboleth for marginalizing the inner-city experiences of African American children as "impoverished," "providing poor parental models," and containing "no language." The invocation of King, however, also demonstrates the extent to which Deutsch himself was reacting to the new social pressure emerging from forces such as the Black Power movement. Because his book was published one year after the birth of Black Power, he could not but be aware of the new political and economic definitions emerging around Black English.

Leaving Ethnic Paradigm Politics

Perhaps the most immediate response to the ethnicity paradigm's characterization of Black English and black culture emerged from the scholars, poets, and activists engaged in redefining Black English in terms of its African roots. These attempts to recast the meaning and history of Black English were complemented by the work of Lorenzo Turner and Melville Herskovitz. In particular, Herskovitz's *The Myth of the Negro Past* (1958) represented a rejection of arguments that attempted to see black culture as divorced from its African roots. Citing the work of Lorenzo Turner, Herskovitz argues that many of the "mistakes" of Black English have their roots in African dialects and speaking patterns. For instance, Herskovitz traces broader communication patterns, such as the call–response language of African American churches, to tribal practices of western Africa. And while some of his examples, such as linking out-of-wedlock births to polygamy in Africa, tend to perpetuate stereotypes, much of his work demonstrates the impact of Africanisms on the speech habits of African Americans.

For the purposes of this chapter, however, it is probably more important to note the effect Herskovitz hoped to achieve; that is, rather than explicate his data on Africanisms, it is more important to place his intellectual framework within the broader study of the invocation of the ethnicity paradigm. For although Herskovitz cites Africa, it is not automatically clear that his work does not participate in the construction of "blacks" within the ethnicity paradigm. Indeed, funded by the Carnegie Corporation of New York, Herskovitz imagined his work would provide the information without which a "true perspective on the values of Negro life in this country cannot be had, either by the student treating of the larger problems of cultural change or by the practical man seeking to lessen racial tension" (xiii). That is, ultimately it appears that Herskovitz is imagining the discovery of an African past as enabling the assimilation of African Americans into the ethnic tradition of the United States: "[I]n time the concept could be spread that the civilizations of Africa, like those of Europe, have contributed to American culture as we know it today. . . . Would this not, as a practical measure, tend to undermine the assumptions that bolster racial prejudice?" (30).

Only ten years after the initial publication of Herskovitz's book, however, anticolonial struggles had renegotiated that African link; Africa as a sign of ethnic integration had been reimagined as a site of anticolonial struggle. Writing in 1958, Herskovitz noted that Franklin Roosevelt's four freedoms, which stated the right of nations to self-determination, had resulted in a web of new countries "coming into being." Herskovitz cited the Philippines, India, Pakistan, Indonesia, Burma, Ghana, and Ceylon, among others, as examples (xv). As the 1950s and 1960s continued, other African nations besides Ghana, such as Algeria, also waged revolutionary struggles. Since many of these struggles were informed by Marxist ideologies, the image of Black English also became recoded in terms of anti-imperialism. The image of an African-based Black English changed from one of cultural integration to one of African alliances, economic empowerment, and black nationalism. Certainly, in the United States, poets such as Langston Hughes and Amiri Baraka used their poetry to express the need for an economic and political solidarity with Africa, particularly the African liberation movements associated with socialist and communist agendas. During the mid- to late 1960s, Hughes was producing poetry that connected civil rights struggles with liberation struggles in Africa. In *The Panther and the Lash* (1967), Hughes presents poems that express anger at white liberals and ask why African Americans must find models of liberation in Third World struggles. In poems such as "Africa, Africa, Africa," Baraka argues that African Americans are in essence "African." Elsewhere, in poetry such as "The 'Race Line' is a product of capitalism," Baraka argues for the need for an alliance of workers brought together by capitalist oppression; that is, he argues for an interracial alliance under the terms of Marxism.

As noted earlier, SNCC President Stokely Carmichael had also employed colonialist metaphors to explain the economic plight of African Americans. Carmichael understood the retention of Black English as a form of resistance by African Americans to becoming "American." For Carmichael, this resistance was a sign that African Americans were aware of the economic oppression being perpetuated upon them by the "speakers of standard English." For instance, in 1965, Carmichael taught a class on the politics of English at the Work-Study Institute, Waveland, Mississippi.[2] As recorded by Jane Stembridge (1966), the class clearly understood that English as spoken in Mississippi by the lower class does not follow the rules dictated by "England," maintained by Harvard, and supported by those who are a minority yet are in control. Carmichael takes this understanding and demonstrates how an interracial class politics could emerge. During the class, Carmichael delineates certain black speech patterns, such as the use of *s* and dialect choices such as "reddish," as those spoken by African Americans. In doing so, students also come to understand how this dialect is similar to lower-class "southern English" in general. Carmichael concludes from these shared features that what marks both dialects is the class oppression of lower-class southern English speakers by those speaking standard English. There is, then, a potential interracial and class-based community that could redefine what standard English represents. For Carmichael (and the NUC), it is from this altered view of the standard as a means of class oppression that a leftist politics can grow from the English classroom. (This is not to say that Carmichael would endorse interracial working-class alliances, at least, not during this time period.)

The work of placing a class-based analysis of Black English into a classroom and political organization was taken up by the Black Panthers. As had Carmichael, the Panthers' national officers and offices represented the situation of African Americans in terms of class struggle. As enunciated in their ten-point program, the Black Panthers demanded an education that would "teach the decadent nature" of the United States. In speaking about the youth associated with their "liberation schools," an article from *The Black Panther* cited in *The Black Panthers Speak* (Foner 1995, 171) states:

The youth understand the struggle that's being waged in this society. It's evident by their eagerness to participate in the program. They understand that we're not fighting a race struggle, but in fact a class struggle. They recognize the need for all oppressed people to unite against the forces that are making our lives unbearable. . . . The beauty of socialism is seen through their daily practice while involving themselves in the program.

Recounting what classroom practices emerged from this insight, the article continues:

They are eager to learn and exchange ideas, because the curriculum is based on true experiences of revolutionaries and everyday people who the children can relate to. One Mother of five told me that her children made satisfactory grades in school, but when she saw the work they were doing in the Liberation School, such as; choosing articles and writing about them or giving them an oral report about an event that happened in the world, she smiled with pride; she said "their work shows that they can relate to what is happening to them and other poor people in the world." Some of the children who can't even write, try because they understand that we are there to help each other. (172)

This class is hardly the image set forth by Deutsch, who imagined African American children as not possessing a language, nor do the grateful children of Johnson's classroom seem in attendance. And while connections are indirectly made to other countries, African cultural heritage is not seen as the common bond. The ethnicity paradigm's attempt to define Black English has been left behind. Instead, what is created is an image of the student (even the very young student) as recognizing through their writing and engagement with written materials the extent to which a common economic oppression links them with other individuals around the world; "Africa" has become subsumed under the language of socialism. What the Black Panthers leave unarticulated, yet most likely was the case, is that these insights are expressed in the language of inner-city black children. It might be argued that the language of socialism and class struggle had become the "Black English" of the Black Panther Party.

Mainstreaming Black English

SRTOL participant Geneva Smitherman's article "Black Power Is Black Language" in *Black Culture: Reading and Writing Black* (1972) is accompanied by a photographic negative of an African American man (possibly Huey Newton) wearing a leather coat and Black Panther beret and holding an automatic machine gun, complete with ammunition belts hanging across his chest. The book itself is a collection of writings by poets and critics who argue that black speech represents the condensation of African influences in the U.S. context. As such, it argues, black speech represents a valuable and important heritage. Following sections titled "A Language of My Own," "Soul," and "Jive," Smitherman's article states,

> The crucial point I wish to make here is that language is the basic instrument of social reality. Created in the human environment, adaptable and subject to change, it is a tool that man manipulates to a desired end. It is power. Black language, though often superciliously termed "non-standard English," contains as much power, complexity, and usefulness as other varieties of American English, including the so-called "standard" idiom. (88)

In making this argument, Smitherman is expanding upon Thomas Kochman's "Language Behavior in the Black Community" (1972), which appears in the earlier "A Language of My Own" section of the same volume. In that article, Kochman details distinct black-community speaking habits, such as "signifying," "sounding," or "copping a plea." Through examining the verbal skills needed to join in such language games, Kochman concludes:

> [I]t ought to be clear to educators that we have missed utilizing the cultural resources that were at our disposal, either because we were unaware that they existed, or felt that they were without value. The time has come to find out what the norms and values of the culturally different are and find some way of incorporating them into the educational process. (55)

In opposition to Deutsch, both Kochman and Smitherman imagine the African American student as possessing a wide variety of language skills and habits when entering in the classroom. In fact, Smitherman's argument would be that Deutsch and his proponents did not even know how to read African American culture.[3]

As a teacher of writing, Smitherman thus wants to alter the terrain of the writing classroom to include the values of Black English. In doing so, she is also simultaneously redefining African American culture away from the political violence and unrest that had marked the 1960s. Smitherman (1972) writes:

> As teachers of written and oral composition, our concerns lie not with our students' linguistic flavoring, but with their linguistic substance, not with sheer grammatical conventions and usage practices, themselves constantly in flux, but with teaching our students to deal with increasingly complex and sophisticated topics in an increasingly sophisticated and powerful way . . . . As we teachers should know only too well, the student's written and oral products like those of the professionals, succeed or fail on the basis of the totality of the language used, not on its degree of mechanical exactness. In short, a paper or speech succeeds as a whole. Faulty logic, poor organization, verbosity, lack of specificity, lack of content—all will produce a weak, ineffective speech or paper whatever the brand of dialect. But language judiciously selected and effectively delivered, *including that of Black dialectical variety,* becomes a weapon capable of the most devastating destruction. Given the contemporary acceleration of "student unrest," we should wish our students black *and* white, to know that language is power. Perhaps then we may convince them that the pen is mightier than the Molotov cocktail. (91)

In imagining her classroom, then, it appears as if Smitherman is positioning herself against violent protests, such as the riots in Watts, Harlem, or Cleveland, and student protests, such as Columbia. Instead she replaces such tactics with an argument about the benefits of black-articulated political messages. She states: "Many black historians credit Malcolm X with igniting the spark that has led to the current thrust for black self-determination. Listen to Malcolm's 'Message to the Grass Roots' for a powerful piece of rhetoric with participle endings dropped, front-shifting of stress ('po-lice') and other features of Black English" (89). In her later work, such as *Talkin and Testifyin: The Language of Black America* (1977), Smitherman focuses on how cultural heroes such as Martin Luther King Jr., Jesse Jackson, and Malcolm X gain power from their use of Black English: "For instance, Malcolm X's heavy sig on the non-violent revolution: 'In a revolution, you swinging, not singing.' (Referring to the common practice of singing 'We Shall Overcome' in Civil Rights marches and protests of the sixties)" (146). She writes that if the Black Power rhetoric is understood from a black communication context, it would be understood as a case of "woofin":

> The black idiom expression "selling woof [wolf] tickets" (also just plain woofin) refers to any kind of strong language which is purely idle boasting. However, this bad talk is nearly always taken for the real thing by an outsider from another culture. Such cultural-linguistic misperceptions can lead to tragic consequences. Witness, for instance, the physical attacks and social repression suffered by black spokesmen of the 1960's, such as the Black Panthers. "Death to the racist exploiters!" "Off the pigs," "Defend our communities by any means necessary!"—the white folks thought the bloods was not playing and launched an all-out military campaign. These aggressive moves resulted in part from White America's sense of fear that radical rhetoric (much of which was really defensive, rather than offensive) constituted more than idle threats. The whites were not hip to braggadocios and woof tickets; at any rate, they wasn't buying any. (83)

It would seem that to dismiss such threatening rhetoric, particularly given the violent attacks on the Black Panthers, as mere "idle boasting," is to devalue the commitment of the participants. Further, while it is true that individuals such as Stokely Carmichael were not violent, Malcolm X's phrase "by any means necessary" has taken on a life that does imply a force behind it. That is, rhetoric without powerful social or political forces behind it can ignite nothing. Political organizing certainly played a part in the vitality of Black English as a social force.

In Smitherman's attempt to revalue the Black Power movement for the writing classroom, she seems to have disconnected it from the socialist or leftist organizations working for African American empowerment. Or rather, she has rhetorically positioned these forces as nonthreatening to the political status quo of coalition politics, mass marches, and nonviolence. While such a critique should not be heard as stating that the Black Panthers, for instance, were only about the possibility of violent counterattack, it does not seem that she effectively translated the most radical language politics of the Black Power movement into the classroom. (Nor does it account for whether socialism was also a case of "woofin" by the Panthers.) That is, unlike the NUC's commitment to reframing the classroom as a potential site of interracial class struggle, Smitherman does not imagine that Black English being utilized in the classroom will lead to the policies being articulated by Black Power advocates. Despite the imagery of the Black Panther photograph accompanying Smitherman's 1972 article, it would be incorrect to place Smitherman's work in alignment with the Black Panthers or the socialist elements of the Black Power movement.

This is not, of course, to say that Smitherman was not concerned about economic justice, only to place her work in terms of previously stated cultural positions. Certainly, like Baraka or Carmichael, Smitherman is attempting to reinvent Black English as a vibrant aspect of African American culture. Like Carmichael, she is arguing that the writing classroom must alter its terrain to allow a greater concept of language use to take hold. That is, she is participating in the transformation of black speech from a language of cultural deficiency to a legitimate form of political speech. Like Herskovitz, Smitherman expands her linguistic study of Black English to encompass its African world view. According to Smitherman, this viewpoint places a large emphasis on community and storytelling. Within African culture, for Smitherman, emphasis is laid upon a community structure that values the opinions and wisdom of elders (76). Additionally, citing the work of numerous African scholars, Smitherman concludes that the preslavery period was illuminated by the concept of Nommo, "the magic power of the word":

'All activities of men, and all the movements in nature, rest on the word, on the productive power of the word, which is water and heat and seed and Nommo, that is, life force itself. . . . The force, responsibility, and commitment of the word, and the awareness that the word alone alters the world.' . . . So strong is the traditional African belief in the power and absolute necessity of Nommo that all craftsmanship must be accompanied by speech. (78)

In fact, for Smitherman, it is out of this valuing of the word that language habits of the African American community, such as cappin', have grown. As did Herskovitz, then, Smitherman is clearly arguing for a philosophical attitude embedded in Black English that is African in its origin. Indeed, it is out of the world view of African culture that Smitherman begins to articulate a progressive politics. Smitherman argues that features of Black English reflect an amalgam of Africa's emphasis on community culture. In *Talkin and Testifyin* (1977), she writes, "The Black communication system is actualized in different ways . . . but the basic underlying structures of this communication network are essentially similar because they are grounded in the traditional African world view" (74). To the extent that such a communitarian world view represents an economic critique of capitalism's individualist ethic, she is also beginning the process of enunciating a critique of U.S. culture through Black English. That is, Smitherman should not be seen as unconcerned about social justice. She does not, however, overtly utilize these African-based community politics to critique the larger dynamics of U.S. capitalism; unlike the Panthers or NUC, she does not make the leap to Black Panther socialism, nor should such a leap be the litmus test for progressive politics.

Smitherman, however, was not the only linguist whose work was being shaped by the emerging image of Black English or the increased attention to the social politics of language instruction. Nor was she the only language scholar attempting to use Black English as a means to express a different political vision of the African American community. William Labov, whose work would circulate among both NUC and CCCC activists, published "The Logic of Nonstandard English" (1972) as a direct response to the work of linguists like Deutsch. His article is framed as a response to proponents of the deficit theory when it is renamed as "verbal deprivation." He acknowledges that under such a name,

African American children are represented as being unable to "speak complete sentences, do not know the names of common objects, cannot form concepts or convey logical thoughts" (179). In fact, Labov argues, such images invoke racist ideas of "the primitive mentality of the savage mind" (207). Labov argues that such a concept has "no basis in social reality":

> [I]n fact, Negro children in the urban ghettos receive a great deal of verbal stimulation, hear more well-formed sentences than middle-class children, and participate fully in a highly verbal culture; they have the same basic vocabulary, possess the same capacity for conceptual learning, and use the same logic as anyone else who learns to speak and understand English. (179)

Labov bases this refutation of Deutsch on the inability of previous studies to understand the power relationship between white interrogators and black children. He argues that it is not surprising that such children often fail to be responsive to questioners' prompts; after all, they are well aware of how previous situations have led them to be considered "special," "different," and "deficient": "The child is in an asymmetrical situation where anything he says can literally be held against him. He has learned a number of devices to *avoid* saying anything in this situation, and he works hard to achieve this end" (emphasis in original, 185).

In making his case for the linguistic skill of speakers of Black English, however, Labov also constructs an image of such speakers as positing a social and economic critique of the United States. In one example, Labov represents John Lewis and Larry H., "a fifteen-year-old core member of the Jets," discussing God. When confronted with the question of where his soul is going after death, Larry argues that it will go to hell:

> Why [will my soul go to hell]? I'll tell you why. 'Cause, you see, doesn' nobody really know that it's a God, y'know, 'cause I mean I have seen black gods, pink gods, white gods, all color gods, and don't nobody really know it's really a God. An' when they be saying' if you good, you goin' t'heaven, tha's bullshit, 'cause you ain't goin' to heaven, 'cause ain't no heaven for you to go. (194)

Larry argues that since there is no proof of heaven, people must go to hell. When confronted with the fact that there is also no proof of hell, Larry responds, "I mean—ye-eah. Well, let me tell you, it ain't no hell, 'cause this is hell right here, y'know" (196). Larry expands this point. When asked, if there were a god, what color would he be, Larry responds:

> JL: . . . [J]us' suppose there is a God, would he be white or black?
>
> Larry: . . . He'd be white, man.
>
> JL: Why?
>
> LARRY: Why? I'll tell you why. 'Cause the average whitey out here got everything, you dig? And the nigger ain't got shit, y'know? Y'understan'? So—um—for—in order for *that* to happen, you know it ain't no black God that's doin that bullshit. (196)

The speaker who emerges in Labov's text is articulate, socially aware of his circumstances, and knowledgeable about his situation. In fact, within his argument, Labov goes on to invoke this image and this speaker as representative of a culture:

> Larry also provides a paradigmatic example of the rhetorical style of NNE [Non-standard Negro English]: he can sum up a complex argument in a few words, and the full force of his opinions comes through without qualification or reservation. He is eminently quotable, and his interviews give us many concise statements of the NNE point of view. One can almost say that Larry *speaks* for NNE culture. (emphasis in original, 194)

Perhaps it is in the nature of Labov's work that he does not attempt to cast this child's language into the larger community and community organizations with which it interacts. The NUC, however, would take this image of the student concerned with how race and class merge to create oppression and embed it within their own institutional documents. In fact, in documents such as "Who(m) Does Standard English Serve? Who(m) Does Standard English Hurt?" (Knowles et al. 1969), the NUC cited Labov's work as indicating a larger class-based substratum in classrooms through which an oppositional politics can arise. Further, the linkages that the NUC attempted to make between itself and the

Black Panther Party's ten-point program (see chapter 1) are also made available by this image. The dialect speaker's awareness here of race and class build the possibility of interorganizational alliances between the NUC and the Black Panther Party. In this way, Labov's work offers institutional moves blocked by Smitherman's focus on Nommo and communitarianism.

In fact, in a move similar to the NUC and Black Panthers, Labov himself uses this new image of the Black English speaker to critique the school system. If the language and the speaker are not illogical or deficient, Labov concludes that it is the school system which must be at fault:

> At present, these deficiencies are said to be caused by his home environment. It is traditional to explain a child's failure in school by his inadequacy, but when failure reaches such massive proportions, it seems to us necessary to look at the social and cultural obstacles to learning, and the inability of the school to adjust to the social situation. Operation Headstart is designed to repair the child, rather than the school; to the extent that it is based upon this inverted logic, it is bound to fail. (208)

Notably, it is this connection between the social structure of public schools and the failure rate of African American children which would be picked up by the NUC. The NUC, however, in OUTS, articulated this critique in terms of a larger economic program designed to reframe the responsibility of corporations to education. Obviously, Labov's work itself should not be read as endorsing the politics of the NUC or Black Panther Party. Instead, I am arguing that its formation of a particular type of dialect speaker created the possibility of political and academic alliances.

Indeed, Labov's own position seems closer to the moderate politics of the ethnicity paradigm than to the NUC, for in *The Study of Non-Standard English* (1969), which was originally prepared for the Office of Education of the U.S. Department of Health, Education, and Welfare, revised for the Center for Applied Linguistics, and published by NCTE, Labov offers a different dialect speaker. As in his later publication, Labov centers his discussion around the voices and attitudes which he believes represent "Negro culture." This time, however, Labov chooses a young man named Junior. As Labov is quick to point out, like

Larry, Junior has a history of discipline problems, that is, failing to conform to the dress code, speaking out of turn, refusing to rewrite essays, fighting, and truancy. From these facts, Labov feels the image emerges of the stereotypical problem student. Under such a rubric, the cultural deprivation model would point to his family life or poor language skills. Instead, Labov demonstrates to the reader that Junior, like Larry, is very aware of his social situation and possesses the linguistic ability to express that understanding. In response to the question of whether high school diplomas were necessary, he argues with a friend, Ronald:

> RONALD: And I'm 'onna tell you; I'm 'onna tell say *why* what they say you have to have a high school diploma. Some whitey's probably ain't got a high school diploma, and he still go out to work. My father ain't got a high school diploma.
>
> JUNIOR: Your father ain't no whitey, is he?
>
> RONALD: No, but he has no high school diploma, but he go out there and work, right?
>
> JUNIOR: O.K.! . . . But . . . I'ma tell you, you're wrong in a *way*— cause ev'ry whitey—ev'ry whitey, if they out o' school, they went through *high* school. If they didn't go to college they went through *high* school. If the whites didn't go through high school, how come they got everything? . . . 'Cause they had the *knowledge*. (53)

In this moment, Labov is tempering the image of the Black English speaker. Unlike Larry, who clearly indicts white power structures (this is hell on earth), Junior distances himself from the racial reading of his situation. Instead, he invokes the standard American myth linking education and upward mobility. In effect, Junior claims the fact of "whitey" having "everything" is directly related to education, not to racism, economic coercion, or other forces to which the NUC or the Black Panthers would point as causes. Although Ronald is allowed to express the opposite view, Labov seems by his commentary to diminish such an opinion:

> In this dialogue, Junior seems to express very well the values of middle class society. He shows a full cognitive awareness of the importance of education. It comes as something of a shock

then to learn that at the time of his interview he was in the
eighth grade and his reading score was . . . more than three
years behind grade. (53)

By framing Junior in this way, Labov reinscribes the speaker of
Black English within a national narrative. While recognizing the
ability of Black English to articulate a viewpoint, he also makes
the student appear to want the very values that the earlier student had questioned in Labov (1972). In other words, the rhetorical effect of this text is to appease the then-growing concerns
that the inner-city African American was rejecting the "American dream."

The attempt to link Junior's dialect with American values, a
gesture absent in his other article and negated by Deutsch, is
furthered by Labov's linguistic understanding of Black English.
According to Labov (1969), "Negro English" represents a particular version of English; that is, it is not a different nor an illogical language. When speaking about the double negative of
Black English, he points out that it is "merely an extension of the
standard rule of literary English which gives us *Never did he see
it*, or *Nor did anybody see it*" (40). According to Labov (1969),
standard English and "Negro English" exist upon a pan-dialecti-
cal grammar, a grammar that contains all the possible variations
of the English language. "Negro English" merely demonstrates
different elements of a common deep structure: "[N]o matter
what historical explanation we give for some of these directions
of development, we are plainly dealing with a dialect of English
which is not, in the larger view, very different from other developments within the language" (42). Consequently, Labov argues
that instead of language drills, "Negro English" speakers should
be given lessons in mitigation skills. Using Junior as an example,
Labov argues that if Junior had known how to properly address
the teacher, many of the discipline problems would have van-
ished. As opposed to Smitherman, who would agree with the
general thrust of Labov's work, Labov does not fully explore the
connections between African dialect structures or speech games
and "Negro English." It is possible to argue that his very use of
the term "Non-Standard Negro" represents a distancing from
the larger social movements then occurring. In fact, it was this

distancing that enabled more moderate SRTOL advocates to cite his work as endorsing their own position; that is, Labov's work would be splintered and dispersed along many political and academic networks.

Finally, not every linguist was comfortable with the politics that grew out of an increased acceptance of Black English. For instance, whereas J. L. Dillard's *Black English: Its History and Usage in the United States* (1972) echoes many of the themes within Smitherman's work, he is decidedly uncomfortable over what he perceives as a growing black nationalism. Similar to Smitherman and Herskovitz, Dillard uses his work to place Black English firmly within African culture and the history of European maritime expansionism. His work places great emphasis on the effects of introducing the West African pidgin English spoken by African slaves into the United States. The effect of his argument is to displace the American–European nexus which had previously anchored linguistic studies of American English. Dillard argues that linguists have to take into account not only the copious history of Black English dialects outside the United States, but the history of immigrant dialects within the United States as well. For if the paradigm that has restricted the understanding of Black English falls, the concept that European languages are the primary influence on American English will also fall. Consequently, Dillard argues for a diverse linguistic terrain as the beginning for language use in the United States:

> [T]he history of New World dialects will need to be altered greatly. It may be necessary to deal in the social dynamics of migration, in mutual influences between the koines, the pidgin/Creole and other contact varieties, and the languages spoken by the aboriginal populations of the New World. Instead of expecting to find reflection of white settlement history, we may rather look for the cultural ties which survived into—and, especially, were forged in—the Americas. . . . Liberation of the Black dialects from Eurocentrism may be the first step in the eventual reevaluation of the white varieties. (25)

In other words, he does not see the different dialects necessarily working toward some natural standard. Instead, it is through the interaction of differing dialects that language change in America can be seen. That is, by removing the European and American framework, the development of particular standards can be seen not as representative of a myth of America, but of immigrant–ex-slave–native–settler colonialist interaction. Like Smitherman, Dillard thus makes an argument to introduce African culture and colonialism into the history of American English. For Dillard, a history of Black English would also demonstrate the usefulness and importance of such a framework. In fact, the implication of Dillard's work is to turn the relationship between American English and Black English on its head: "It may be possible to know the white speech community of the New World better through the insights which we gain from studying the Black communities" (25).

Politically, however, Dillard seemed unwilling to deny the political efficacy of a widespread normative standard. In response to the emergence of Black Power, forces which denied the myth of the ethnicity paradigm, Dillard felt that, linguistically, the nation stood the chance of falling apart. Given that his work also went against the grain of the homogenizing idea of European ethnicity, his work could be used to defend the idea of America as a series of independent group identities, meeting only in the contact zones of language. Consequently, at the end of his book, he attempts to close the lid on the implications of both his theory and the separatist nature of the Black Power movement. He argues that network standard English

> almost seems like the last alternative to Black Separatism in language and behavior—a pattern which is already widely advocated in the Black community but could have serious consequences to the nation as a whole. . . . There always remains the possibility, hinted at already, that the Black Community, disenchanted with pretenses at desegregation and with the white man's attempts—futile and weak even on the part of liberals—to bring about social justice, may stop seeking to adjust itself to mainstream (white) culture. In that case, the teaching of Standard English to Black Speakers may be rejected no matter what the method. (293)

The manner in which the development of a linguistic concept, established through linguistic proof, intersected with the emerging racial and political conflicts of the time is thus clear. It was not just that Black English, as a concept, acted as a corrective to the linguistic strategies and paradigms previously used, but that its acceptance by academics gave credence to the idea of different linguistic groups existing in the country. Such an argument creates a space for the emerging economic and racial politics being pushed by Black Power advocates, such as Stokely Carmichael or the Black Panthers, to enter the academy. It is for this reason that the use of "Black" by Dillard versus "Negro" by Deutsch also represents the ways in which a political position can be derived from a text. It is not accidental that in a text using Negro and ignoring African roots, Deutsch dedicates his work to Martin Luther King Jr. Nor is it happenstance that in a book concerning the African origin of Black English, the author ends with a concern about black nationalism. The question became, Which version of "Black English" would the SRTOL argue should enter the writing classroom?

Conclusion

This chapter demonstrated that the political struggles occurring in the civil rights movement and in the New Left over the role of the liberal welfare state, the role of the professional scholar, and the role of the student had a counterpart in the struggle over Black English. Deutsch's student is clearly positioned differently to issues of social justice than the Black Panther's student. Indeed, it has become evident that the confrontation between the NUC and CCCC was primarily over what political framework defined the student in the classroom. For the NUC, students were necessarily involved in struggles for racial and economic justice. Linking its efforts with the Black Panthers, the NUC hoped to use the issue of dialects as a means to alter the role of the university classroom. For the NUC, then, Black English and the African American student became the symbol of that struggle. What will become apparent in the remaining chapters, however, is the way in which the attempt to formulate such a movement for social and economic justice through the image of the dialect speaker was recoded by the CCCC into the ethnicity paradigm. Links between race and class were supplanted by a vision of the United States as ethnically diverse; liberation schools became university classrooms that recognize diversity. That is, as with the King–Johnson dynamic, the ability of a conceptualized student to reach his or her institutional potential depends on a political organization's or caucus's ability to infiltrate and alter the entire structure of debate. As will be shown in the remaining chapters, the CCCC, not the NUC, would ultimately win this struggle. To understand how an interracial class movement seemed to vanish as a goal through which to understand writing instruction, it is necessary to discuss how the various forces and social movements discussed within these first three chapters locked horns in the development and writing of the SRTOL language statement.

---

1. In fact, to some extent, Martin Luther King Jr. participated in this idea of assimilation through education. The first paragraph of *Stride Toward Freedom* (1958) reads:

> On a cool Saturday afternoon in January 1954, I set out to drive from Atlanta, Georgia, to Montgomery, Alabama. It was a clear wintry day. The Metropolitan Opera was on the radio with a performance of one of my favorite operas—Donizetti's *Luci di Lammermorr*. So with the beauty of the countryside, the inspiration of Donizetti's inimitable music, and the splendor of the skies, the usual monotony that accompanies a relatively long drive—especially when one is alone—was dispelled in pleasant diversions. (1)

This representation of a culturally assimilated speaker is markedly different from the opening cultural moment of *The Autobiography of Malcolm X* (1965):

> When my mother was pregnant with me, she told me later, a party of hooded Ku Klux Klan riders galloped up to our home in Omaha, Nebraska, one night. Surrounding the house, brandishing their shotguns and rifles, they shouted for my father to come out. My mother went to the front door and opened it. Standing where they could see her pregnant condition, she told them that she was alone with her three small children, and that my father was away, preaching, in Milwaukee. The Klansmen shouted threats and warnings at her that we had better get out of town because "the good Christian white people" were not going to stand for my father's "spreading trouble" among "good" Negroes of Omaha with the "back to Africa" preaching of Marcus Garvey. (1)

2. The full text of "Notes About a Class Held by Stokely Carmichael" (Jane Stembridge 1966, 130–136) appears as follows:

> The most important class was "Stokely's speech class." He put eight sentences on the blackboard, with a line between, like this:

I digs wine	I enjoy drinking cocktails
The peoples want freedom	The people want freedom
Wheninsoever the policemens goes they causes troubles.	Anywhere the officers of the law go, they cause trouble.
I wants to reddish to vote.	I want to register to vote.

> Stokely: What do you think about these sentences? Such as—
> The peoples want freedom.
> Zelma: It doesn't sound right.
> Stokely: What do you mean?
> Zelma: "Peoples" isn't right.
> Stokely: Does it mean anything?
> Milton: People means everybody. Peoples means everybody in the world.
> Alma: Both sentences are right as long as you understand them.
> Henry: They're both okay, but in a speech class you have to use correct English.
> *(Stokely writes "correct English" in the corner of the black-board.)*
> Zelma: I was taught to use the sentences on the right side.
> Stokely: Does anybody you know use the sentences on the left.
> Class: Yes.
> Stokely: Are they wrong?
> Zelma: In terms of English, they are wrong.
> Stokely: Who decides what is correct English and incorrect English?
> Milton: People made rules. People in England, I guess.
> Stokely: You all say some people speak like on the left side of the board. Could they go anywhere and speak that way? Could they go to Harvard?
> Class: Yes . . . No. Disagreement.
> Stokely: Does Mr. Turnbow speak like on the left side?
> Class: Yes.
> Stokely: Could Mr. Turnbow go to Harvard and speak like that? "I wants to reddish the vote."
> Class: Yes.
> Stokely: Would he be embarrassed?
> Class: Yes . . . No!
> Zelma: He wouldn't be, but I would. It doesn't sound right.
> Stokely: Suppose someone from Harvard came to Holmes County and said, "I want to register to vote?" Would they be embarrassed?
> Zelma: No.

Stokely: It is embarrassing at Harvard but not in Holmes
    County? They way you speak?
Milton: It's inherited. It's depending on where you come from.
    The people at Harvard would understand.
Stokely: Do you think the people at Harvard should forgive
    you?
Milton: The people at Harvard should help teach us correct
    English.
Alma: Why should we change if we understand what we mean?
Shirley: It is embarrassing.
Stokely: Which way do most people talk?
Class: Like on the left.
*(He asks each student. All but two say "left." One says that
Southerners speak like on the left, Northerners on the right.
Another says that Southerners speak on the left, but the majority
of people speak like on the right.)*
Stokely: Which way do television and radio people speak?
Class: Left.
*(There was a distinction made by class between Northern
commentators and local programs. Most programs were local
and spoke like on the left, they said.)*
Stokely: Which way do teachers speak?
Class: On the left, except in class.
Stokely: If most people speak on the left, why are they trying to
    change these people?
Gladys: If you don't talk right, society rejects you. It embar-
    rasses other people if you don't talk right.
Hank: But Mississippi society, ours, isn't embarrassed by it.
Shirley: But the middle class wouldn't class us with them.
Hank: They won't accept "reddish." What is reddish? It's Negro
    dialect and it's something you eat.
Stokely: Will society reject you if you don't speak like on the
    right side of the board? Gladys said society would reject
    you.
Gladys: You might as well face it, man! What we gotta do is go
    out an become middle class. If you can't speak good
    English, you don't have a car, or anything.
Stokely: If society rejects you because you don't speak good
    English, should you learn to speak good English?
Class: No!
Alma: I'm tired of doing what society say. Let society say
    "reddish" for a while. People ought to just accept each
    other.
Zelma: I think we should be speaking just like we always have.
Alma: If I change society, I wouldn't be free anyway.
Ernestine: I'd like to learn correct English for my own sake.
Shirley: I would too.
Alma: If the majority speaks on the left, then a minority must
    rule society? Why do we have to change to be accepted by
    the minority group?

(Lunch time.)
Stokely: Let's think about two questions for next time: What is
    society? Who makes the rules for society?

3. Consequently, it is important to note the extent to which the SRTOL,
while obviously about a student's language, is also concerned with the education needs of writing teachers. The resolution states, "We affirm strongly
that teachers must have the experiences and training that will enable them
to respect diversity and uphold the right of students to their own language."
This need for teacher education as a key aspect of the SRTOL was reiterated by both Richard Lloyd-Jones, writer of the SRTOL-CCCC, and Geneva
Smitherman at the 1993 CCCC Convention.

CHAPTER 4

Locking Horns:

The NUC Encounters the MLA, NCTE, and CCCC 1968–1972

CCCC and NCTE meetings and CCCC and NCTE Executive Committees should work actively to make non-standard dialects acceptable in all schools from kindergarten on and create an active articulation between the elementary schools, secondary schools, junior colleges and universities to deal with this problem. Linguists and English teachers should concentrate not on trying to teach everyone to speak and write upper middle class white dialect but rather on changing the attitude of society that discriminates against other dialects. Their efforts should be devoted to teaching the truths that all dialects are effective and valuable and that no dialect is any more indicative than any other of intelligence or even language ability on the part of the speaker.

NEW UNIVERSITY CONFERENCE RESOLUTION,
presented to the CCCC Executive Committee, 1969

By the time Neal Resnikoff appeared at the CCCC, the NUC possessed an agenda and a way of speaking that represented an alternative politics to those of traditional academic organizations. Yet as the NUC attempted to exert its influence, it became clear that the institutional "mass" of the MLA, NCTE, and CCCC was formidable. Long-standing internal debates, interorganizational conflicts, and policy shifts all had the ability to rearticulate and reframe NUC efforts. Demands for the MLA to criticize the

Vietnam War produced policies to restrict militant activity. Resolutions concerning racial and class oppression perceived in the teaching of standard English became wrapped up in CCCC/NCTE organizational struggles. Attempts to organize two-year college faculty were usurped by existing institutions. In the face of such opposition and appropriation, the NUC found itself powerless to project its own agenda.

At this point, then, a shift in focus is necessary. Having developed the social terrain surrounding students' rights, it is now possible to examine how existing organizations responded to New Left pressures. In this chapter, I examine the path of the NUC from engaging with the MLA to its attempt to reform the CCCC and NCTE. In doing so, I demonstrate how these institutions worked against NUC objectives either through policy changes or through redefining the context of the goals of the New Left. It is out of these institutional maneuverings that the SRTOL would finally emerge. As will be evident, the development of the SRTOL was about to step onto a "long and winding road."

The Modern Language Association

Advertising its presence in New York as an opportunity to "stir things up at the [MLA] convention," the NUC declared its intention to be part of the efforts to raise "questions about the response (and responsibility) of [the] profession to the demands of a society—and a university—in need of radical change" (Bloland and Bloland 1974, 68). Indeed, the NUC intended to force the issue of radical change through a series of politically motivated resolutions. These resolutions called for the MLA to condemn the practice of withholding fellowship support from politically active students and to condemn university cooperation with the Selective Service program. Resolutions were also presented which called for the immediate end to the Vietnam War and the Selective Service system. Since SDS itself had only recently taken such positions, the NUC was attempting to position the MLA in line with leading New Left organizations.

The MLA Convention was unprepared for what followed. In the past, the business of the MLA had been the presentation of

scholarly papers. To outsiders, the MLA appeared to be a congenial hodgepodge of interests and ideas coexisting peacefully. This
congeniality also marked the elections of MLA officers. An MLA
committee nominated "outstanding" candidates who usually ran
for office unopposed. These officers reinforced the image of congeniality by consistently avoiding political issues. As a consequence, attendance at MLA business meetings was usually quite
sparse. At the 1968 business meeting, however, due in part to
NUC activism, over four hundred people were in attendance. All
but one of the NUC resolutions passed.[1] The NUC also succeeded
in a sense-of-the-house motion calling for the MLA to move its
1969 convention out of Chicago. (A previous attempt by mail
ballot to move the convention had failed.) Finally, the NUC broke
the hold of MLA-nominated candidates. NUC activist Louis
Kampf was nominated from the floor for the office of second
vice president of MLA. By a vote of 292 to 187, Kampf was
elected, ending a fifty-year run of MLA-nominated candidates
winning office. He was now in line to become MLA president.

The NUC also used individual sessions to develop a politically informed classroom practice for its members. As noted earlier, the NUC had based its initial actions as an organization upon
a strategy of linking a general critique of U.S. economic and foreign policy with particular university and public school practices.
At the NUC-MLA High School Teaching of Language and Literature workshop, participants attempted to articulate how such
insights could reform the classroom: How could literature and
language instruction intervene in the current political struggle?
In summarizing the discussion, Neal Resnikoff (1968b) wrote:

A number of questions were raised:

a. How can we get blacks or whites to experience literature?
Suggestion: start with feelings and interests; use sensitivity training or T-Group techniques.

b. Are T-Groups and similar techniques really so good since it
is not enough to feel or have people turned on; conscious analysis is what is needed; this can be seen when feelings are out in
the open as they often are with fascistic types as shown by
many of the New York teachers who were on strike?

c. What are works that stimulate attitude change? *Huckleberry Finn, One Flew Over the Cuckoo's Nest*, "Student As Nigger" were suggested.

d. What can we do about counteracting the pernicious political influence of many basic language texts? German texts, for example, tend to be anti–East Germany with Middle German texts implying that Middle Germany is not East Germany. Also in most basic texts stories tend to be about consumption and tourist training. Perhaps good texts by Mann or Brecht can be substituted in German classes.

As recorded, the group's first concern was the pedagogical problem of how to "get [students] to experience literature." By "experience," however, is meant the attempt to read literature for its political content. The effect of reading literature must transcend individual emotions and lead to conscious analysis of the reader's situation. This is why "feeling" or being "turned on" is not enough. The NUC's use of *Huckleberry Finn* in "Who(m) Does Standard English Hurt?" (Knowles et al. 1969) has already been discussed in chapter 2. At this moment, however, the NUC text did not exist. Consequently, Resnikoff often distributed Farber's "Student as Nigger" (1970) to exemplify NUC classroom practice.[2] This move would affect how NUC actions and language resolutions were perceived at MLA .

In "Student as Nigger" (1970), Farber analyzes a university education by comparing the situation of university students to "niggers" in slavery: "Students are niggers. When you get that straight, our schools begin to make sense" (90).[3] Students are "enslaved" in two ways. Socially, university policy commonly separated faculty from students through dress codes or dining facilities. Intellectually, students are given no choice as to course offerings or course content. The faculty members themselves, however, are also under the control of the university administration and state governments:

The teachers I know best are college professors. Outside of the classroom and taken as a group, their most striking characteristic is timidity. They're short on balls. Just look at their working conditions. At a time when even migrant workers have

begun to fight and win, most college professors are still afraid
to make more than a token effort to improve their pitiful economic status. In California state colleges, the faculties are
screwed regularly and vigorously by the Governor and Legis-
lature and yet they still won't offer any solid resistance. They
lie flat on their stomachs with their pants down, mumbling
catch phrases like "professional dignity" and "meaningful dialogue." (94)

Farber concludes, "What I'm getting at is that we're all more or
less niggers and slaves, teachers and students alike. This is a fact
you might want to start with in trying to understand wider social
phenomena, say, politics, in our country and other countries"
(99). As with other texts discussed, Farber seems unaware of how
such metaphors distort both the situation of students as well as
the political forces of Black Power. To this extent, Farber's text is
very similar to those of Hoffman (1968), Knowles et al. (1969),
Macrorie (1970), and Friedrich and Kuester (1972).

Additionally, as had other process texts, Farber also fails to
indicate how such metaphors translate into actual activism. Instead of initiating a political program, Farber argues that students and faculty should draw from personal experience to escape
this "slavery." He writes: "At a very early age, we all learn to
accept 'two truths.' . . . Outside of class, things are true to your
tongue, your fingers, your stomach, your heart. Inside class, things
are true by reason of authority" (92). While it is not necessarily
the case that such essentialism is unpolitical, Farber's analysis
does not lead the student to collective action with other students.
Instead, students are led toward self-discovery. In a reflective essay written much later, "Learning How to Teach" (1990), Farber
describes his classroom practice at that time:

> For a few years my own approach tended to be head-on and at
> full speed: "Your authenticity or your life!" Long, long silences.
> Zen weirdness. Classes held in people's living rooms. Dancing.
> Darkness. It was a fruitful period actually. But there was this
> eternal focus on process. I felt like those couples who did noth-
> ing but discuss their own relationship; what I wanted to do
> was get on with it. What I wanted to do was teach compara-
> tive literature. And writing. And to do it as though the revolu-
> tion had already been won. (135–136)

Notably, freedom for faculty and students meant the ability to teach comparative literature—an odd form of freedom at best. What is missing from Farber's argument, then, is the effort to turn the classroom into an NUC workshop for the "movement," that is, there is no effort to push students to collective action against U.S. corporate and educational systems. There is little discussion in "Student as Nigger," for example, of how to link concerns about literature or writing to social issues concerning the United States. In fact, through Farber's appeals to a core humanity, the social and economic analysis then emerging in the NUC is negated. That is, it is difficult to build a political program from such intuitive insights.

In this sense, Farber's (1970) essay is more like Macrorie's *Uptaught* (1970) than the later NUC essay "Who(m) Does Standard English Serve? Who(m) Does Standard English Hurt?" (Knowles et al. 1969). The NUC essay had explicitly challenged any call to eliminate dialect differences as representing a racist and anti–working class bias. Unlike Farber's essay, it also rejected the attempt to frame nontraditional students as "noble savages." In doing so, the authors invoked the student's political subjectivity. Like Macrorie, however, Farber invoked the political only as a pedagogical tool to help students achieve personal growth. This elision of race and working-class politics is important, for later the NUC would also present the following resolution on dialects (cited in Resnikoff 1969a):

> That the MLA establish a Commission on Dialects, mandated and sufficiently funded to reeducate teachers in the politics of dialect, to develop materials for teaching white children how to understand black English, to advance the understanding of cultural differences, and to work out means for language teaching that aims to liberate individual students and the larger society from race and class. (1)

Surrounded by the language of Farber, the resolution could be read by some as arguing for liberation as consciousness raising or personal growth. That is, key goals such as liberating individual students were not put in the context of a larger political program. Left as individual insights, the NUC's resolution could be interpreted as not fundamentally challenging the nature of the classroom or the role of the teacher. Professionals could be brought into the NUC with a sense that a liberal politics was being endorsed.

At this moment, however, the NUC was increasingly taking on the language of socialism.[4] For instance, in *Classes and Schools: A Radical Definition for Teachers* (1970), prepared by the Teacher Organizing Project of the NUC, it was argued that the goal of educational reforms should be understood within a struggle for socialism:

> A struggle for educational change must culminate in a struggle for socialism. Still, there is much that teachers must do now to win educational reforms and to build a socialist movement. We can develop programs which interfere with the ability of the educational system to fulfill its functions of tracking, socialization and discipline. And we can, here and there, win some resources of the educational establishment away from the service of capitalism to the creation of a movement for a new society. (11)

These organizing efforts would not separate teachers into their particular departments nor, as a consequence, into particular disciplinary organizations. Rather, teachers should focus on altering the capitalist system in which they all teach. Therefore, while there is emphasis within *Classes and Schools* on altering the content of courses and the "race, sex, and class biases of textbooks," emphasis is also placed upon open admissions, community control of schools, exposing the biases of the counseling system, and women's liberation (11). To return to the work of Macrorie (1970), it is possible to imagine Macrorie endorsing an end to tracking and supporting an open admissions policy, yet it is impossible to imagine either Macrorie's text producing an argument for the end goal of socialism. His work (along with others such as Murray 1969) ultimately endorse key concepts of American democracy or American exceptionalism. Consequently, as was stated earlier, their work represents a more traditional and liberal understanding of the goals of education.

This ability of the NUC to appeal to both liberal and radical leftists enabled much of its success at MLA. It was able to straddle competing camps, simultaneously endorsing the teaching of comparative literature and the formation of a socialist politics. To this extent, the NUC was clearly attempting to build a coalition of professionals in the hope that once on board, individuals would endorse the larger political program of the organization. In fact, given the success of the NUC at the MLA business meeting, the development of a language resolution focusing on class and race, and its success in attracting an audience to its workshop, the next *NUC Newsletter* brimmed with confidence. In "What Success at the MLA?" (1970), Florence Howe writes:

> From any viewpoint, NUC at MLA was an incredible success
> . . . . How could we, six weeks ago, have thought in terms of
> changing so enormous a bureaucratic structure as the Modern
> Language Association. . . . [W]e assumed that professionals
> were ready for change; in fact, we underestimated the quality
> and quantity of that readiness.[5] (1)

It is important to note, however, that to a great extent, the NUC victories were short-lived. A closer examination of the nature of the NUC led to questions about its ability to represent a broad-based coalition within the MLA. Furthermore, as NUC actions became known, moderate and conservative MLA members argued that the votes of 292 individuals for NUC's Kampf did not adequately represent MLA's 30,000 membership. Marginally supported NUC resolutions, they argued, should not be the basis for MLA actions. As a result, structural reforms were put in place to limit the ability of "cadre organizations" to seize control of the MLA agenda. Mail ballots were increased. In 1969, for instance, the 1968 NUC resolution against the Vietnam War was defeated by mail ballot. A 1971 NUC proposal for the MLA to endorse the anti–Vietnam War "People's Peace Treaty" was also defeated by mail ballot. Finally, a resolution was approved that forbade the MLA to commit "the language profession to any position on [current] issues unless they are directly connected with the promotion of literary or linguistic scholarship or are necessary to preserve professional integrity" (Bloland and Bloland 1974, 71).[6] After 1970, the business meeting itself was replaced with a 232-delegate assembly whose members were elected by mail ballot. According to Bloland and Bloland (1974), only twelve members of the new delegate assembly could be considered "radicals" or sympathetic to the NUC. By 1972, the end result of the NUC efforts was to strengthen the "bureaucratic structure" of the MLA against the ability of cadre organizations to affect its institutional image or politics. As a consequence, these efforts drastically cut back on the ability of the NUC to "reform" the MLA.

Leaving the MLA Convention in 1968, however, the NUC could feel confident that the connections between social policy and educational reform were being taken up by English professionals. The leadership of the NUC could feel confident about the ability of the organization to attract both liberal and radical-leaning members. In fact, the NUC High School Teaching and Language Workshop had recommended that the NUC continue its work and had specifically requested that the NUC attempt to organize at the Conference on English Education[7] and CCCC.[8] Given such support, the NUC saw itself as able to initiate a series of actions which would have an even greater impact than those initiated at the MLA. They would soon discover, however, that the institutional mass of the CCCC, like the MLA, was not overly interested in radical reform.

1969

As it had at the MLA, the NUC held a series of workshops at the 1969 CCCC Convention focusing on the relationship between language and society. Among these sessions were a "Workshop on Oppressive Linguistics," "Composition as Death," "Cultural Bias," "Teachers as Political Beings," "The English Teacher and Student Rebellions," and "Reactionary Biases Our Curricula Promote" (Bird 1977, 12). Notably, these sessions attracted only about one hundred participants. An additional forty-two people signed a sheet asking for further information, a list which included Lou Kelly (future SRTOL critic) and Mina Shaughnessy. A separate sheet also has the name of NUC member Walker Gibson, but its origins cannot be attached to any specific meeting.[9] Although NUC members Louis Kampf, now MLA second vice president, and Richard Ohmann, editor of *College English*, were in attendance, it did not initially appear as though the NUC was gaining much support.

Instead, it appeared as if the CCCC had successfully integrated the social concerns that the NUC was trying to represent. As had the NUC, the CCCC organized panels on how the freshman composition course could situate itself in light of the "student rebellion." Garland Cannon's "Language Study in the Composition Course" (CCCC 1969) for instance, recognized that "old certainties are shaken; the open policy of the community college has admitted a militant, unprepared, but not uneducatable student." In response to this situation, Cannon would revise traditional grammar education to better prepare the new student in standard English. (Cannon would later reject the SRTOL.) The issue was also raised of whether the composition course should even be the tool for the dialect speaker to learn standard English. "Freshman English as a Happening" would toss aside grammar and stylistics altogether if the student was "communicating" (CCCC Workshop Reports 1969). Yet neither workshop appeared to place freshman composition or dialects within a social or political agenda. Unlike the NUC's goals, the political reasons or effects of such change were left unarticulated. As had Macrorie's (1970) text, these panels seemed to endorse a politics that stopped at the classroom door.

At the panel titled "Freshman English Teacher in the 1970's," the difference in the positions of the NUC and CCCC panels was made evident. In his presentation titled "Must We Have a Cultural Revolution," Louis Kampf (1970) argued that "the disease of composition is not a matter of pathology, but a natural consequence of our educational—and, therefore, social—system." The freshman composition course, he argued, had very little to do with enabling students to gain a better sense of themselves and "how institutions have shaped their identities and their speech" (249). Instead, reiterating for composition the general viewpoint of Davidson's critique in "A Student Syndicalist Movement" (1966), Kampf argued that the goals of freshman composition represent the interests of U.S. corporations for a literate population. In arguing for freshman English teachers to resist such corporate pressures, Kampf focused on the need for freshman composition to respect a student's language: "Freshman English courses should become part of a resistance culture giving students a sense of a different world; of social arrangements which do not transform our skills—our very language—into a source of labor value" (249). Kampf's politics were markedly different from Murray's and Macrorie's. They were also different from the lines of diversity being articulated in CCCC panel discussions. But the use of "resistance" or "students' language" at that time could be read as an endorsement of process education. Or rather, it could be read as a use of process education that moved beyond just "students' language" to the social environment from which it originated. In this way, the NUC was beginning to embed itself within the mission of the CCCC.

The NUC's political redefinition of the process movement, however, did not go unnoticed. In fact, at the April 19, 1969, CCCC Executive Committee meeting, questions were raised about the relationship of the NUC to the CCCC. As discussed in chapter 1, for most of the 1950s, the Executive Committee had been discussing what should be the goals of the CCCC as an organization. These discussions had typically revolved around whether the CCCC should expand its concern to include high schools and literature. Only in the past year had the Executive Committee confronted the emerging social politics symbolized by the New Left. Consequently, the NUC represented a different type of work for the Executive Committee. The NUC would ask the CCCC to come out against the war, the draft, and corporate America. It would link such issues directly to writing instruction. For these very reasons, CCCC Executive Committee members wondered "whether the purpose of CCCC includes what the NUC seems to feel is relevant, and to what extent the NUC convention program reflects the interests of CCCC and its members" (CCCC Secretary's Report No. 61, 16 April 1969).

In fact, even Bob Ross, first interim president of the NUC, expressed doubts about the role of the NUC at the CCCC. In a letter to Neal Resnikoff dated April 8, 1969, Ross writes about the goals of organizing at the CCCC. As can be seen, there is little consideration given to the implications of teaching writing in the classroom and the "composition group" (the CCCC):

There is by now a rather large backlog of notes from you asking advice, suggestions, etc. on your organizing efforts with NCTE and the composition group [CCCC].

In particular, I have nothing much to say about the problems internal to these fields in which you're working. Nor, that much about specific tactics at these meetings. I do have some thoughts on tone, style, and political strategy.

I think we should beware of being sheep in sheep's clothing. At meetings of teachers of English or composition we should present ourselves as interested in "more relevant" classroom materials, period. Our substantive position is that of radical leftists; our analysis of the university as an institution and the university experience as a process is not discontinuous with our analysis of contemporary warfare-welfare capitalism. What I am saying is that there should not be a reception of us which implies you are honestly trying to better the institution. Of course it's okay if we're easy to talk to, and we should always be reasoned, but we should not . . . put down . . . the radical student movement.

My second thought concerns strategy of work in the professions. I think our objectives should be these; to transform the self-identification of teachers from that of being "professionals" who relate to other colleagues in a field to that of being politicals whose most important relationships are to comrades who may or may not be in their field; attendant to that goal is the need to raise substantive issues about these institutions—the raising of these issues done in such a way to persuade new people that they can break out of professional stagnation to a more activist identity; to, therefore, recruit people to the left, and to aid in the creation of an organized left constituency where previously there had been, perhaps, only left sympathies. But politics remains in the fore. What I think we should avoid is the notion that here is a group of like-minded friends banded together to make their professions more relevant. In general, though there are obvious exceptions, many of the specific struggles and fights within the professional organizations tend to be tempests in academic teapots; they engulf us in the trivia of organizations and issues which are not that important. Especially in these early months when building NUC on a firm basis is so important. (1–2)

Obviously Ross was not endorsing an image of the NUC which had been created at the MLA. The NUC should not be seen as concerned with disciplinary or institutional reform, but with creating a different network for academics to organize. That is, what is clear from this letter is that to a great extent the NUC was not concerned with the development of the CCCC as an educational institution. As has been discussed in earlier chapters and is reiterated in the letter, the NUC was concerned with creating a political relationship among academics, not with the reformation of a particular discipline's organization. Within that goal, the classroom also served similar purposes. The rhetoric of Louis Kampf (1970), then, about the need for a cultural revolution was quite sincere; the goal was a reformed society, not a reformed CCCC. Consequently, the Executive Committee can be seen as correct in its hesitation toward and concerns about the intent of the NUC.

As had the MLA, the CCCC moved to limit the ability of cadre organizations to influence the internal politics of its organization. William Doster recommended that the CCCC set up a procedure which would require outside organizations "to submit the proposed program in writing to the officers and Executive Committee in time for consideration at the November meeting" (CCCC Secretary's Report No. 61, 16 April 1969). This move effectively gave the CCCC Executive Committee veto power over any outside organization's participation, for such a resolution can be read as empowering the CCCC to distance itself from any New Left group which attempted to organize at its conference or as an attempt to limit the scope of the CCCC. In fact, given the quick pace of political events and the quick creation and disintegration of political groups, the CCCC resolution would effectively exclude organized political activism. Speaking in response to these moves, Raymond Liedlich stated that he "hoped this did not mean the program chair would not be sensitive to incorporating a variety of ideas in the program by leaving such new ideas up to other groups to propose" (CCCC Secretary's Report No. 61, 16 April 1969). That is, having effectively placed certain political organizations outside of the CCCC, it appeared that the next logical move was to place the actual political concerns outside of the CCCC as well. The Executive Committee quickly stated that this was not the intention of the resolution (CCCC Secretary's Report No. 61, 16 April 1969). Either reading of the resolution's intent, however, effectively demonstrates the attempt by the CCCC Executive Committee to gain control of an increasingly expanding conference.

Several months later, however, the CCCC would again have to return to the subject of the NUC. Based upon the 1969 CCCC workshop "The Future of CCCC: An Informal Discussion," Resnikoff presented resolutions to the CCCC Executive Committee. In a memo titled "The NUC at CCC and a Look ahead to NCTE" (Resnikoff 1969b), Resnikoff reports that the resolutions developed as follows:

> 1. In light of the influence of CCCC and NCTE on teacher certification requirements, we urge that CCCC and NCTE work to include preparation for student teachers which will lead to black studies for black students, working class studies for working class students, women's studies, etc.

> 2. Because as English teachers we constitute the sole market for a certain group of textbooks, it seems reasonable that we should seek to shape the nature of these books. We should study the existing anthologies for implicit racism and discrimination against subordinate groups, including women, in order to issue guidelines for the individual teacher seeking to make choices.
>
> Furthermore, CCCC and NCTE should insist that publishers not have racist texts on their commercial displays at CCCC and NCTE conventions. Even better CCCC and NCTE should not allow publishers who have racist books in their catalogs to have bookstalls at CCCC and NCTE meetings. Also, the CCCC and NCTE should be highly concerned with and active about the individual teacher-author's conflict with publishers over what can be printed.

> 3. As people whose careers are affected by the spending of federal funds, we ask CCCC and NCTE to study the patterns and consequences of their allocations so as to take stands on these decisions that shape our destinies.

> 4. As teachers whose current or former students are often taken from the classroom by the draft, and as human beings who must give grades that help determine who may be killed, we ask CCCC and NCTE to take a position against the nature of that grading system, that draft, that war, and that foreign involvement that may lead to other Vietnams in Latin America and elsewhere.

5. [T]his organization must be open and democratic. Workshops should be listed for any member or members who have a topic they want to discuss and act upon. There should be a general meeting at the end of each convention where each workshop can present its proposals for the deliberation of the body and subsequent action.

6. CCCC and NCTE meetings and CCCC and NCTE Executive Committees should work actively to make nonstandard dialects acceptable in all schools from kindergarten on and create an active articulation between the elementary schools, secondary schools, junior colleges and universities to deal with this problem. Linguists and English teachers should concentrate not on trying to teach everyone to speak and write upper middle class white dialect but rather on changing the attitude of society that discriminates against other dialects. Their efforts should be devoted to teaching the truths that all dialects are effective and valuable and that no dialect is any more indicative than any other of intelligence or even language ability on the part of the speaker. (1)

In presenting these resolutions to the Executive Committee, there is evidence that the NUC felt CCCC chair Wallace Douglass was among its ranks, for in response to Resnikoff, Douglass "noted that the CCCC was founded on specific professional and administrative issues and is now being invited to expand [its] range of concerns" (CCCC 1970). Earlier Douglass had argued that the NUC was "an example of issues which force us into thinking about CCCC and the state of this profession as well as the organization and its relationship to other groups." (CCCC Secretary's Report No. 61, 16 April 1969). In a CCCC workshop, Douglass had also argued that composition instructors "must adopt a political attitude toward the schools since the schools now simply maintain the class system in America" ("The Future of CCCC: An Informal Discussion" 1969). In addition, Bob Ross, NUC president, named Douglass as an NUC contact person. Another NUC document actually lists Wallace Douglass as an NUC member and NUC contact person, someone who could be contacted by others to find out about the organization ("Regional Contacts of NUC, 1969"). It appeared that, as with Kampf in the MLA, the CCCC had a chair who would advance the efforts of the NUC. In fact, Douglass would become a pivotal figure in the success of the NUC at the CCCC, for Douglass moved NUC resolution 6 (which was stated as resolution 1 in the meeting) concerning nonstandard dialects from the status of interest-group politics to official CCCC Executive Committee status.[10]

> In response to the resolutions proposed by the NUC, the Chairman of CCCC [Wallace Douglass] be directed to appoint a committee that will formulate a statement for the use of CCCC and the Executive Committee concerning the relationship between language and social attitudes, especially in the case of teachers and to suggest a direction toward which CCCC can develop. The motion passed unanimously. (CCCC 1970)

Given the emerging importance of the process movement and its emphasis on a student's language, it is perhaps not surprising that the language resolution concerning nonstandard dialects attracted the most discussion at the Executive Committee meeting. Nor is it surprising that Douglass was able to make this move on the language resolution rather than other NUC proposals. Success was not unambivalent for the NUC, however. In taking up the resolution, the CCCC placed the resolution within its own paradigm. Whereas the NUC supported the need for structural change of the social and economic system, the CCCC foregrounded "considerations [concerning] . . . the attitudes of teachers and the complexities of socio-linguistics" (CCCC 1970). To proceed on the resolution, the CCCC thus removed the NUC emphasis on the relationship of education to the corporate and social structure of the United States. The sheer fact that the resolution had spawned a formal CCCC committee, however, represented a success for NUC.

The NUC-CCCC resolution, then, produced the Ad Hoc Committee on Social Dialects chaired by Wallace Douglass. John Asmead, Juanita Williamson, and Richard Young were committee members (CCCC 1970). Douglass had firmly supported NUC efforts and envisioned a more activist CCCC. Williamson would later endorse the guidelines for junior college teachers which strongly supported respect for student dialects. Asmead had endorsed Macrorie's *Uptaught* (1970), although it is difficult to know how this might have affected his opinions toward the committee's mission.[11] From the outset, then, there was the possibility that the committee might produce a progressive statement.

But there were also institutional reasons beyond the NUC for the CCCC to develop a forward-looking language resolution at that time. By 1969, the NCTE's Committee on the English Language (CEL) had already drafted two resolutions concerning the "new student" and her or his dialect. The CEL was a recent creation. According to Richard Lloyd-Jones (1991), its purpose was to monitor NCTE public statements about linguistics. As related in Wilson (1967, 129), this was particularly important, since linguistics had achieved a new prominence in composition. Chaired by Sumner Ives, a partial list of CEL committee members includes Harold Allen (who would later lead the committee to consider a new language statement for the 1980s), Raven McDavid (who had opposed the connection between Black English and African roots), Albert Marckwardt (author of NITE), Rosemary Wilson, and Kellogg Hunt. The first CEL resolution recommended that NCTE realize that "because of the large amounts of public and private funds being expended in these efforts" and "the lack of professional training" of project guides, NCTE "prepare guidelines for conduct and evaluation of such projects." In a second resolution, the CEL recommended that the NCTE "explore calling a national conference on teaching English to speakers of non-standard dialects" (Committee on the English Language 1969). At the time of the formation of the CCCC's Ad Hoc Committee on Social Dialects, the CEL was also in the process of preparing a new "Statement on Usage" (CEL n.d.).

When one realizes that the CEL usage statement was intended to direct NCTE efforts concerning dialects, channel the direction of funds, guide the evaluation of projects, and frame orientations of conferences, it becomes evident the way in which the NCTE's understanding of dialects could affect composition's attitude toward pedagogy, research, and curriculum. It has already been noted how the NCTE's previous efforts, such as NITE, had affected the study of writing nationally. Recognizing the power of the NCTE, the NUC had submitted the following resolution in December 1969 (NUC 1969):

As organizations whose members have their work affected by the spending of federal funds, we ask NCTE to create a committee of nine to study the patterns and consequences of their allocation so as to take stands on these decisions that shape our destinies. A report should be circulated through NCTE journals by March 1.

Unlike its CCCC resolutions, no action was taken upon this resolution. At the March 1970 Executive Committee meeting, however, Richard Larson stated that any statement by the CCCC Ad Hoc Committee on Dialect's resolution should then be presented to the NCTE Committee on Resolutions. In this way, the CCCC would be able to preempt automatic approval of NCTE's statement. Since the NUC advocates appeared to have an ally in Douglass, the endorsement of the CCCC resolution by the NCTE would serve similar purposes to the preceding NUC-NCTE resolution. Indirectly (and perhaps unintentionally), then, Larson was pushing the agenda of the NUC.

The CEL's "Statement on Usage" (n.d.) soon became a site of controversy between CCCC, NCTE, and NUC. Initially, this might not appear to be the case. Written by Sumner Ives, the "Statement on Usage" seems to make a strong argument for the rationality of all languages: "All regional and social varieties of language are equally legitimate as language, that is, as a means of verbal communication among members of a community" (4). The social dynamics of the late 1960s, however, had surrounded any statement endorsing the legitimacy of all languages with a radical content. For this reason, the CEL attempted to address the concerns of "parents, employers, administrators, and other molders of public opinion . . . that the policy recommended is not anything goes" (7). That is, the document does not endorse the right of all languages to exist in the classroom or in the social world with prestige equal to standard English. The policy is also far from an endorsement to alter the dynamics of a composition classroom. Recognizing "the position of standard English among American dialects," it states, "[I]t is a responsibility of the schools to help children add standard English to their repertory. . . . The fact that public life requires a mastery of one variety of English should not alienate anyone from a possibly different variety spoken in his home or his neighborhood" (3). This argument that the acquisition of another dialect does not distance the student from a "native dialect" echoes the position of the Dartmouth Conference.

The pragmatic implications of such a document also contradict the emerging role of the composition classroom as a site of resistance to the social and economic pressures faced by students. Kampf (1970) had spoken against using the classroom to turn a student's language into labor value. Macrorie (1970) had positioned his classroom as a site where students could escape the pressures causing them to write "Engfish," yet in the "Statement on Usage" (CEL n.d.), Ives writes that "a command of standard English is required for many jobs, especially for the clerical, sales, and service jobs that are available in a complex society" (1). (Little did Ives know how plentiful service jobs would become in the 1980s when the manufacturing base of the United States suffered serious setbacks.) The effect of such a statement for classroom practice can be seen in Ives's "The Relevance of Language Study" (1966):

> I suppose we can agree that we could teach writing better if we could talk about writing more specifically: I am not referring simply to the correction of errors such as dangling modifiers and violations of agreement. Our freshman classes are filled with students who can write more or less standard English but who write it poorly. They write such sentences as "This problem of assuring employment and the work force would be released as a result of the sudden reduction of demand for war materials and products is of paramount importance." Correction is simple; just bring the head of the subject nominal closer to its verb. . . . The problem is how to tell the student what to do. For this, as in any other instruction, we need a vocabulary of technical terms, and a pedagogically adequate grammatical description provides such terms. (134)

Both Macrorie and Kampf would have asked the student to work on the content of the essay. They would have focused on the ways in which writing could empower the writer's self-image as either an individual or political being. Ives, however, leads the class into to a discussion, embedded in grammar, of style. The political sentiment expressed in the student paper or a general discussion of politics does seem not part of Ives's writing class. That is, the role of writing instruction envisioned by Ives would limit any political discussion to a greater emphasis on questions of style or "pedagogically adequate grammatical descriptions." When placed within the context of dialect diversity in a classroom, the image emerges of a class which features an increased respect and tolerance for a variety of personal languages coupled with the necessity to subordinate those personal languages to standard English. While this is certainly an improvement over traditional writing courses, it does not go as far as advocates of the NUC would suggest.

Further, the CEL usage statement effectively erases Black English as a distinct dialect. Instead, it points to the need to study "standard English . . . in all its regional and functional varieties" (1). Thus, while the document discusses the need to recognize Chicagoan, Bostonian, or San Franciscan dialects, it does not mention Black English. When using an example that might be Black English, the "Statement of Usage" argues: "Someone who says 'I seen him yesterday' is not dropping have; he is using seen as his common form for both simple past and past participle, just as walked is the form for both in Standard English" (5). To understand this emphasis on regional dialects instead of Black English, it is important to reflect upon the members of the CEL committee, Raven McDavid and Albert Marckwardt, who helped write the document. Both McDavid and Marckwardt argued that American English was a derivation of British English. Under this paradigm, research into linguistic change consisted of tracing aspects of American dialects back to their "British" origins. Broadly, this paradigm led to a study of the development of American English from its arrival in New England to its arrival in California.[12]

Consequently, both Marckwardt's and McDavid's work saw the study of urban Black English as an interruption to the scholarly study of American English. In "Planning the Grid" (1971b), McDavid discusses how regional research should follow a geographical grid, arriving at the inner cities in due course. According to McDavid, this scholarly grid was interrupted by Lyndon Johnson:

Such an orderly progression, however, was rendered impossible by the very circumstances that prompted the development of social dialectology in the United States. Under the presidency of Lyndon Johnson, attention was drawn as never before to problems of the large number of poorly educated and low skilled, displaced from rural areas as agriculture became industrialized, and drawn to the big cities. It became apparent that the differences between the speech of the migrants (usually non-standard Southern) and the local varieties of the standard constituted one of the obstacles to the employment of the new arrivals and success in school for their children. Consequently, metropolitan school systems sought and often obtained large sums for the study of speech differences, in the hope of improving teaching materials and methods of instruction. Although, from the point of view of research in sociolinguistics, the first grants might have been better allocated to such communities as Bamberg, South Carolina . . . such communities could not dramatize their case nearly as effectively as could the mayor of New York city, nor did they have local universities with traditions of social research and officers trained in the art of soliciting funds for it. As it was, so much money was allocated through urban school boards, and so few were the scholars with the competence in field research in language variety, that it was often necessary to use inexperienced investigators and try new methods, some more successful than others. (20)

Unlike Resnikoff and Macrorie, then, McDavid does not valorize the African American student or Black English speaker. Even though Black English certainly would have been spoken in Bamberg, South Carolina, for McDavid, the Black English speaker is a disruption of scholarly research. Even when speaking of the northerly migration, McDavid does not mention the fact that many of the migrants were African American. His use of the term "non-standard Southern" serves to erase the issue of race entirely. Finally, as is evident, McDavid is also bemoaning the very shift in emphasis, the community research, that the NUC appears to endorse (although the work of Deutsch indicates the ways in which "community research" did not always produce the most positive images of African American speech).

Given the CEL's usage statement, it is not surprising that the NUC would have concerns about the ways in which the NCTE would spend any federal research money it acquired. The reintegration of Black English into a traditional linguistic paradigm would limit the ability of the NUC to use the English writing classroom as a site to initiate race and class politics. In November 1969, the NUC had attempted to set up a special committee within the NCTE to address their concerns. In a letter to the NCTE, Resnikoff (1969b) submitted the same resolutions, slightly revised, that were earlier presented to the CCCC. The language statement presented to the NCTE reads

> All NCTE and section meetings and Executive Committee shall work actively to make "non-standard" dialects acceptable in all schools from kindergarten on. We realize that this cannot be accomplished unless social realities are taken into account. Therefore, we urge linguists and English teachers to concentrate on changing the society that discriminates against various peoples and their dialects. The linguists' and teachers' efforts should initially be somewhat focused on teaching the truth that all American dialects are effective and valuable and that no dialect is any more indicative than any other of intelligence or even language ability on the part of the speaker; this should be accompanied by analysis of what has caused the discrimination by classes. Only with this in mind should teachers and linguists help provide students with "survival space" by teaching them how to speak and write upper middle class white dialects as secondary dialects.

With its endorsement of both standard English and the workings of the U.S. economy, however, the CEL statement represented a strong rejection of the goals the NUC had articulated. As a consequence, the NUC would have little success in arguing its case to the NCTE. The NUC's call for "linguists and English teachers to concentrate on changing the society that discriminates" was largely ignored. The success of NUC's efforts, at this point, rested with the CCCC and its Ad Hoc Committee on Dialects.

The CCCC would respond to the NCTE-CEL usage statement at its November 1970 Executive Council Meeting. At this meeting, it became evident that the CCCC Executive Committee was not only responding to the usage statement, but also using it to redefine the parameters of its power within the NCTE. For while the meeting started with a discussion of the CEL usage statement, concern soon focused on why the CCCC positions were not represented in the CEL. As a consequence, the CCCC

Executive Committee began to argue for increased representation. The minutes from the meeting detail these concerns:

> Freeman asked the group to consider co-operation with the NCTE Commission on Language and continue working on the project, begun last year. Douglass was charged to keep in touch with the Commission and to have Juanita Williamson express her views on any document it issues; there will be a presentation of the matter at the 1971 meeting in Cincinnati. Concern centers on what may be said about dialect differences and levels of language. The officers agreed that CCCC should discover all it can about the NCTE statement in order to decide if CCCC can endorse it.
>
> [William] Irmscher moved and Douglass seconded the following: The CCCC Officers resolve that CCCC should have on each NCTE Commission an official voting representative who will be nominated by the Executive Committee. . . . The motion passed unanimously.
>
> [William] Irmscher asked that in the event this request is refused, that CCCC be given an explanation of the reasons for the NCTE refusal.
>
> After further discussion, it was agreed that CCCC should characteristically be more generously represented officially on major bodies of NCTE (CCCC officers meeting, 22–23 November 1970).

It is significant, then, that Wallace Douglass was nominated to be a representative to the College Section of the NCTE. He had pushed for an expanded role for the CCCC in English studies as well as for the CCCC to become an organization which endorsed certain values. Finally, he had appointed the original Ad Hoc Committee. At this moment, not only was the Ad Hoc Committee formulating the theoretical future of the CCCC, but it was also being used as a wedge to split and reform the relationship between the NCTE and the CCCC. In wanting to carve out a space for its own resolution and its own organization, the CCCC was taking a theoretical stance and also attempting to direct the NCTE's attitudes about what conclusions should be drawn from the new students entering universities and colleges.

1971

A participant at the March 1971 open discussion meeting held at the CCCC Convention in Cincinnati stated that he hoped "CCCC would not become a politically oriented organization." Another participant "spoke against CCCC becoming involved in political activity" (Open Discussion Meeting 1971). Given the tenor of the meeting, it is easy to see why participants believed the CCCC was becoming "political." The open meetings had allowed organizations such as the NUC, or activists such as Gregory Cowan, to circumvent the April 1969 Executive Committee decision to monitor the activity of outside organizations. At that meeting, for instance, NUC members Bob Blackwood and Robert Saalbach presented a series of resolutions for endorsement by the CCCC membership. All of the resolutions echoed NUC policies:

> 1. Resolution on Political Repression: The heightening struggle of oppressed peoples against the institutions which hold power has brought with it heightened repression. Many teachers who have expressed some concern for these struggles have found themselves in difficulty with department chairmen and administrations; an increasing number are being fired.
>
> Repression in the academy has become a way of life, and prevents many teachers from performing their duty toward their students. Firings and harassment are not the acts of a few misguided and stupid people; repression and the use of force are the only means by which the U.S. government can keep the American and foreign peoples under control.
>
> Be it resolved that: The CCCC will utilize its good offices to oppose political firings wherever they occur and work for the reinstatement of any teacher fired for political reasons. Furthermore, any such cases will be documented in the publication of the CCCC.
>
> 2. We, the CCCC, deplore the imperialist aggression in Viet Nam, North Korea, South Africa and against our own people, black, brown, yellow, and red, which our government considers more important than the educational, economic and social good of the people. The [continued support] for the corporate war expenditure of the federal regime has expanded a crisis in educational student enrollment increases while faculty personnel remains the same or even decreases.

We, the members of the CCCC, demand both an immediate end to this colonialist aggression and immediate dedication of government funding to the needs of the people.

3. Resolution on Women: The status of women in the English profession reflects the status of women in society at large. They are assigned to what are deemed "inferior" roles, such as teaching composition, are virtually ignored in curricula, perpetuating the assumption of male supremacy, have difficulty being hired by elite institutions, are tenured very seldom in proportion to their numbers, often receive less pay than their male counterparts, often cannot work at schools at which their husbands are employed, and often cannot work at all, although adequately trained, because of child-care responsibilities.

The oppression and exploitation of women must be brought to light and then rectified. To this end, be it resolved that the CCCC use all the influence and power it can wield to:

1. Support the MLA Commission on Women in its study of women in the profession.

2. Remove nepotism rules at member colleges.

3. Support and encourage curricula relating directly to women.

4. Publish in its journal articles and data relating to the status of women in the profession.

5. Provide day care centers at its annual conventions. . . .

6. Investigate and reveal any disparities in institutional salary schedules between men and women. (NUC 1971)

Additionally, through procedural moves and sense-of-the-house motions, Gregory Cowan was able to put the CCCC in the position of endorsing the "People's Peace Treaty." Such resolutions probably did not represent the majority of the CCCC membership. If the concerns over teaching and writing instruction that dominated Executive Committee meetings are taken into account, the concerns of the NUC do appear to be outside the mainstream of the CCCC. Therefore, while the Executive Committee had successfully distanced itself from the NUC, it was unable to distance the CCCC as a whole from New Left political activity. (This failure is important because when the CCCC's SRTOL was finally produced, it would be read by many as a statement from the "activists." Unlike the aforementioned resolutions, the NUC resolution on dialects had been accepted by Douglass and placed for development by a committee designated by the Executive Committee. Therefore, it had an institutional status different from these resolutions, yet since it grew out of the context of these resolutions and the NUC, it would be read as a de facto coup d'état by the militants within the CCCC.)

It was within this environment of political activity, then, that the CCCC Executive Council responded to the CEL's "Statement of Usage." The response occurred one day after the CEL had given the document final approval. As the minutes of the Executive Committee meeting detail, the usage statement was not received enthusiastically by the NCTE's Executive Committee or its Council on Composition. In a letter to the CEL (cited in McDavid 1971a), Ives states: "The matter has stirred up considerable discussion, and there seems to be some idea that it should be tied in with a more general discussion of language and composition teaching, involving composition folk as well. Walker [Gibson] will [be] meeting with us to discuss the matter Wednesday morning. I asked him to do so."

By choosing Gibson, Ives was selecting an advocate of the process classroom but without the larger social politics of a Douglass, Resnikoff, or the NUC. (Although as noted, Gibson was listed as an NUC member.) In his letter to the committee, which was quoted by Ives, Gibson (1971) wrote:

> [A]s I read the various papers in the Composition booklet (The Student's Right To Read) together with the one on usage, I was struck by the parallels, the agreements, the general sense of purpose. . . . To put it in one quick sentence, from my own point of view, what I'd like to see is a serious effort to redefine the teaching of writing, away from graded themes, proof reading, and all the ills we know so well, and toward the goals of self-discovery and linguistic play.

Notably Douglass had expressed concern over the Right to Read document almost a year earlier.[13] While Gibson represented a liberalization of traditional teaching values, he did not represent the values of the militant wing within the CCCC, particularly the progressive aspects within the NUC.[14] Further, it was exactly

Gibson's failure to examine social problems that Douglass was attempting to force into the NCTE "Statement on Usage." Finally, in choosing Gibson, Ives was bypassing the Ad Hoc Committee entirely. In fact, as soon as his role was announced, Douglass stated:

> [I]n light of CCCC statements and concerns over the past few years, there ought to be a strong statement indicating that the CCCC Executive Committee will not tolerate anything short of a lucid statement indicating the linguistic and social problems that are involved in current teacher attitudes toward the language of their students. (CCCC Secretary's Report No. 64, 24 March 1971)

The Executive Committee further stated its sense of frustration by noting that while the CCCC Executive Committee was willing to work with NCTE in forming a strong statement "concerning teachers' attitudes toward usage and dialect . . . [i]f a strong sensible statement does not come from the commission soon, the CCCC Executive Committee will issue its own statement" (CCCC Secretary's Report No. 64, 24 March 1971). The motion was forwarded by Lawrence Freeman, seconded by Juanita Williamson, and passed with twenty-five ayes and two abstentions.

The First CCCC SRTOL

It is at this moment that the two-year college forces begin to enter the debate. In 1965 the CCCC Executive Committee had voted to sponsor seven regional conferences on English in the two-year colleges. Given the success of these conferences, the Executive Committee appointed "a full-time NCTE-CCCC conference director of the program, and [sponsored a] planning conference to be held in NCTE Headquarters in 1966" (Wilson 1967, 130). This "planning conference" produced the bylaws of a permanent organization in the same year. These efforts to organize two-year as well as junior college faculty represented an attempt by the CCCC both to expand its membership base and to recruit minorities, particularly minorities from urban areas.[15] Richard

Lloyd-Jones argues that the growth of two-year and junior college faculty shifted the internal politics of CCCC (author's interview with Lloyd-Jones at the CCCC convention, 1991). The new members had greater experience teaching minority and working-class students. As a consequence, they came to the CCCC with a strong sense that their students' language needed to be validated. Whereas Ives's "Statement on Usage" ignored Black English, according to Lloyd-Jones, Black English was an important concept to the two-year and junior college faculty (author's interview with Richard Lloyd-Jones at the CCCC convention, 1992).

The CCCC was not alone, however, in attempting to organize two-year and junior college faculty. During its 1970 national convention, the NUC would officially commit itself "to organizing efforts in community colleges" (NUC 1970). As analyzed by Richard Rothstein (1969a), executive secretary of the NUC,

> [T]he junior college system is an important arena for higher education, because in it the contradictions of this society are highlighted with special viciousness. The crisis in public finance confronts the exploding need for technical education and the mobility desires of working class kids; from this confrontation stems the proletarianization of teachers in Jr. colleges, the perennial budget crisis within them, the irrationality of the things taught and learned. The class inequalities of the society, on the one hand, and the false consciousness of consumerism on the other, are all acted out in the day-to-day life of the junior college. I believe that transformation of education towards egalitarianism and towards education that serves the people will see these institutions and their constituencies—teacher, community, and student—take an important role.

The NUC believed that its programs, such as the OUTS agenda discussed in previous chapters, would have resonance in the community colleges' predominantly working-class and minority student populations. Black Power, however, had seemed to place barriers around biracial coalitions. As a consequence, NUC efforts would focus mainly on "community and junior college campuses, primarily in white working-class communities."[16] While the NUC was attempting to have the CCCC endorse its language statement, it thus was also attempting to organize community college instructors. That is, a language statement which emphasized the problem of class discrimination might successfully demonstrate the commitment of the NUC to the white students in two-year colleges.

It should be noted, however, that the NUC was relatively unsuccessful in its attempts at recruiting two-year and junior college faculty. Part of the reason for this failure within the CCCC is that the NUC was unable to move beyond its image as an organization for "elite" institutions. This seems to be admitted by NUC member Tom Hecht, who argued that the NUC did not have the knowledge necessary to organize at these institutions:

> [O]ur success has only been marginal. At no time in the organization's history were more than 25% of the members in [community colleges]. The political center of the organization remained at elite schools or resided in individuals whose political teeth were cut in the campus politics of the 1960s. We did not have the kind of collective experience in the arenas our ideology designated as critical. We were very foreign to the turf for which we were attempting to develop our strategy. (Hecht n.d.)

Finally, while its politics were sympathetic toward working-class and African American students, the emerging cultural backlash against "student activist" politics hindered the NUC's attempts to integrate itself into the two-year college CCCC mainstream.

Prior to the November 1970 meeting, however, the CCCC had set up a committee to prepare a set of guidelines for preparation of junior college teachers. The chair of the committee was Gregory Cowan, who at the aforementioned March 1971 Convention asked the CCCC to endorse the "People's Peace Treaty." (Cowan, however, does not appear to have joined the NUC.) As part of its guidelines, the committee stated a position on how to consider the variety of languages and dialects these teachers would confront. As reported in the Executive Committee meeting notes (CCCC Secretary's Report No. 64, 24 March 1971), the discussion went as follows:

> Cowan presented the "Guidelines for Junior College English Teacher Preparation Programs"... and there was discussion of the content and use of the document. Freeman moved that the

CCCC Executive Committee endorse the document "with enthusiasm": Fairclough seconded the motion. There was discussion about the wording of competency #4 (on levels of language and dialects) and it was felt that this should be a strong statement "to offset the pernicious influence of programs advocated by people like Engelmann, Bereiter, and Bernstein." Davis requested that her "Amen" to that statement be recorded in the minutes. Further discussion centered on the general tone and rhetoric of the document, the generality of the recommendations, and the wording of individual items.

Williamson moved to substitute wording so that competency #4 would read "recognize that all levels of language and all dialects are equally valuable and that academic insistence on a so-called 'standard' English for all situations is an unrealistic political and social shibboleth based on unsound linguistic information." Campbell seconded the motion. In the ensuing discussion, Degnan spoke strongly against the motion. The vote on the motion was 27 aye, 1 no.

McPherson moved that the following statement by Douglass be added between the paragraphs headed "Linguistic". . . . "recognize that, historically, Standard English is a term that refers to the fact that Southern or South Midland English attained primacy over other official (regional) dialects in the 14th and 15th centuries, that there is no such comparable dialect in American, that there are certain chiefly phonological and morphological items in American English, that there are very widespread, that there are others that are associated with various localities, cultures or classes, and that the choice between one item or another is a matter of sociology and etiquette, not of grammar or linguistics."

Baden seconded the motion. Degnan voiced his objection to the motion, but it passed by a vote of 26 aye [to] 2. . . .

Douglass moved the previous question, i.e., Freeman's motion to endorse the Guidelines with enthusiasm. Campbell seconded the motion and it passed. The vote on Freeman's motion was then taken and it passed with 24 ayes, 1 nay, and 2 abstentions.

The statement seems to follow the goals that the NUC had articulated two years prior, particularly when placed within the context of Cowan's previous actions and the emergence of advocates for Black English. This statement would gain added importance over the next year. For despite the potential generated by the NUC, the Ad Hoc Committee would apparently never publish a report.[17] For the SRTOL to move ahead, then, the NUC would have to rely on new figures, constituencies, and events pushing their resolution forward. At this point, however, what constituted progress on the NUC agenda would be open to debate.

Conclusion

If the NUC imagined that the opening moments of its work in the CCCC had gained broad support, the response of professional organizations would soon indicate the difficulty of translating that support into actual change. At every turn, the NUC would see its resolutions, protests, and activities pulled into institutional politics which had little to do with its goals. Indeed, the NUC became positioned as the counterexample to correct professional behavior. Institutionally blocked at the MLA and CCCC, it would have to rely upon the actions of NUC members placed on boards, councils, or committees. These members, however, by necessity also had to respond to the needs of the organizations which they also represented. A resolution could not produce results. The development of the SRTOL, then, is not the story of a cadre of individuals pushing through radical reform, but the ability of organizations to usurp progressive politics into the mainstream. It is the story of the difficulty of individuals producing radical change. As the next chapter testifies, without a strong base of collective action, many of the progressive politics endorsed by the NUC vanish.

---

1. The only resolution to fail called for the elimination of the MLA's Center for Editions of American Authors.

2. In *Student as Nigger: Essays and Other Stories* (1970), Farber recounts the history and effect of his essay:

> Early in 1967, I wrote "The Student As Nigger" and published it in the Los Angeles Free Press. The article was an outgrowth of my attempts to be a good teacher. After several years in the English Department of the L.A. State College, I had decided that there were limits to how well you could teach in an authoritarian and dehumanized school system. So I thought I would do my bit to help change the system.

When the "Student As Nigger" appeared, I hoped that a few other underground papers would pick it up but I had no idea that it would arouse the interest that it did. The article, particularly its central metaphor, embodies ideas and feelings that had been around for a long time but were then working their way rapidly up to the surface. I don't know exactly how often it has been reprinted; I would guess about 500 times. It has appeared in several papers, in a book, in almost all of the underground papers, and most frequently, in student newspapers and pamphlets on hundreds of campuses in the United States and Canada. (13)

3. In "Relevant 'Relevance'"(1968), Deena Metzger writes about her use of "Student as Nigger" to demonstrate to her students their "inferior, oppressed status." In an echo of Mario Savio's defense of the FSM movement, Metzger writes: "My students who are not, for the most part, black, soon see that black students are not the only ones oppressed." That is, as a theme being traced throughout these chapters, students are asked to imagine themselves in the subject position of African Americans.

It should be noted that soon after using "Student as Nigger" and a poem titled "Jehovah's child," Metzger was suspended from her teaching position at Los Angeles Valley College by the Los Angeles Junior College Board of Trustees. The charges against her, based upon her use of these texts, were "immoral conduct" and "evident unfitness for service." The 1971 open discussion meeting of the CCCC Executive Committee endorsed a resolution by Robert Saalbach of Indiana State University at Terre Haute against political firings and recommending that the CCCC support legal appeals by faculty. The resolution passed 48 to 17. (This resolution was later overturned by the CCCC Executive Committee for lack of quorum.)

4. It should be noted that the opening statement of the NUC announced its socialist tendencies. Further, as was detailed in OUTS, an "American socialism" had been the goal of the NUC. With *Classes and Schools* (Teacher Organizing Project 1970), however, this language would become more pronounced.

5. One year later, Howe herself would win an election for the second vice president.

6. As might be expected, the NUC argued against the use of a mail ballot. In part, the NUC understood that its proposals would not have gained widespread support. It countered, however, that by removing important decisions from the MLA Convention, the most active members of the organization were having policy dictated by inactive members who voted only from a distance. These arguments, however, did not carry the day.

7. In opposition to the "coup d'état" strategy inadvertently employed at the MLA, the NUC participation in the Conference on English Education (CEE) in March 1969 actually laid the groundwork for a more sustained institutional struggle within the NCTE. In a flyer advertising the meeting (NUC n.d., "A Call to Meetings"), the NUC represented its presence as follows:

Possible Topics: Teachers as political beings, the positive aspects of student rebellions, reform of literature teaching, revolutionary demands for literature teaching, New Left Literary Criticism, bringing the Third World into the Schools, the cultural elitism of our curricula, the war in Vietnam, institutional racism, differences between radical and liberal analyses of social issues and solutions, building campus democracy, the dilemma of teacher as authority, the bias of professionalism.... Why should we teach the "western tradition," which seems disastrous in so many ways, to white and black students?

As with the MLA, NUC efforts seemed to garner widespread support:

Although CEE members in NUC doubted that there would be much response to an NUC presence at the CEE convention, as things turned out there was considerable interest in the questions, ideas, and organization we talked about and the materials at the NUC table.... The Friday noon meeting sponsored by NUC revealed unexpected interest by CEE participants in examining the decision-making structure of NCTE and its subgroups (e.g. CEE). This resulted not only in the crowded Friday evening meeting with Dr. Margaret Early, Program Chairman of the fall NCTE meeting in Washington and Mr. Robert Hogan, Executive Secretary of NCTE, but also produced a small-group Saturday afternoon meeting with Mr. Hogan.

At this meeting, NUC members found out how to submit extra proposals to the "'confrontations' (program sections with a new format—brief statements of position followed by open discussion)," how to elect a Program Chair, and obtained space at the upcoming Washington Conference. (Resnikoff n.d.)

In speaking of the purpose of focusing on professional institutions, Richard Ohmann had stated that what was important at such meetings

is the membership. Radicals want to get to people in the MLA—because people are what count, because teachers of language and literature have great impact through their work on the acculturation of young people.... [R]adicals see serious politics inhering in the effort to change peoples' beliefs and actions, not in parliamentary maneuvering or elitist power plays. (cited in Bloland and Bloland 1974, 70)

However, what the CEE meeting demonstrated was the extent to which an organization dedicated to "teachers as political beings" could become dominated by issues of "parliamentary maneuvering." In part, this was because such maneuvering was an easier and more recognizable achievement, but also because the MLA "counterrevolution" demonstrated that bureaucratic institutions could effectively limit the ability of radicals for self-expression. In leaving the meeting to prepare for the CCCC and NCTE, it was perhaps out of a sense of frustration that Resnikoff reminded participants that much as we are interested in moving NCTE, we should not forget that we must give primary attention to working at the community level to get as many as possible involved in making the changes needed in our schools and society. New University Conference is one national vehicle to help us do these things. (Resnikoff 1969b)

8. See Resnikoff (1968a).

9. See Workshop on Oppressive Linguistics Attendance Sheet (1969), Composition as Death Attendance Sheet (1969), and Workshop on Cultural Bias Attendance Sheet (1969).

10. Neither Richard Lloyd-Jones, author of the SRTOL, nor Richard Larson, CCCC chair who reinitiated the SRTOL movement in 1971, however, believed that Douglass would have joined such an organization. Consequently, instead of a neat causal connection, what emerges, as with the process rhetoric, is a cross-hatching of concerns that in 1969 mutually supported increased attention to and respect for a student's language in the composition classroom.

11. Asmead is quoted as writing that *Uptaught* is "a classic of its kind—every new college teacher should know it. . . . It tells us what we can and must do in the way of loving and cherishing student creativity . . . the way to the best education, a mutual enjoyment passionately shared by teacher and student" (Macrorie 1970, back cover).

12. In *American English* (1958), Albert Marckwardt writes,

> One must remember, however, that no matter how striking the differences between British and American English may be, the similarities far outweigh them, for it is in grammatical structure and syntax—essentially the operational machinery of a language—that the difference is negligible.

And in a statement that erases the "colonialist history" to standard American English, he continues:

> It is neither exaggeration nor idle chauvinism to say that the English Language, with the exceptional past behind it, appears to be on the threshold of a still greater future. Moreover, this future is to a considerable extent in the hands of those who regularly speak and write the language. What can they do to insure and even to further the development that lies ahead? (182)

13. See CCCC officers meeting minutes, 22 November 1970.

14. It was Gibson who wrote the CCCC's statement on why the CCCC Convention would be moved from Chicago. In response, the New University Caucus (1969, 238) had written:

> One aspect of [the CCCC's] explanation is fine: "We take this stand that our concern for rhetoric is also a concern for the world." But this is undercut by: "What is wrong with Chicago, what is

wrong with our society is its expression of values. As teachers of English, we are in the business of trying to improve our society's expression of values. . . . [We] rededicate ourselves to our belief in just language . . . we state our opposition to the language of the nightstick, and restate our commitment to the language of words in their auspicious places."

This concentration on "expression" and forms seems to avoid the facts of our situation in the U.S. Can we deny that evil values are the primary problem and not the way in which these values are expressed? . . . Thus our effort should not stop at criticizing the expression, the symptoms of evil. Rather, we should look beyond these superficial symptoms of wrong to the more fundamental problem of inhumane goals (e.g. the desire to impose U.S. interests on Viet Nam or Latin American countries.)

Let us not spend too much time and effort with the problem of "society's expression of values." Let us work primarily to foster human values themselves as the rhetoric of humanities in college catalogs and elsewhere asserts we are doing. This requires even more action than the gesture of not going to Chicago. It requires organizing ourselves to foster change, fundamental change, in the country."

15. In 1965 the CCCC Executive Committee, recognizing the lack of two-year affiliated committee members, recommended that the nomination committee construct future ballots such that two-year faculty competed against two-year faculty, thus ensuring continued representation. (CCCC officers meeting minutes, 25 November 1965). In 1967 the CCCC Executive Committee "requested Robert Hogan, Darwin Turner, and Virginia Burke to develop a list with particular attention to Negro members who had not yet appeared on CCCC and NCTE programs" (CCCC officers meeting minutes, Louisville, Kentucky, 4 April 1967).

16. See Rothstein 1969a.

17. This conclusion is based upon research in the NCTE archives and discussion with CCCC members active in the committee and organization at that time. It does not preclude that such a statement might exist. Indeed, it is likely that the very name "a student's right to his own language" might have emerged from this committee. I have been unable to verify this fact, however.

CHAPTER 5

The Students' Right to
Their Own Language
1972–1974

*We affirm the students' right to their own patterns and
varieties of language—dialects of their nurture or whatever dialects in which they find their own identity and
style. Language scholars long ago denied that the myth
of a standard American dialect has any validity. The claim
that any one dialect is unacceptable amounts to an attempt of one social group to exert its dominance over
another. Such a claim leads to false advice for speakers
and writers, and immoral advice for humans. A nation
proud of its diverse heritage and its cultural and racial
variety will preserve its heritage of dialects. We affirm
strongly that teachers must have the experiences and training that will enable them to respect diversity and uphold
the right of students to their own language.*

"The Students' Right to Their Own Language"

I f the CCCC business meetings were becoming increasingly politicized and polemical, the Executive Committee continued to
officially distance itself from the leftist political activity of the
1960s. For instance, at the November 1971 Executive Committee meeting, officers discussed what action should be taken concerning four sense-of-the-house motions passed at Cincinnati. As
discussed in the previous chapter, these motions had included
strong statements concerning firing teachers for political activity,

the "imperialist Vietnam War," support for the role of women in the profession, and the inclusion of African American interests in CCCC programs. Since the meeting, mail ballots had been sent concerning the first two resolutions. As reported by CCCC Chairperson Edward Corbett, "only 40 people responded to the mailing." A resolution was passed that "[i]n the light of the fact that only 40 people responded to the mail ballot, the results of the ballot cannot be considered representative and the Executive Committee can take no stand based on the responses, either approving or disapproving the resolutions" (CCCC Secretary's Report No. 65, 24 November 1971). As had happened at the MLA Convention in 1968, the policies of the NUC and the New Left had been blocked through a mail ballot.[1] Notably, the SRTOL would pass with just seventy-nine votes, only thirty more than the antiwar resolution had taken to pass and only thirty-nine more than the aforementioned mail ballots. As discussed later, however, the SRTOL would be sufficiently scrubbed of New Left policies; its low vote total would not be used to dismiss its passage.

The Second SRTOL

Indeed, the whole SRTOL matter might have remained unresolved if Executive Committee member Richard Larson had not stated that the CCCC should "make another effort at a statement affirming the student's right to his own language." (The title had not yet been made gender neutral.) It is clear from the outset, however, that this new effort saw itself as principally opposed to the NCTE's previous statements. As recorded in the minutes, committee member Richard Lloyd-Jones "reminded the group that the Commission on Language had issued a very mild statement" (CCCC Secretary's Report No. 65, 24 November 1971). In response, Corbett appointed a new committee consisting of Richard Lloyd-Jones as chairperson, with Geneva Smitherman, Darnel Williams, Myrna Harrison, and Ross Winterowd, among others, as committee members. The committee was appointed "to examine the statements of the Commission on Language and the Commission on Composition [and] . . . to report to the Executive Committee in Boston [in November] its judgment about whether the CCCC should endorse an existing statement on language (from one of the NCTE Commissions) or propose its own" (CCCC officers meeting, 25 November 1971).

Even prior to Boston, however, Elisabeth McPherson reported at the CCCC officers meeting that the SRTOL committee was corresponding and "developing a CCCC statement on language." Further, McPherson reported that a subcommittee of Blyden Jackson, Walker Gibson, Betty Petola, and herself was recommending that CCCC "recommend acceptance of the [NCTE CEL "Statement on Usage," but only the] part stating that teachers should know about the nature and structure of language, including information about dialects, but that the Executive Committee [of CCCC] reject the rest of the report of the Commission and refuse to publish it" (CCCC officers meeting, 5 March 1972). It is important, then, that the subcommittee argued for an endorsement of only the general claim of a need for increased linguistic awareness. The subcommittee was not endorsing the CEL's argument about standard English nor its vision of how standard English should be used to supply students to the U.S. economy. That is, the subcommittee was leaving open what types of knowledge would be necessary to be linguistically aware, as well as the implications of the NCTE "Statement on Usage" for the writing classroom. The CCCC accepted these requests and, in effect, began the process of finding a new linguistic and nationalist paradigm through which teachers could understand dialect difference. Consequently, when approximately two weeks later Richard Lloyd-Jones reported to the full Executive Committee that the SRTOL committee believed its role was to decide whether the CCCC needed to develop its own language policy, it appears that the CCCC officers had already decided.

The Executive Committee's concern now focused on the makeup of the committee which would be writing the SRTOL. According to the minutes (CCCC Secretary's Report No. 66, 21 March 1972), Marianna Davis stated that the committee ought to include black linguists. This suggestion, however, seemed to be part of a larger concern about racial representation. Soon after this, the minutes reflect that both Davis and Douglass argued that the committee needed to represent a larger cross section of the CCCC constituency and to include a greater representation of minority groups. Additionally, they argued that a clearer committee charge was needed. Both of these objections were overridden. McPherson, who was now CCCC chairperson, is positioned in the minutes as arguing that any statement by the committee could be modified, rejected, or accepted; black linguists were not needed. Hogan, Nelson, and Campbell argued for the efficacy of a small group working on the project and then allowing the full Executive Committee to see its way through as a body. Consequently, McPherson ordered the committee, as currently organized, to report the next day (CCCC officers meeting, 21 March 1972).

The failure to produce a clearly stated charge, however, would come back to haunt the future status of the SRTOL, for the following day Lloyd-Jones reported that the committee now understood that the goal of the committee was to provide a brief statement on language, adding that such a statement would be *a guide to teachers on all levels and under a variety of local conditions*. In making the committee's mission include *all* teachers, the committee created the opportunity for future participants in the development of the SRTOL, such as Harold Allen, to argue that the SRTOL was properly under the domain of the NCTE. Furthermore, Lloyd-Jones added that the draft of the SRTOL statement about to be distributed "was not the report of his total committee nor did it represent consensus by the committee; it was being presented to determine if the ideas in it illustrated the general framework on the sort of statement the Executive Committee wanted" (CCCC Secretary's Report No. 66, 21 March 1972).

It is, of course, difficult to assess what transpired in the meeting. Nor is it possible to state positively what individual motivations shaped the document. Within the cultural, political, and historical context developed throughout this volume, however, it is possible to read how different versions of the resolution placed CCCC within the time period. It appears that faced with an unclear committee charge and an unclear consensus among its members, the SRTOL committee argued that the previously endorsed guidelines for junior college teachers be endorsed as the general policy of the CCCC. As recorded on a handwritten note, one of the original SRTOL's statements read as follows:[2]

> The Executive Committee of CCCC affirms the student's right to his own language—the dialect of his nurture in which he finds his identity and style. Claims that only one dialect is acceptable should be viewed as attempts of one social group to exert its dominance over another not as either true or useful advice to writers nor as moral advice to humans. A nation which is proud of its diverse heritage and of its cultural and racial variety ought to preserve its heritage of dialects. The Executive Committee affirms strongly the need for teachers to have such training to enable them to support this goal. (SRTOL [handwritten copy] n.d.)

This draft seems in line with the goals of the junior college guidelines as written by Gregory Cowan. As discussed in chapter 4, these guidelines had argued for the recognition "that all levels of language and all dialects are equally valuable and that academic insistence on a so-called 'standard' English for all situations is an unrealistic political and social shibboleth based on unsound linguistic information" (CCCC Secretary's Report No. 64, 24 March 1971). To that extent, the CCCC was not being placed in a position of endorsing a new viewpoint.

The initial revisions by the committee seem to further position the SRTOL within historical precedents. For instance, the committee moved to add spoken language as a protected right, yet the Dartmouth Conference had already articulated such a view. Given this strategy, the committee chose to speak on behalf of all CCCC members instead of just the Executive Committee. As amended, then, the resolution read as follows:

> **We** affirm the student's right to his own language—the dialect of his nurture in which he finds his identity and style. The claims that only one dialect is acceptable should be viewed as attempts of one social group to exert its dominance over another not as either true or sound advice to **speakers or** writers nor as moral advice to human beings. A nation which is proud of its diverse heritage and of its cultural and racial variety ought to preserve

its heritage of dialects. We affirm strongly the need for teachers to have such training as will enable them to support this goal. (SRTOL [handwritten copy] n.d.)

Looking at the comments made on the draft, these changes appear to have occurred without much discussion or debate. This was not the case when it came to the role of the teacher, a role which had developed conflicting political significance as the 1960s progressed. As noted earlier, the Dartmouth Conference had created an image of the composition teacher simultaneously respecting a student's native dialect while teaching standard English. Citing Ellison, the Dartmouth Conference argued that such a pedagogy could lead to a lessening of social tensions and a greater opportunity for equality. Further, McPherson herself had stated to the Executive Committee that writing teachers needed to gain a background in linguistics if a student's dialect was to be understood. To this extent, the SRTOL was merely a weaving of a new linguistic paradigm into preexisting disciplinary insight and CCCC policy. The goal of the teacher appearing clear, "this goal" in the last line was amended to reiterate "this right":

> We affirm strongly the need for teachers to have such training as will enable them to support **this student's right to his own language.**

Since 1966, however, the concept of student rights, particularly surrounding a person's dialect, had become permeated with issues of anticapitalism and Black Power. As noted earlier, Stokely Carmichael and the Black Panthers had tried to link Black English to a general critique of U.S. society. The amended last line, then, could appear to place teachers as potentially aligned with these more radical forces concerned with rights and language politics. To clarify the relationship, this right is placed under the rubric of cultural pluralism. Two different version of this phrase exist:

> We affirm strongly the need for teachers to have such training as will enable them to support **this part of our cultural pluralism.**

> We affirm strongly the need for teachers to have such training
> as will enable them to support **this feature of our cultural plu-
> ralism.** (SRTOL [handwritten copy] n.d.)

Traditionally, *cultural pluralism* was a term intended to demonstrate a common American ethic beneath all the different ethnic
and racial heritages. Given the strong rejection of the ethnicity
paradigm then occurring, such language appeared to bring the
concerns under an ethnicity paradigm which had been rejected
by New Left forces. Additionally, through the use of "this part"
or "this feature," the resolution is also indirectly endorsing standard English instruction as the "other" part or feature of a
teacher's work. Thus, the language represented a deliberate attempt to distance the resolution from the more radical aspects of
the 1960s. That is, the Executive Committee appeared to need
language which would invoke the United States as a multiracial
and multiethnic country but would not necessarily align teachers
with the more radical implications of such language. Ultimately,
however, it appears that invoking "cultural pluralism" went too
far in the other direction. Consequently, the final language eliminates "cultural pluralism" entirely and settles for "diversity" at
the same time that it reasserts the "students' rights."

> We affirm strongly the need for teachers to have such training
> as will enable them to support **this goal of diversity and this
> right of the student to his own language.** (SRTOL [handwrit-
> ten copy] n.d.)

This phrasing merely reiterates the idea of "a nation proud of its
diverse heritage." Since this "nation" is not named but merely an
abstract idea, the CCCC effectively erases the resolution's immediate relationship to the competing images of the United States
then occurring. That is, the SRTOL is not necessarily speaking
about the history of the United States, but merely making a moral
argument about diversity. Nor, despite its invocation of "students'
rights," does the resolution invoke other loaded terms which
would position the meaning of these rights within then-current
debates. In effect, this gesture removed the teacher from the immediate terrain of the 1970s classroom. It offered no concrete
meaning for teachers facing an increasingly varied and politi-

cally active student population. Nor did it offer a specific linguistic or nationalist paradigm through which to understand the resolution's intent. (It was this lack of specificity which would later spur CCCC to attempt to produce teacher guidebooks concerning the resolution.) The effect of such a revision, particularly if read as a revision of the NUC's original version, is to systematically translate the protest language of the 1960s into a seemingly ahistorical, unlocatable classroom. Or rather, to ensure the consent of the Executive Committee, the original NUC resolution had to be moderated and made into a general statement about student–teacher dynamics.

At the conclusion of the discussion, it was decided that the SRTOL committee should revise the statement as suggested.[3] As presented by Lloyd-Jones, the amended version of the SRTOL statement read as follows:

> We affirm the student's right to his own language—the dialect of his nurture in which he finds his identity and style. Any claim that only one dialect is acceptable should be viewed as attempts of one social group to exert its dominance over another, not as either true or sound advice to speakers and writers, nor as moral advice to human beings. A nation which is proud of its diverse heritage and of its cultural and racial variety ought to preserve its heritage of dialects. We affirm strongly the need for teachers to have such training as will enable them to support this goal of diversity and this right of the student to his own language. (CCCC officers meeting, 22 March 1972)

Gaining CCCC approval was risky. Composition teachers would not necessarily follow the Executive Committee's lead in endorsing a resolution which seemed to validate languages other than standard English. In fact, during discussions preceding the vote on the revised resolution, the minutes (CCCC Secretary's Report No. 66, 21 March 1972) reflect that it was agreed that any resolution would have to be part of a larger document which would explain to CCCC members the background of the statement, the necessary linguistics supporting it, and what its implementation would entail for teachers. This seemed crucial, since it was the role of teachers within the resolution which had created such trouble. Therefore, despite misgivings and the admitted need for further explanation, the resolution was passed by a vote of 22 to 1, with 1 abstention. Finally, Davis moved that McPherson appoint a subcommittee for the "purpose of working on an explanation and methods of implementing this statement and that such a group be given funds for travel" (CCCC Secretary's Report No. 66, 21 March 1972). The motion passed.

Beyond the passage of the resolution, this meeting also set in motion rule changes which would allow the ultimate approval of the SRTOL. That is, an attempt was made to alter the rules regarding what constituted a quorum at CCCC business meetings. At the Executive Committee meeting proper, Sophia Nelson had argued that the bylaws of the business meeting should be altered to allow fifty eligible representatives to constitute a quorum, as opposed to the current requirement of one hundred. After some discussion, the resolution failed by a vote of 7 to 14. Several months later, at the November 22, 1972, Executive Committee meeting, James Barry, who was in charge of a committee to develop guidelines for business meetings, gave his report. He proposed that two thirds of the voting members present should be necessary to pass any resolution and that one hundred eligible voters were necessary to pass any resolution. In the course of discussion, however, Larson recommended that, instead of two thirds, "[a] vote of the majority of members present constitutes adoption." This passed unanimously. Immediately afterward, Davis moved that "50 voting members will be considered a quorum." Cowan, who had earlier pushed through antiwar amendments concerning the "People's Peace Treaty," only to see them disputed through a mail ballot, seconded the motion (CCCC officers meeting, 22 November 1972). Although the vote total is not recorded, this motion also passed. Consequently, it was now possible to put the CCCC on record as endorsing a resolution with as few as twenty-six members voting in its favor. In contrast to the MLA, which through procedural moves had blocked the ability of small cadres of individuals from positioning it as a political organization, the CCCC was now open to a broad series of initiatives. As will be seen, a little over a year after the CCCC had decided to place its executive and business meetings at its conventions and open up the voting procedures, it would find itself subject to the type of politics the conservative elements of the MLA had tried assiduously to avoid.

Whereas It Is at Least Arguable . . .

If the Executive Committee postponed a public discussion of how the SRTOL would impact teachers' duties, one possible formulation of these duties would be supplied by Wallace Douglass at the business meeting several days later. Anticipating the future rule changes, the first official act of those in attendance was to amend the quorum rules. It was moved and passed that the business meeting rules be amended to allow fifty members to constitute a quorum. The effect of this rule change was soon evident, for the amended quorum allowed resolutions concerning race to be approved which otherwise might have not been accepted. For instance, Marianna Davis, with the second of Wallace Douglass, presented a statement in support of the resolution of the College Language Association Black Caucus. While supporting the implementation of Black Studies programs, the resolution argued:

> We are distressed . . . at the apparent ease with which ill-conceived programs, directed by persons with limited experience with Black people and their history and often prompted by questionable academic and social motives, seem to receive ready approval. In contrast to this, Black institutions and their faculties are being by-passed in the general rush to redress an imbalance of which we are most direct witnesses.
>
> We are especially distressed by the funding policies of the major foundations, which are proceeding in this matter in a manner which can only be described as neopaternalistic. Accordingly we are calling upon the directors and trustees of these foundations to include knowledgeable Black scholars at all levels in the formations of policies relating to Black people and studies based on them, and warn that many directions are now being pursued which are dangerous and will lead to disaster. (CCCC business meeting, 25 March 1972)

The second motion concerned the current role of publishers in printing African American writers:

The recent surge of interest in Black people in the United States has brought about, inevitably, an energetic redirection and expansion of activity in the world of publishing, particularly in the realm of textbook production. The members of the College Language Association, most of whom have spent many years teaching in predominantly Black institutions, have long been concerned, along with colleagues in other disciplines, with the Black experience. We now take note with some indignation that expansion into the field of Black studies has not entailed the abandonment of an essentially colonialist attitude held by the publishing industry in respect to Black teachers and scholars.

Many books now appearing have been prepared by "instant" experts and have apparently been seen only by such experts before they reach publication. CLA calls for nothing less than a decolonization in the field of publishing in which the talents, background, and experiences of those who have long labored, without reward, in this area will be drawn upon on the same favorable terms so readily available to white writers. (CCCC business meeting, 25 March 1972)

Both of these resolutions called for the larger publishing and academic communities to respect the historical role of the black college and black faculty. As had Stokely Carmichael and the Black Panthers, both of these resolutions invoke images of colonialism and decolonization. Rhetorically, at least, these resolutions appear to participate in larger social arguments concerning the role of African Americans in the United States, yet since neither of these resolutions called for the CCCC to take a stand on public policy concerning African Americans, neither generated much opposition. However, later in the same meeting, Wallace Douglass made a motion concerning "Executive Interference in Integration." The resolution stated:

Whereas it is apparent that the national executive has begun a formidable attack on the federal judiciary and

Whereas it seems that the Congress is likely to pass legislation prohibiting busing of children to achieve integration and

Whereas it is at least arguable that learning in English in its widest sense depends on children having as broad an experience with the various dialects or styles used in this country

> Therefore be it resolved that the annual business meeting of the Conference on College Composition and Communication express its support of the Supreme Court decision in Brown vs. Board of Education of Topeka, Kansas, that furthermore it also express the hope that all deliberate speed may now, after eighteen years, be devised as including any and all means that are necessary to achieve the effective integration of the school systems of the United States. (CCCC business meeting, 25 March 1972)

While Executive Committee member Richard Clark spoke in support of the resolution, the minutes also reflect that some members stated that the motion was not the concern of CCCC. (As noted in chapter 4, earlier activities by the NUC had also been argued to be outside the CCCC mission; the ways in which the organization was having to confront its self-image as simply a teacher and researcher organization are evident here.) Mary Campbell stated that such a resolution would polarize the CCCC members. Another member spoke in favor of the resolution, stating that it was not about busing, but about achieving integration. Finally, Douglass himself argued that the resolution was aimed at deploring executive interference in the judicial process. In effect, however, Douglass was asking the CCCC to stand against the emerging conservative New Right forces taking control of the political debate in the United States.

Indeed, during the period in which the SRTOL was being developed within the CCCC, roughly from 1969 to 1974, the political climate was rapidly changing under Richard Nixon's presidency. During Nixon's administration, the southern states were given almost unprecedented political power. In an attempt to court favor with the South during his presidency, Nixon made efforts to reduce funds for school desegregation from $1 billion to $75 million as well as to block "enforcement of integration laws, even sending Justice Department lawyers down to sue for the suspension of court-ordered school integration in Mississippi" (Sale 1975, 244). In fact, Nixon aide Robert Haldeman ordered that "no official anywhere in his Administration was at any time for any reason to make a statement that might upset and antagonize the South" (Sale 1975, 244). His administration also argued against busing and against the Voting Rights Act, cut funds for

Justice Department lawyers working on civil rights law enforcement, and decided "that all challenges to existing voting laws would have to be decided by protracted lawsuits" (Sale 1975, 244–246 passim).

Beyond his efforts to block busing, Nixon also attempted to influence the type of education that students would receive. Under the leadership of Sidney Marland, who was Nixon's Commissioner of Education, a series of academic reforms were implemented which would push for "career education." As discussed by Ira Shor in *Culture Wars* (1986), Marland's attempt to push career education in public schools and community colleges was an attempt to limit the number of students exposed to a liberal arts education and to slow the production of overeducated college students with no jobs to fit their degrees:

> Soft disciplines in the humanities, arts, and general studies, along with autonomous programs in experimental education, were undermined by the thrust towards courses most open to direct job-training. The broad critical learning possible in liberal arts, women's courses, minority programs, interdisciplinary studies, etc., represented the political problem of the 1960's which careerism in the 1970's helped to solve. Marland not only saw career education as an antidote to campus unrest, but he also gladly agreed to its vocational character, despite his "career" tag. When one voc-ed advocate suggested that with career education vocationalism finally went "big time," Marland happily agreed. (35)

For instance, during Marland's tenure, community colleges received $850 million to fund occupational programs for three years. (This influx of money was occurring at the same time that Gregory Cowan was attempting to push for implementation of the junior college guidelines, which contained some elements of the SRTOL.) Notably, the guidelines moved English instruction away from a strictly utilitarian function. As a result of this increased funding, as well as Nixon's campaign against antiwar demonstrators, four-year colleges and universities also began to examine the relevance or appropriateness of programs.

Consequently, in offering the resolution on "Executive Interference," Douglass was attempting to get the CCCC to stand for its recent history of supporting the government's duty to ensure equality in educational access. The CCCC, he seemed to be saying, should not be seen as even implicitly supporting the sea change in civil rights policy and education. Furthermore, by linking this duty to language, Douglass also seemed to be indicating that the SRTOL and its endorsement of a heritage of diversity demanded a statement on social politics as well. Whereas the SRTOL held the students' language as a right which blocked some moves by a teacher in a writing classroom, Douglass's statement argued that to support diversity in dialects demanded that busing or school integration be supported and worked for by the CCCC. That is, whereas the SRTOL steered clear of taking a stance on public policy, Douglass's statement demanded that the very endorsement of dialect differences (and the need to increase students' awareness of those differences) demanded that school desegregation occur.[4] Despite its endorsement of an expanding role in the liberal welfare state, this particular resolution was thus in many ways more in the spirit of the NUC than the emerging SRTOL. Indeed, this resolution passed by a vote of 83 to 12. The SRTOL only had 79 votes in its favor. Notably, neither would have passed without the altered quorum rules.

The Third SRTOL

As CCCC chairperson, McPherson attempted to represent the SRTOL as a significant accomplishment. In her 1972 report to the NCTE (McPherson 1972a), she stated, "Perhaps the most important thing CCCC did this year was to adopt . . . 'The Students' Right to Their Own Language,'" yet she had to be aware that such a statement would not go unchallenged. To allay the fear of CCCC members, McPherson informed them that a longer report explaining the resolution and its meaning was being produced. In a memorandum addressed to CCCC members, McPherson (1972d) states:

> When the Executive Committee of the Conference on College Composition and Communication met in Boston at the end of March, the members of that committee passed the following

resolution on the Student's Right to His Own Language. . . . At the same meeting, on March 22, the Executive Committee agreed that a committee should be created to write a longer statement providing the members with the linguistic background on which the resolution rests. The committee is in the process of formation now, and we hope it will have at least a preliminary report when the Executive Committee meets in November.

The promise of a forthcoming report which would supply the linguistic background for the statement, however, could not blunt the negative reaction. In October, CCC began to print the reactions of CCCC members to the resolution. William Pixton (1972) criticized both the logic and the probable outcome of the resolution. In particular, Pixton indirectly demonstrates that the Executive Committee's attention to the language of diversity and cultural pluralism was well placed. Stating that it is sound advice to inform students of the need to learn standard English, Pixton wrote that the SRTOL, in contrast,

> will result in a chaos of dialects that will hamper communication and promote ignorance, a situation to be brought about by teachers who, abrogating their responsibility to teach English, substitute in its place the cultivation of individual verbal eccentricity. America will become Babel, and a man traveling from New York to California will be forced to seek the assistance of thirty translators. (300)

Beyond endorsing a belief in the power of English teachers slightly out of touch with rationality, Pixton is positioning the SRTOL as taking English teachers outside of their traditional roles of teaching standard English. The refusal of other CCCC members to take seriously the resolution's endorsement of the validity and logic of all languages is best demonstrated by John R. Hendrickson (1972):

> Praiz be for I hav liv to see grandpas personl-type tibetan-Amurican inglish vindikated. at last igdorence has took its riteful plas in the world if olny grandpa hadnt of bin in such a hury to check out he cood og got a job tiching inglish most anywheres from the plow tot the compozi9shyun clas in yoost won yump . . . . This is muy dilect and I'god its gonna be perservd even if

itmeens the deth of the bestest anglo-imperialist fashistrtriting that was ever rote. Beowulf had his day and he coodnt even talk inglish but now its mine and what I say it teibetanamunicans arise you aint got nuthin to loose but other piples funny inglish. (301)

This counterstatement continues Pixton's disdain for social or political attempts to counter linguistic prejudice toward other dialects. In fact, in this instance, the prejudice is so extreme that differences get translated into simple spelling errors (*olny* for *only*). In contrast to the work of Smitherman or Labov, Hendrickson does not even consider that nonstandard dialects might have their own logic or consistency. He also fails to consider how dialects might be usefully invoked in a classroom setting. Hendrickson's viewpoint demonstrates the refusal to consider how a teacher could reconfigure knowledge in the classroom so that different dialects could lead to both an increased understanding of language *and* the acquisition of dialects of wider communication.

In part, both Pixton and Hendrickson assume that the right accorded to students negates and invalidates the teacher's knowledge of standard English. Following the militant image of the student then emerging, these writing teachers seem to be unable to imagine a student who, while maintaining the right to his or her own language, would also choose to learn the dialect of wider communication. (As noted in chapter 2, even Vernon of *It's Mine and I'll Write It That Way* [Friedrich and Kuester 1972] had reasons for wanting to learn standard English over Friedrich's objections.) Finally, in his invocation of imperialism, Hendrickson also mocks the emphasis of the original motivation of groups such as the NUC and thus participates in the larger social movement of the New Right to discredit the language of the liberal and progressive left. That is, in part, these responses demonstrate the extent to which the political and educational work of the 1960s was unable to fully dethrone the negative images of dialect speakers and their ways of speaking; when the political climate began to edge toward the right, these diffuse symbols could be rearticulated with other conservative elements into a reinvigorated hegemonic structure.

In this environment, McPherson found herself having to argue that the SRTOL's endorsement of all languages was supported by traditional academic standards and was not an abandonment of standard English. For instance, in a letter to an upset CCCC member (McPherson 1972c), she began her defense by reiterating the SRTOL as a call for a higher standard of education for both current students and future teachers:

> First, it is largely because the Executive Committee does feel strongly that, just as a chemistry major should understand chemistry thoroughly, so should an English major, and especially a major who plans to teach English, understand thoroughly the nature of language, the nature of dialects, and the way a student's language habits affect his view of himself and of the world. Second, the committee feels strongly that if education is not to remain the privilege of an elitist few, we must recognize that dialect differences do not by themselves prevent students from getting on with the real business of a college education: the understanding of real chemistry, for instance, or indeed, the more important business of "English"—organization of ideas, specificity of expression, support for generalizations, appreciation of literature. Third, there is no real evidence that correcting student papers for so-called errors has any effect other than eliminating from a chance at education those students whose language choices differ from our own.

For McPherson, the SRTOL is a call for future teachers to become educated in all aspects of the English language: literary forms, dialect forms, and so on. Further, taking aim at those who value writing instruction only for its economic usefulness, she supports a view of education for all, not just the elite. That is, much like Friedrich and Kuester's (1972) text, the English classroom becomes a place where writing, in the sense of communication, dominates. Echoing Smitherman's "Black Power Is Black Language" (1972), McPherson also defines the effectiveness of communication as more important than whether that communication is written in standard English. It is significant that all of these individuals had spoken about the need to listen to students who want to learn standard English.

McPherson's letters, however, did not seem to be a forceful enough response. Facing criticism of the resolution for both its practical effects and scholarly support, the Executive Committee apparently decided to amend the resolution. Richard Larson states that at its November 22, 1972, meeting, the committee made several changes (SRTOL 1974, cover). After these amendments, the resolution reads:

> We affirm the students' right to their own **patterns and varieties of** language—the dialects of their nurture or whatever dialects in which they find their own identity and style. **Language scholars long ago denied that the myth of a standard American dialect has any validity. The claim that any one dialect is unacceptable amounts to an attempt of one social group to exert its dominance over another. Such a claim leads to false advice for speakers and writers, and immoral advice for humans.** A nation proud of its diverse heritage and its cultural and racial variety will preserve its heritage of dialects. We affirm strongly that teachers must have **the experiences and training that will enable them to respect diversity and uphold the** right of students to their own language. (SRTOL 1974, 2–3)

The most obvious change, which is not highlighted, is the removal of "his" for the gender neutral language of "their." More substantially, the resolution makes two key moves. First, instead of a right to one's *own language,* the resolution personalizes language to individual "patterns and varieties." If this right was not later put in terms of "one social group" dominating "another," this personalization might be seen as an attempt to remove any remnants of the group rights and identity which had characterized Black Power discussions of language politics. Instead, while group identity is maintained, the authority to claim group identity is now placed in the hands of linguists, who have proven the invalidity of any standard. That is, the statement's moral stance on language rights is now portrayed as the result of linguistic research. At the outset, "The claim that any one dialect is unacceptable" was written as "Any claim," but now the resolution precedes this phrase with backing from linguistic research ("Language scholars long ago . . . "). This gesture returns the SRTOL back to its mission of responding to the NCTE CEL. The rhetorical effect of such an addition, however, is to turn a general moral belief into a consequence of research (or as McPherson had written in her letter to CCCC members, the result of "linguistic background.") Such a move weakens the political and ethical strength of the resolution. Consequently, although the body of the resolution is significantly more aggressive in tone, the cumulative effect of these revisions is to weaken the moral impact of the statement. Ultimately, what had been a moral duty of teachers has become the moral outcome of academic research. Perhaps as important, the positions that advocates of the New Left and Black Power student activists were making about social justice in the classroom also are recoded as depending on academic research.

Obviously, the resolution had traveled far from its inception in the NUC. Much of the social and economic politics undergirding NUC efforts had been eliminated. Moral critiques of the liberal welfare state, Vietnam War polices, institutional racism, and class stratification also appeared to be left behind. The confrontational images of the student invoked by these organizations had been recast into a classroom where language scholars and teachers define students' rights, rights which had very little traction with the actual activities of student protesters. Douglass's attempts (CCCC business meeting, 25 March 1972) to link the resolution's intent with social movements such as busing seem to have failed.

Within the context of the NCTE and CCCC, however, the radical nature of this resolution should not be underestimated. That is, the resolution can be seen as a politically radical response to the CEL's "Statement on Usage" (n.d.). That document (discussed in detail in chapter 4) was clearly embedded within a linguistic tradition which supported the exclusion of Black English. It had clearly stated the need for teachers to recognize "economic reality" and prepare students in standard English. This version of the SRTOL (1974) is significant, then, for what it does not do: It does not position teachers as producers of future workers; it does not endorse the nationalist paradigm of Marckwardt or McDavid; it does not call for the necessity of standard English; it does not denigrate other ways of speaking. In that sense, its lack of specificity speaks volumes about what it was against: the CEL and figures such as Pixton and Hendrickson. Within this oppositional context, phrases such as "a nation proud of its linguistic and racial variety" clearly position the CCCC within a set of linguistics and politics which, if not radical, were certainly liberal. Even the more conservative version of the NUC's original prompting resolution, then, was progressive. That is, within the NCTE–CCCC dynamic, it represented a political and linguistic departure from the Cold War definition of composition, for it was, in fact, arguing for the right of students to refuse instruction by empowering student acts of civil disobedience.

The final meaning of the resolution, however, was not yet decided. With the language of the resolution now complete, the Executive Committee approved the drafting of a language statement which would make clear its "meaning and intent."

Defending the Right

When the SRTOL was first passed by the Executive Committee, the committee also resolved to produce a longer document, a language statement, which would explain the resolution to CCCC members. The resolution had produced quite a bit of controversy. Consequently, it is not surprising that in McPherson's request to Melvin Butler to chair the SRTOL language statement committee, she argues that the committee's work "will be extremely important to college English instructors and to the students they teach" (McPherson 1972b). In effect, the SRTOL language statement committee needed to explain that the SRTOL resolution was not an abandonment of the traditional role of instructors to teach standard English and to secure an economic future for their students. It is not accidental, then, that the SRTOL language statement committee[5] focused its initial efforts on explicating the effects of the resolution on future graduates.

At the same Executive Committee meeting where the resolution was amended, the language statement committee reported that the audience for the statement should include "business people as well as professional educators." In particular, the committee decided that "post-schoolroom concerns (training of teachers, students' lives after they leave high school or college, concerns of business people)" would warrant their own section (CCCC Secretary's Report No. 67, 22 November 1972).

Indeed, in correspondence between March 1 and March 11, 1973, the SRTOL language statement committee, now under the guidance of Richard Lloyd-Jones,[6] began to discuss how the resolution situated students in relationship to the economy. That is, almost immediately, the committee was confronted with an argument about the relationship between linguistic theory and economic reality. Under the section titled "How Does Dialect Affect Employability," a draft of the document discussed the implications of spoken dialect:

> Many employers expect a person whom they consider for employment to speak whatever variety of American English the employers speak, or believe they speak. Consequently, many speakers of divergent dialects are denied opportunities that are readily available to the applicants whose dialects more nearly approximate the speech of the employer. But a plumber who can sweat a joint can be forgiven confusion between "set" and "sat." (SRTOL 1974, 14)

In response, Ralph Long stated that the initial draft of the resolution and background statement were "quite unsatisfactory." Long (1973) argued that the emphasis on

> dialects [is] quite out of proportion for teachers of composition. [I agree] that we should "leave" spoken language alone as much as possible—totally so in composition classes, but [for] the purposes of expository writing standard English is indispensable—even, sometimes, for plumbers, as the experience of an old friend long active in the plumber union showed. standard English is not "mythical"; it is absurd to regard EAE (Edited American English) as a reality but standard [English] as a myth.

On the same date, however, McPherson (1973) was writing to Lloyd-Jones that the document should not be read as an endorsement to teach standard English until employers become more tolerant. She writes,

> [One section] seems to say that until employers change their minds, we must continue to teach "standard," and that's not what anybody meant. Could it read something like: "As teachers determined to affirm the students' right to their own language, we must work toward seeing that employers stop discriminating against prospective employees who speak a divergent dialect."

Expanding upon this idea, McPherson asks if the following paragraph might be included:

> The people who insist that English teachers must deliberately impose a new and different "school dialect" ignore the ways in which situation motivates versatility, and, perhaps, overrate the possibilities of external "teaching." When students move into new situations—other school classes, new jobs, community projects—the situations themselves will "teach" far more effectively than a classroom can, and students whose school experiences have given them a sense of confidence in themselves and their language, rather than a sense of ineptitude and inadequacy, will be ready to "learn" from the new situation.

Arguing that "this whole document is a strong protest" against the emerging social consensus, McPherson stated that the English classroom was not a just a site for turning students into marketable workers. In fact, turning the argument about the need for career education on its head, she appears to be arguing that it is up to the particular businesses to train their employees in the language of the job, a muted endorsement of similar claims made in NUC's *Open Up the Schools* (1972). To this extent, McPherson also shares common ground with Davidson's (1966) student syndicalist paper. Unlike Davidson, however, McPherson would not embark upon an argument that such practices make the students unproductive for the corporate economy. Instead, it would be the businesses' role to make the students "useful." That is, she would ask writing teachers to suspend their belief that the teaching of standard English was the goal of teachers and not of particular businesses. She was asking teachers to consider how writing instruction could be used to allow students to invent their own relationship to the larger society. Moving to summarize the implications of her additions within the same rubric, McPherson (1973) also suggested the following statement:

> We must encourage students to concentrate on the crucial exactness of words and ideas, and persuade our colleagues to discard their own biases about dialect long enough to recognize and respect this better kind of exactness.

The impact of these additions on the document was to frame the SRTOL statement as endorsing a composition classroom where the relationship between dialects (including standard English) and their individual usefulness were the topic. In doing so, McPherson gave body to the SRTOL resolution as a call for teachers to do more than participate in the production of future workers; instead, teachers would participate in the formation of individually empowered speakers and writers. Such a stance was in stark opposition to the emerging Nixon doctrine of career education and earlier NCTE documents (such as NITE), as well as against the wishes of the factions of CCCC previously discussed. Although little of McPherson's language is incorporated into the document, the moral dilemma she articulates is included:

> The attitudes that [tomorrow's employers] develop in the English class will often be the criteria they use for choosing their own employees. English teachers who feel they are bound to accommodate the linguistic prejudices of current employers perpetuate a system that is unfair to both students who have job skills and to the employers who need them. (SRTOL 1974, 14)

The potential for such statements, however, is muted by the nationalist landscape in which they are embedded. That is, much more in the spirit of the CEL than the NUC, the SRTOL language statement produces an image of the United States as a harmonious country. In particular, an initial reading of the completed document makes it appear as an endorsement of the ethnicity paradigm and integration politics that had earlier characterized the civil rights movement of Martin Luther King Jr. As detailed in chapter 3, King had argued that the Montgomery bus strike had produced a sense of the African American community which created a cross-class alliance representing the unfilled promise of the Declaration of Independence and the Constitution of the United States. With the African American as a symbol of such a possibility, King seemed to argue that a harmonious community was possible within a capitalist state if citizens lived up to the heritage and meaning of U.S. democracy. Differences could be accommodated by capitalism. In fact, capitalism could benefit from these differences.

As was evident in the CCCC's SRTOL resolution from its outset, the resolution is also a call for the United States to live up to a certain standard: "A nation proud of its heritage and its cultural and racial variety will preserve its heritage of dialects" (SRTOL 1974, 2–3). As noted earlier, however, the SRTOL as written does not actually claim that the United States has acted in accordance with this precept. Within the SRTOL language statement, however, the United States is represented as a place where, in everyday situations, tolerance and understanding are the norm. In particular, it is the relationship between a banker and a farmer through which this tolerance is announced:

> It is not surprising to find two or more social dialects co-existing in a given region. In small towns where a clear social cleavage exists between the wealthier, more educated portion of the population and the mass of people, the difference may be reflected in their speechways. The local banker whose dialect reveals his group allegiance to the statewide financial community still is able to communicate easily with the local farmhand who may rarely cross the county line and whose linguistic habit patterns reveal different allegiances. (SRTOL 1974, 3–4)

In NUC documents, such as the previously discussed "Who(m) Does Standard English Serve?" (Knowles et al. 1969), this recognition of a class-based linguistic difference was used to argue for an interracial class alliance among nontraditional students and workers. Here the difference is used to demonstrate a latent understanding which can be appealed to for the sake of linguistic diversity. That is, the farmer does not take this difference as an alienating economic factor, but as an underlying confirmation of equality. Generalizing from the interaction of these two individuals, the statement argues that a similar situation exists in the metropolitan United States as well.

> In many larger American cities, people of the same ethnic origins tend to live in a single neighborhood and have a common culture and thus share a dialect. Through their clothing, games, and holidays, they may preserve the values and customs of the "old country" or "back home." And in their restaurants, churches, schools, and homes, one may hear the linguistic values and customs of their heritage preserved. For example, a

neighborhood group's cultural orientation may encourage its members to differentiate between action and intention in the immediate future and in a still-further immediate future through "I'm a-do it" and "I'm a'gonna do it." Yet, a neighborhood is not a country, so speakers of several dialects may mingle there and understand each other. Visitors with yet another heritage may render an approximation of such differentiation through "I'll do it now" and "I'll do it soon." Pride in cultural heritage need not lead either group to attack the other as they mingle and communicate. (SRTOL 1974, 4)

Notably, such an image of U.S. cities can work only if the then-recent riots in Watts, Harlem, and Newark are ignored. These riots, particularly for Bobby Seale's vision of the Black Panthers, had led to an increased call by black activists for black economic empowerment. In the particular case of Stokely Carmichael, such empowerment was a direct critique of how class works in the United States, yet the SRTOL language statement acts as if capitalism's recognition of differences will ameliorate fundamental class and social inequity. Consequently, the rhetorical structure of the document works to minimize or displace the NUC's attempt to link racial and class politics. As was seen earlier and will be reiterated later, in the SRTOL language statement, economic concerns are cast principally in light of how to expand acceptable dialects within corporate capitalism, not how to use dialects to question it.

Indeed, the SRTOL language statement creates an image of dialects as a cultural problem which can be solved by the raised consciousness of its citizens. That is, the answer to the question of why different dialects are not accepted is the personal attitudes of the listener. When "speakers of a dialect of American English claim not to understand speakers of another dialect of the same language, the impediments are likely to be attitudinal. What is really the hearer's resistance to any unfamiliar form may be interpreted as the speaker's fault" (SRTOL 1974). Given the endorsement of a traditional view of the United States and its citizenry, the SRTOL is a call for individuals to live up to the moral character which, the SRTOL language statement implies, has historically characterized U.S. citizens.

In addition, the SRTOL language statement also seems to be positioning itself closer to the work of Marckwardt and McDavid than was implied by the resolution alone. This is particularly evident in the final draft of the language statement's discussion of American English and its historical development. When tracing the development of English in the United States, the SRTOL language statement excludes many of the recently discovered African influences on American English. As noted in chapter 3, linguists such as Herskovitz argued that the roots of Black English were actually international. Dillard in particular represented Black English and its history as a way to reimagine American English, yet, as in the work of McDavid or Marckwardt, the SRTOL language statement argues for an essentially British origin of American English.

> When the early American settlers arrived on this continent, they brought their British dialects with them. Those dialects were altered both by regional separation from England and concentration into sub groups within this country as well as by contact with the various languages spoken by the Indians they found there and with the various languages spoken by the immigrants who followed (SRTOL 1974, 5).

After recounting the development of New England English as the standard idiom, the section "The History of English and How It Continually Changes in Vocabulary, in Syntax, and in Pronunciation" of the document states:

> From its earliest history, English has borrowed words from the other languages with which it has come in contact—French, Latin, Spanish, Scandinavian, Yiddish, American Indian—from sources too numerous to list. (SRTOL 1974, 15–16)

The language of Black English is reduced to "sources too numerous to list" and to several recorded instances within the text. Within the SRTOL language statement, then, a version of the ethnicity paradigm is reinvoked that serves to bracket out certain historical experiences (or linkages) through which dialects might gain oppositional meaning. While the document openly rejects the cultural deficit models endorsed by Deutsch and Bereiter, the document does not offer positive models of Black English's impact on standard American English.[7] That is, in a resolution and a document clearly initiated by NUC activists to speak on behalf of African American and working-class students, it would appear that there is little demonstration of what their culture, language, or history represents about the historical development of English in the United States. Here the conservative nature of the ethnicity paradigm, as diagnosed by Omi and Winant (1994), becomes evident, for with the invocation of that paradigm, an NUC attempt to create an argument of social and economic justice has been effectively eliminated from the meaning of the SRTOL.

The document's call for a respect of different cultures or dialects must be read within this overarching conservative paradigm. For instance, within a document painting the social fabric of the United States as harmonious, the statement reads, "Our pluralistic society requires many varieties of language to meet our multiplicity of needs" (SRTOL 1974, 5). It further states, "Since dialect is not separate from culture, but an intrinsic part of it, accepting a new dialect means accepting a new culture; rejecting one's native dialect is to some extent a rejection of one's culture" (6), yet the potential opening up of diversity along leftist lines, which was at least possible in the resolution, is effectively muted by the collapsing of a race- and class-based politics into the ethnicity paradigm. Within the potential pluralism of the United States, the activation of different dialects within a student's possibility can now safely be ascribed as the new goal of education: "No one can ever use all of the resources of a language, but one function of the English teacher is to activate the student's competence, that is, increase the range of his habitual performance" (6). It is within this validation of the ethnicity paradigm that the SRTOL statement can ultimately endorse language as representing the pluralistic nature of U.S. society. While appearing to articulate the goal of many 1960s New Left and Black Power organizations, the SRTOL statement thus falls closer to the emerging New Right politics in its articulation of what those dialects represent about the United States or what questions they might cause the United States to ask about itself.

Ultimately, the angry student who protests the idea of a pluralist America from a New Left or NUC perspective is replaced by a student "eager to come to the aid of his country." That is, the SRTOL statement is careful to represent the ability and willingness of dialect speakers to learn standard English. In contrast to earlier rhetorical moments where the black-dialect speaker is brought in to validate a particular political position, here white men are brought in to validate the potential assimilation of urban black and Chicano students. The SRTOL language statement argues that minority dialect speakers are equally as capable of learning standard English as those with more classically recognized regional dialects, that is, southern or New England dialects. The section titled "Does Dialect Affect the Ability to Write" states,

> In fact, if speakers of a great variety of American dialects do master EAE—from Senator Sam Ervin to Senator Edward Kennedy, from Ernest Hemingway to William Faulkner—there is no reason to assume that dialects such as urban black and Chicano impede the child's ability to learn EAE while countless others do not. (8)

Nonstandard speakers' acquisition skills are historically represented as part of a larger national Cold War effort:

> And experience tells us that when speakers of any dialect need a new word for a new thing, they will invent or learn that needed word. Just as most Americans added "sputnik" to their vocabularies a decade or more ago, so speakers of other dialects can add such words as "periostitis" or "interosculate" whenever their interests demand it. (9)

In such a scheme, the nonstandard dialect speaker comes to represent both the ideal ability of a united citizenry participating in the utopic image of the United States and the international benefits such participation brings to the nation. To this extent, then, the document could be read as conservative. Unlike the political and economic motivations behind the NUC's attempts to recognize dialect differences as the first step to a social reformation of U.S. society, here recognition comes to stand for further incorpo-

ration of the nonstandard dialect speaker into traditional economic and cultural roles and into an emerging global responsibility.

Such a reading of the document necessarily leads to the
SRTOL's invocation of Langston Hughes. For within the SRTOL
language statement, it is the voice of Hughes who represents the
proper attitude toward language difference. In particular, Hughes
is brought in to support the traditional idea of the ethnicity paradigm. Through the protocols of the text, the image given of
Hughes is similar to the representation of Ralph Ellison in
Dartmouth Conference documents. As addressed in chapter 2, in
the work of Muller (1967) and Dixon (1966), the image of the
English teacher was of someone who could manage different dialects within a writing classroom to produce social harmony.
Within that dynamic, the voice of Ralph Ellison was cited as representing the possibility of relieving tension: "[I]f you can show
me . . . how I can cling to that which is real in me, while teaching
me the way into the larger society, then I will . . . drop my de-
fenses and hostility" (cited in Dixon 1966, 19). Approximately
ten years later, the SRTOL appears to use the voice of Hughes to
argue that a proper tolerance toward language diversity will result in individuals who "dig all jive":

> I play it cool and dig all jive
> That's the reason I stay alive.
> My motto as I live and learn
> Is to dig and be dug in return. (SRTOL 1974, 2)[8]

In citing Hughes, however, the SRTOL language statement appears to conclude the SRTOL resolution's long march
from progressive politics to a traditional, nationalist statement
about diversity, for it is important to note that the Hughes poem
comes from his 1967 collection of poetry *The Panther and the
Lash*. As discussed in chapter 3, *The Panther and the Lash* is an
argument against the ethnicity paradigm. That is, in various poems, Hughes positions African Americans outside the parameters
of the traditional U.S. history. In a poem called "American Heart-
break," Hughes writes:

> I am the American heartbreak—
> The rock on which Freedom
> Stubbed its toe—
> The great mistake
> That Jamestown made
> Long ago.

Commenting on the need to find heroes outside the American historical landscape, in a poem titled "Angola Question Mark," Hughes writes:

> Don't know why I
> Must turn into
> a Mau Mau
> And lift my hand
> Against my fellow man
> To live in my own land.

Reiterating and expanding on the idea of "digging jive," Hughes discusses the murder of James Powell. Written in the form of a riddle, "Death in Yorkville" asks "How many bullets does it take / To kill a fifteen-year-old kid" (15). The poem then goes on to retell the history of African Americans as the violent repression and murder of their race and culture. For Hughes, invoking U.S. history would not liberate African Americans; only an international understanding would accomplish this goal. As Hughes notes at the end of his poem concerning Powell, "Death aint No jive" (21). While African Americans may have to "play it cool / And dig all jive" to "stay alive," such conditions were not conducive to African American self-respect or long-term survival. That is, Hughes will only "dig all jive" if he is "dug in return"; otherwise, trouble will ensue.

This use of Hughes within a conservative argument must also be placed within one of the other moments when race is discussed. In the section titled "What Do We Do About Handbooks?" the following scene is represented:

> By discussions of actual student writing both students and teachers can learn to appreciate the value of variant dialects and recognize that a deviation from the handbook rules seldom

interferes with communication. The student who writes, "The Black Brother just don't believe he's going to be treated like a man anyway," is making himself completely clear. Students and teachers can go on to discuss situations in which adherence to handbook rules might actually damage the effectiveness of the writing (SRTOL 1974, 11).

As did Labov, this example uses a nonstandard writing example to express a social critique of the current status of African Americans. Unlike the utopic image of the United States, represented earlier, this example interrupts and argues that race is a category unrepresented and oppressed within the ethnicity paradigm of the United States. If race is used as the controlling metaphor for the United States, it seems to say, an image of injustice and oppression emerges. Using this image, one could imagine a critique of "handbook rules" which would lead to points very similar to Stokely Carmichael's English class; that is, only when the African American student gains control of the language defining American history will that student be able to reimagine a new, liberating subject position. Within such a paradigm, McPherson's argument about the need to alter the dynamics of business and dialect could have taken on a potentially more radical meaning, yet, similar to Sumner Ives's reaction to a student paper on the Vietnam War (discussed in chapter 4), the document asks the teacher only to speak in terms of "effectiveness." Consequently, within the parameters of the SRTOL language statement, it is difficult to imagine any of the this discussion occurring. That is, more confrontational or nontraditional approaches to race or the politics of dialects are effectively muted in the document. Ultimately, the inclusion of Hughes marks the absence of a radical economic educational critique more than its endorsement.

To say that the SRTOL language statement is a conservative document when placed next to the militant politics of the New Left, however, is not to denigrate its importance within the shifting relationship between teachers and students, NCTE and CCCC, or New Left and New Right debates about education. Just as the SRTOL resolution could be considered radical when placed next to the CEL statement, in the emerging conservative climate of the 1970s, any statement which appeared to accord students rights or dethrone standard English was "radical" at the moment of the New Right's emergence. That is, one reading of the SRTOL would be to see it as an instance of the radical margin being incorporated into a traditional center. While this is certainly true, it is also important to remember that political terrain upon which the imagined center–margin binary exists is constantly shifting. As a document created in the meantime between the New Left and the New Right, then, the SRTOL offers one attempt to negotiate the new emerging social context.

We Affirm Strongly . . .

By November 1973, the SRTOL resolution and language statement were ready to be submitted to the Executive Committee. The committee's response to the language statement, however, was mixed and somewhat confrontational. According to the minutes, William Irmscher, who would later figure in the movement to overturn the SRTOL, stated that the language statement was meant to be a "means of understanding the resolution," yet in the discussion that followed, complaints were made that the statement was ambiguous:

> [Was it] an endorsement of bi-dialecticism or [an] endorsement of tracking in education; [it had] a glib treatment of handbooks; what language options [are meant]; young teachers [will be] hard put to know what to do with the document. (CCCC Secretary's Report No. 69, 21 November 1973)

Some unidentified members even argued that the "previous resolution as written is not acceptable." Committee members questioned "the rhetoric used [and] the political implications." In fact, "the controversial nature of the background statement [led to] Mr. Bain's question of whether the Language Committee had considered rewording the resolution." Ross Winterowd explained that it was not within the charge of the language committee since they had "no mandate to change it" (CCCC Secretary's Report No. 69, 21 November 1973). McPherson, however, argued that the committee should accept the language statement. In fact, it was argued by some that the language statement was more a "whereas" than an individual document. Consequently, the Executive Committee had an obligation to accept or reject the preamble to their own resolution. Initially, a motion was made that the Executive Committee "accept and transmit the Resolution and Background Statement to the membership of CCCC for their study and consideration and a vote on this resolution be taken at the Anaheim Conference in 1974" (CCCC officers meeting, 21 November 1973). This motion passed by a vote of 14 to 4, with one abstention. Cowan then moved that the resolution be embedded in the letter sent to CCCC members, expressing the approval of the Executive Committee and encouraging acceptance. This motion passed by a 12–4 vote.

Consequently, soon after the Executive Committee meeting, Richard Larson, now CCCC chairperson, sent a letter to the CCCC members. In the letter, Larson (SRTOL 1974) avoids the political beginnings of the SRTOL in New Left activism. Instead, he dates the beginning of the SRTOL with an oblique reference to "a series of discussions begun in 1969." Positioning the document as a linguistic, new rhetoric statement, Larson argues that it incorporates the "current findings of linguists and rhetoricians about dialects and usage." Further, Larson points out that the language statement, if not the resolution, "has won the praise of linguists who have examined it; it is, in my judgment, a major accomplishment and probably the first extended statement prepared to assist the deliberations of members on a major issue since the CCCC was founded" (SRTOL 1974). It was not possible, however, to use such a disciplinary argument to shield the SRTOL against political interpretations of its meanings.

Even prior to the SRTOL resolution and language statement's formal distribution, members of the CCCC community began reacting to the recent events on a grassroots level. For instance, in April, Constance Weaver, who would later serve on the committee to revise the SRTOL, would ask for copies of the SRTOL language statement. In doing so, she hoped to "persuade the Linguistics Committee of the Michigan Council of Teachers of English to introduce . . . a resolution that the MCTE endorse the CCCC resolution" (Weaver 1974). In June, Nancy Prichard (1974) circulated a statement of support from the Institute for

Service and Education which argued that the statement does not grow out of a need to "smash tradition, rather it is a positive extension of the fundamental educational issue arising out of the 1960's: how can we effectively teach language skills to students who come from diverse backgrounds?" Consequently, she argues,

> The position statement is comprehensive and extraordinary in that it not only examines some of the assumptions underlying the teaching of English, but it provides some contemporary linguistic thought and findings concerning some of these assumptions. Clearly, if we have any commitment at all to providing educational opportunity, we have no alternative to our affirmation of the students' right to their own language. . . . [We] also hope that those who attend the convention in Los Angeles will not allow the fantasy of Disneyland to obscure the importance of affirming the students right to their own language. (Prichard 1974)

Other people, however, used the possible political associations created by an endorsement of the SRTOL to discredit it. In May, Evelyn Miller, of Manchester Community College (MCC), wrote to Richard Larson that "the Proposed Position Statement [is] totally unacceptable [since] it is based upon the tendentious assumption that what is called Standard English is merely a dialect" (Miller 1974a). In response to the statement, Miller (1974b) circulated a memorandum calling for her English Department "to take a firm stand in favor of Standard English in all our composition courses at MCC." In support of her position, Miller cites Stephen Koch's "Hard Times for the Mother Tongue." In the excerpt she provides, Koch attacks the politics of individuals who would draw moral conclusions from linguistic insight:

> Listening to the current polemics, one might gather that Standard English is somehow highly literate and the mandarin of upper-crust speech. It is nothing of the kind. It is simply more or less correct English. . . . Correctly spoken, it easily encompasses an internal array of regional dialects. . . . There is nothing fancy or overwhelming about it. Its fundamental structural habits are very simple, and (except perhaps for children born into the most extreme of the illiterate English dialects) there is no reason why it should not be second nature to anyone of

normal intelligence by the age of fifteen. . . . It is the fundamental—and indispensable—basis for educated speech, writing, and thought in the English Language.

Indispensable? The American universities are currently
crammed with students who have no command over it what-
soever. And this fact, grounds for despair, is being promoted
by some as grounds for celebration. . . . [T]he fact is that a
grotesque proportion of students coming from the secondary
schools are close to being functional illiterates. Even middle
class students who speak Standard English habitually cannot
write it: many remain stuck in the pre-literate language of infantilism. They are only slightly better off than their less-pam-
pered conferees from outside the middle class, whose teachers
sometimes seem divided between hostile hailers and people who
think correct English (or almost any other kind of education)
is a class insult. . . .

Now as the universities drown in the inundating ignorance
produced by these attitudes, their irritated and pressed staffs—
the ranks of the professors swollen by many brilliant people
who have absolutely no pedagogical or scholarly calling, but
who are busy evading the "real world"—began to be infected
with [America's historical anti-intellectualism] and to ramify it
in more fancy versions. Standard English? Since it is possible
to demonstrate that the illiterate dialects of English have their
own coherent grammar and structure, that it is quite possible
to "conceptualize" in them, who needs it? No teaching [Stan-
dard English] is a viscous cultural imperialism, an arbitrary
humiliation rigged by the middle class to flatter itself—and to
baffle and stultify what are called its class and racial enemies
. . . . Around the educational catastrophe swirls the numbing
fog of a politicized and mysticized ideology of illiteracy. (cited
in Miller 1974b)

It should be noted that Koch writes into his argument many of
the racial stereotypes which had surrounded Black English. Speakers of nonstandard dialects are "stuck in pre-literate languages
of infantilism." Individuals who cannot grasp the fundamentals
of standard English are only those who come from the "most
illiterate of households." Negating all the linguistic scholarship
that demonstrated structural differences between Black English
and standard English, Koch argues that the learning of standard
English is easily acquired. The image of the nonstandard-dialect
speaker that emerges is of either a lazy individual who refuses to
learn or an individual so damaged by his or her culture that he or

she is unable to learn. In addition, he attaches any opinion that would claim a legitimate status for Black English to the anti-imperialist or class-war ideologues. While he is certainly correct in drawing these two domains together, he obviously does so to further weaken the possibility of resolutions such as the SRTOL. Clearly this argument shows the weakening or near collapse of the legitimacy of the New Left rhetoric as the 1970s continued.[9] Further, it demonstrates that the CCCC and Larson were unable to contain the associations the SRTOL would accrue during its history.

Given the range of grassroots responses, it seemed that the business meeting at Anaheim would be packed and contentious. Unlike previous years, however, the Anaheim convention would have an attendance of only eight hundred people, lower than any other convention of the previous six years. Additionally, to a great extent, the "business" agenda of the CCCC, particularly the business meeting, was increasingly dominated by the need to respond to the changing political and social climate. Unlike in the 1960s, when the business meeting served as a forum to push forward a progressive and liberal agenda, that agenda was now under attack both politically and economically. As noted previously, Nixon had forcefully argued against the New Left, painting the "silent majority" as the true repository of social values. It was also his administration which "cut and impounded university funds for liberal arts, libraries, and scientific research, [and] eliminated most grants for graduate education (down from 51,400 to 6,600 in the Nixon years)" (Sale 1975, 250). The effect of the new rhetoric and government policies was to lead universities to cut back or remodel their liberal arts programs. This shift also led to the abandonment of full-time faculty for the cost effectiveness of part-time faculty. Consequently, it should not be surprising that the business meeting addressed the effects of these policies. Among the resolutions presented was one directly relating to the new economic troubles facing English departments:

Resolution III:

BACKGROUND: Lower enrollment, or the fear of lower enrollments; decreased budgets, or the threat of decreased budgets; community pressures; and legislative demands for economy and accountability have led some colleges and universities to dismiss faculty members with little or no notice, ignoring the obligations of tenure and bypassing the procedural safeguards intended to protect untenured faculty. Because English departments are especially vulnerable to such administrative retrenchment, the method by which these dismissals are handled becomes a special concern of CCCC.

RESOLVED, first that CCCC express its condemnation of the arbitrary abrogation of tenure, the mass dismissal of untenured staff, and the elimination of due process; and second, that CCCC strongly urge that all retention and tenure decisions, whether or not they involve a reduction in staff size, be securely based on a thorough, balanced professional evaluation of teaching competence, and a consideration of each faculty member's contributions in creative, research, and professional work. (CCCC business meeting, 6 April 1974)

The emphasis on "community pressures" as well as legislative pressures further indicates the extent to which the CCCC found its previously liberal business meetings out of step with the culture.

At the same time that Nixon continued his attacks upon "egghead" academics,[10] there was a growing movement to a "Back to the Basics Curriculum." This reform effort grew out of a conservative attempt to portray liberal curriculum reforms as the reason for the United States' "social decline." They argued for a return to a "traditional education" (Shor 1986, 78–79). According to "Back to the Basics" advocates, proof of their position was the failure of SAT scores to improve; according to New Right advocates, SAT scores were declining. In response, the SAT added a section which would measure a student's ability to identify and correct standard English usage. At a CCCC business meeting at which the Executive Committee was asking the CCCC to endorse the SRTOL, such a move was clearly antithetical. Consequently, the following resolution was passed:

BACKGROUND: Beginning in October, 1974, a new section will be added to the Scholastic Aptitude Test—a 30 minute test of English usage containing questions similar to the objective portion of the English Composition Achievement Test. To make space for this section, fifteen minutes will be taken from the verbal portions of SAT and fifteen minutes from the math portion. The new usage score will be recorded separately, along with the math score and the verbal score, which will be reported in two parts: reading comprehension and vocabulary. This new section was added without consultation or advice from the professional associations most closely concerned, NCTE and CCCC. Although the usage section is said to be an experiment, subject to re-evaluation after two years, the students who are rated by the test between 1974 and 1976 will be permanently labeled by their scores in this section.

RESOLVED, first, that CCCC protest the inclusion of an objective usage test in Scholastic Aptitude Test, on the grounds that such tests are a measure of copy reading skill rather than a measure of student ability to use language effectively in connected discourse of their own composing; such tests place emphasis on mechanical matters of spelling, punctuation and conventions of usage, rather than on clarity, appropriateness, and coherence of thought; such tests tend to discriminate against minority students whose linguistic experiences often lead them to choose answers different from those expected by the test-makers; and the inclusion of such a test may encourage secondary English teachers to teach toward the test at the expense of matters more fundamental to effective writing and sophisticated reading; and second, that CCCC encourage members to resist the use of usage scores in the admission and placement of its students (CCCC business meeting, 6 April 1974)

Unlike other New Left or NUC resolutions passed at a CCCC business meeting, the following day, the Executive Committee decided that Part One of the resolution "be sent to CEEB and ETS, to the Association of College Admissions Officers and the admissions officers of CEEB member schools; and Part Two should be included in Mr. Larson's report to the membership. In addition, the entire resolution should be sent to the CCCC Committee on Testing and the NCTE Task Force on Evaluation and Measurement" (CCCC officers meeting, 7 April 1974). Notably, these measures did not necessarily have as much support as previously passed New Left resolutions.

It is within this emergence of conservative politics that the SRTOL came to vote. Unlike the other resolutions, the SRTOL was not presented with a clear statement of its social or political background. If the language statement proper had provided such information, this would not be notable. In a context in which the right had achieved the political initiative nationally, it appears bringing up the New Left past of the SRTOL would be unwise. Consequently, those in attendance received only the resolution, without context, for discussion. As recorded in the minutes, the SRTOL was presented as follows:

> BACKGROUND: All CCCC members were sent by mail the explanatory statement and bibliography which serve as support for this resolution.

> RESOLVED, that CCCC affirm the students' right to their own language—the dialects of their nurture or whatever dialects in which they find their own identity and style. Language scholars long ago denied that the myth of a standard American dialect has any validity. The claim that any one dialect is unacceptable amounts to an attempt of one social group to exert its dominance over another. Such a claim leads to false advice for speakers and writers, and immoral advice for humans. A nation proud of its diverse heritage and its cultural and racial variety will preserve its heritage of dialects. We affirm strongly that teachers must have the experiences and training that will enable them to respect diversity and uphold the right of students to their own language. (CCCC business meeting, 6 April 1974)

Given the support of the previous two resolutions, it is not surprising that the SRTOL was passed by a vote of 79 to 20. What is noteworthy is that under previous rules, or perhaps in a better attended conference, the SRTOL could not have been voted on and probably would not have passed. As was noted previously, however, the meeting rules had been changed to allow only fifty members to constitute a quorum and majority vote for passage. The low vote total for the SRTOL would hurt its status. Seventy-nine votes were in the approximate range of previous votes endorsing the "People's Peace Treaty," anti–Vietnam War stands, and anti–usage standards measures. Furthermore, over the previous six years the business meeting had become the site of New Left and activist politics. The political context of the resolution, then, automatically made it appear to be a coup d'état by the radical minority rather than a stand taken by the Executive Committee that developed over the course of two years.

It is also unclear whether the resolution would have passed if the CCCC business meeting was held, as previously, at the NCTE Convention, for after the CCCC passed the SRTOL, the NCTE also passed a similar resolution. But perhaps in response to the growing criticism, the NCTE amended its resolution slightly:

> RESOLVED, that the National Council of Teachers of English affirm the students' right to their own language—to the dialect that expresses their family and community identity, the idiolect that expresses their unique personal identity; affirm the responsibility of all teachers of English to assist all students in the development of their ability to speak and write better whatever their dialects; affirm the responsibility of all teachers to provide opportunities for clear and cogent expression of ideas in writing, **and to provide the opportunity for students to learn the conventions of what has been called written edited American English;** and affirm strongly that teachers must have the experiences and training that will enable them to understand and respect diversity of dialects; and
>
> Be it further RESOLVED, that, to this end, the NCTE:
>
> make available to other professional organizations this resolution as well as suggestions for ways of dealing with linguistic variety, as expressed in the CCCC background statement of students' right to their own language; and promote classroom practices to expose students to the variety of dialects that comprise our multiregional, multiethnic, and multicultural society, so that they too will understand the nature of American English and come to respect its dialects. (NCTE 1988, emphasis added)

It is evident that the NCTE statement backs away from much of the moral tone and intent of the CCCC SRTOL. As opposed to a statement which speaks about the immorality and unsoundness of demanding that students learn another dialect, the NCTE statement offers assistance for students to broaden the parameters of individual dialect use. It also ensures that students are given the opportunity to learn "edited American English." To a great extent, the NCTE resolution most clearly matches the more conservative aspects of the CCCC's SRTOL language statement. The NCTE resolution noticeably calls for the NCTE to circulate its resolution, but the CCCC's language statement. The NCTE must have felt that its own resolution most clearly matched the intent of the statement.

Conclusion

In amending its SRTOL resolution, the NCTE was offering, inadvertently, the final requiem for the radical and progressive politics which had first brought student's rights into the CCCC arena. In fact, when the CCCC and NCTE SRTOL documents are combined, the total affect is not unlike the original CEL language statement. Ultimately, however, even the more sedate and restrained NCTE SRTOL would not go unnoticed. In chapter 6, the final decline of the SRTOL as a possible vision for leftist academics is examined.

---

1. In fact, the use of mail ballots had so effectively blunted the ability of the business meeting to act as a catalyst for progressive politics that during the 1980s the Progressive Composition Caucus attempted to pass an amendment which would dictate that the Executive Committee must follow business meeting resolutions.

2. The original version of the SRTOL produced by the committee was approximately two pages long. During a break, however, the statement was edited down by members to approximately one paragraph. In a discussion with the author, Richard Lloyd-Jones stated that the original document contained additional emphasis on the linguistic knowledge needed by teachers. He also stated that he no longer owned a draft of the original two-page statement. Thus, I am more concerned with how the various cultural forces directed the language chosen for the final resolution than with any particular committee member's contribution. My argument, in part, is that the committee acted as a body rather than as individual members in response to the political and social terrain. The role of individual members in constructing the resolution is best left to their memory and their personal goals at that time.

3. At this meeting, Davis suggested that an ad hoc committee or a task force be appointed that would include people not on the Executive Committee. Apparently, there were still concerns that the SRTOL committee, in its makeup and consequent actions, was not strong enough in its support

for the rights and concerns of minority members, or perhaps there was concern that the SRTOL was beginning to lose the political intent and focus originally articulated by advocates of the NUC. In any case, the idea of a task force was rejected.

4. The idea in the SRTOL resolution that students should gain experience with different dialects was translated in the SRTOL language statement, in part, into the idea that the teacher should visit the areas in which those students live but not necessarily endorse policies which would ensure their continued presence in a diverse classroom.

5. As detailed in the published SRTOL (1974), the full committee was chaired by Melvin Butler, and its members were Adam Casimer, Nina Flores, Jennifer Giannasi, Myrna Harrison, Robert Hogan, Richard Lloyd-Jones, Richard A. Long, Elizabeth Martin, Elisabeth McPherson, Nancy Prichard, Geneva Smitherman, and W. Ross Winterowd. (In light of chapter 2, it is interesting to note that Ken Macrorie was invited to be a member of the SRTOL committee but declined.)

6. Melvin Butler was killed during an attempted robbery of his home.

7. The SRTOL clearly positions itself against arguments that minority or underclass students are culturally deprived. In a direct response to the work of Bereiter and Deutsch, the statement argues,

> To cope with our students' reading problem, then, we cannot confine ourselves to the constricting and ultimately ineffectual dialect readers designed for the "culturally deprived." We should structure and select materials geared to complex reading problems and oriented to the experience and sophistication of our students. An urban eight-year old who has seen guns and knives in a street fight may not be much interested in reading how Jane's dog Spot dug in the neighbor's flower bed. Simply because "Johnny can't read" doesn't mean "Johnny can't think." He may be bored. Carefully chosen materials will certainly expose students to new horizons and should increase their awareness and heighten their perceptions of the social reality. (7)

8. As published in *The Panther and the Lash* (Hughes 1967), the poem is reproduced differently:

> I play it cool
> And dig all jive—
> That's the reason
> I stay alive
>
> My motto,
> As I live and learn
> Is
> *Dig and be dug*
> In return.

9. A less confrontational argument about the connection between social politics and linguistic insight was written by graduate students Warren Dwyer, Kent Baker, and Dennis McInerny (1974). They wrote that while the resolution is "in many ways laudable, we find a good deal of inconsistency and factitiousness in the supporting statements." These authors argue that from the simple fact of dialect diversity, the concept of a rich language cannot be implied; the linguistic concept of dialects does not imply any judgment about their worth. Consequently, disputing the overlaid morality, they conclude, "The compassion that obviously motivates the Resolution is commendable, but we believe that any resolution regarding minority students that is not explicitly committed to teaching them standard English is an invitation to the cynicism and neglect that have for so long nourished separateness and deprivation in this country" (Dwyer et al. 1974).

10. This phrase is attributed by Sale (1975, 250) to John Mitchell of the Nixon administration.

CHAPTER 6

A Coup d'Etat and Love Handles

1974–1983

Let love handles and dialects flourish. Operate instead on the culture sick enough to devalue them. That's the surgery the Students' Right To Their Own Language *effects, and that's why many fear it.*

> LOUIE CREW, "Minority Report of the
> Committee on the Advisability of a New
> Language Statement for the 1980s and 1990s"

The SRTOL and its language statement had never garnered wide support. The original Ad Hoc Committee on Social Dialects appeared unable to issue a report. The original version of the SRTOL resolution did not represent the unanimous view of the SRTOL committee. The SRTOL resolution was passed only with a provision that a longer statement detailing its reasoning be provided to members, yet the longer SRTOL language statement itself was also passed with hesitation. Rather than being strongly endorsed, it was considered more of a "whereas" to the resolution proper. Even at its moment of triumph, the resolution garnered only seventy-nine votes. Despite all the hesitation, complaints, and counterarguments, to this day the SRTOL still stands as an official statement by the CCCC on language rights.

The SRTOL exists, however, weakened by the repeated attempts to overturn, amend, or replace it. To a great extent, the

SRTOL has ceased to be a catalyst for political organization and instead had become the symbol of a time past. As a way to summarize the general arguments which organized this work, I now detail the means by which a particular political project for social change within the CCCC came to be fossilized. In these remaining pages, then, I move away from the strategy of tracing connections between alternative political documents and CCCC activities to a more conjectural discussion of the SRTOL's demise. In doing so, I focus on how the SRTOL became "history."

Creating the Void: 1974–1980

In *Open Up the Schools* (NUC 1972), the NUC had imagined the integration of corporate capital into public school and public university classrooms for progressive ends. In articles such as "Who(m) Does Standard English Serve? Who(m) Does Standard English Hurt?" (Knowles et al. 1969), it had also projected an image of the classroom where issues of dialect could be used to educate students concerning the racist and class-based nature of the United States. By the mid-1970s, the NUC was defunct. Corporate capital, however, had indeed entered the classroom. In the same year that the CCCC published the SRTOL language statement, for instance, the Continental Group formed a program to educate Virginia's public school teachers on "how business operates." According to Holmes Brown, director of community and educational relations at Continental, "there [was an] amazing effect on the attitude of the teachers toward business and toward our economic system."(Pines 1982, 58). Writing in 1982, Pines stated, "Today [the program] flourishes at dozens of colleges and universities, influencing high school teacher's attitudes toward economic matters" (58). In fact, other corporations such as Armstrong Cook, Tupperware, Duracell, Kraft, Central Illinois Public Service, and Pacific Gas also started corporate economic education efforts. These education programs ranged from leaflets, posters, or meetings, to full-scale lectures and classes. Dow Chemical Company offered the "Business Money Workshop." As recounted by Pines (1982),

A major aim of the program, the firm candidly admits, is to "demonstrate the superiority of the American Free Enterprise system and the imminent dangers of government socialist programs." [The program is designed to] increase employee and voter awareness that: As more government regulations and taxes emerge, our unique American system is an endangered species. (54)

Within this emerging paradigm of pro-corporate education, the role of the composition teacher also came in for reconsideration. Joseph Williams's "Linguistic Responsibility" (1977) argues that English teachers need to return to their traditional role of preparing students for the work world. During the 1960s, he believes, it seemed inevitable teachers would begin to "feel particularly responsible for doing something about social ills" (8). When faced with dialect discrimination and the resulting bitterness among discriminated populations, English teachers had argued the moral position; students had a right to their own language. "In this country, the expression of linguistic discontent has taken more sedate forms, most recently as a resolution adopted by English teachers that every student is entitled to his own dialect" (Williams 1977, 10). For Williams, such moral stands failed to touch the actual economic motivations behind such discontentment, nor did such morality offer pragmatic pedagogical solutions. Instead of perpetuating discontent through socially correct but economically indefensible attitudes, Williams argues that English teachers need to study how "effective communication occurs." That is, Williams proposes that English departments return their focus to the type of communication skills students will use in the working world. Such skills will alleviate the economic discrimination for which dialect discrimination had become the marker. In particular, English teachers need to understand the world of business. He writes that English professors and writing teachers

know almost nothing about the way individuals judge the quality of writing in places like Sears and General Motors and Quaker Oats. What counts as good writing at Exxon? Are memos with a T-unit–subordinate clause ratio under 0.7 judged immature? Or is the problem excessive "maturity?" It is the

obligation of universities to support research that would tell
us, so that we would know what to teach—or at least what to
teach about—and yet virtually no such research exists. We have
felled entire forests to provide the paper on which to report
how English teachers grade papers higher after their students
have been exposed to transformational grammar or the lyrics
of "Let's Do It In the Road," without knowing whether anything English teachers have to say about writing has much to
do with what their students will be judged on several years
hence. (13)

With such arguments, Williams is attempting to shift the emphasis of writing instruction away from the protection of self-iden-
tity toward a program of instruction that more closely models
the corporate education then emerging as paradigmatic. In doing
so, he is resituating the English classroom as the supplier of trained
workers, a clear reversal of Carl Davidson's student syndicalism.
Later, Williams (n.d.) would author a paper calling for the NCTE
to "set aside the SRTOL Document." (As demonstrated later,
this report would be used to taint the objectivity of the Committee on the Advisability of a New Language Statement for the
1980s and 1990s.)

At this moment, the need to reintroduce a progressive critique of the corporate system seemed to be a necessary and logical move for activists within the CCCC. Clearly, the SRTOL at
its initiation was designed to offer such a critique. Growing out
of a network of academics, social activists, and political organizations, the SRTOL might have become a link between socially
progressive organizations and composition teachers. Instead, as
noted earlier, the SRTOL had applied the imagery of the black-
dialect speaker to reinstate a nationalist paradigm. There was,
however, one remaining opportunity within the CCCC to redefine the SRTOL as overtly against the emerging corporate agenda.
At the same meeting where the Executive Committee had autho-
rized publication of the SRTOL and language statement, a plan
to publish another document surrounding the SRTOL had also
been endorsed. The committee endorsed an ERIC proposal to
fund a "booklet of essays which would present specific classroom applications of theories contained in the special publication *The Students' Right To Their Own Language*" (CCCC

Secretary's Report No. 71). Elisabeth McPherson and Geneva Smitherman would serve as co-editors of the booklet. (CCCC Secretary's Report No. 77, 23 November 1977). Although neither had direct links to the NUC, the role of defining the SRTOL as classroom practice was clearly in the hands of the scholars perceived as part of liberal forces within the CCCC.

Indeed, McPherson had already spoken about what an SRTOL classroom might encompass. In "Notes on Students' Right To Their Own Language" (1974), McPherson discussed the resolution and its classroom implications. As with her earlier articulations of the SRTOL, McPherson states that the resolution was not designed to deny standard English instruction, nor was it meant to deny students access to education that will enable career success. In making these arguments, she provides several assignments which appear to implement the SRTOL resolution:

> We can make students aware of the language shifts they already make without thinking twice about it by role-playing and three-minute play writing. What's the difference between the way people talk at parties and the way they talk at funerals? Between the way Nixon talked on the tapes and the way he talked on television? . . .
>
> We can look for the vocabulary changes that go on around us all the time. We can talk about why "pacification" meant bombing five years ago and why "inoperative" meant lying this year. Turned loose on the daily papers students can find newly coined words—"stonewalled it" for instance—and old words with changed meanings. If they find etymology fascinating, they can discover that OED is a pretty lively volume. (17)

Such strategies have overt connections to the work of Friedrich and Kuester (who dedicated their earlier book to McPherson). In this classroom, the political terminology of the period is opened up and investigated for the ways in which it represents or creates a type of reality. Further, as with the work of Friedrich and Kuester or Macrorie, the type of work being done here creates the possibility of alliance with other leftist organizations. While McPherson does not take the logical next step of articulating how such critiques would necessarily entail an examination of the probusiness rhetoric being produced by corporations like Mobil, the possibility is latent.

Instead of the SRTOL taking on an anticorporate critique, however, McPherson (1974) ultimately places the call for teachers to endorse the SRTOL in terms of African American experience. In declaring that a "nation proud of its diverse heritage ought to preserve its dialects," she writes:

> But it *is* this part of the statement, turned around, that is most frequently and most sincerely, given as a reason for opposing the resolution. *Because,* the argument goes, language differences *are* one way of keeping people down, if we eradicate the differences, everybody can move up. "It's true," people say, "that there's no such thing as a single standard, and that school-room English is not better, and often worse, than other, less prestigious dialects. I'd *like* to support the resolution," these people say, "but I can't change the world. It's those other teachers, in those other departments, who don't know anything about language. *They'll* fail these students, if they write their history tests in funny English, and if we don't fail them first, we'll get the blame." That, of course, is much like what the supporters of slavery told the abolitionists a hundred and fifty years ago: "We know slavery is wrong, but we can't change the world. We didn't create slavery, we just inherited it." And in one way, the slavery supporters had a better case than English teachers have; slavery was a *legal* institution, and language, although it's certainly an emotional issue, is not yet legislated. (6)

Imagining writing teachers as would-be abolitionists is, of course, part of a longer narrative with roots in the Dartmouth Conference or the work of Ken Macrorie. In the social climate of the 1970s, however, such metaphors of oppression were facing a strong challenge from the corporate right. For instance, in a public attempt to discredit liberal and affirmative action programs aimed at African American constituencies, corporate advertisement campaigns were created which featured headlines such as "The greatest war on poverty is a successful corporation" and "How much Federal aid did the pilgrims receive?" (Pines 1982, 80). (By the 1980s, Mobil was spending approximately $5 million on such advocacy campaigns.)

In fact, it is at this moment that the failure of the left in the CCCC to articulate a strong response to the emerging cultural shifts become most apparent. Metaphors based on African American history could not explain the social and economic terrain upon which composition teachers and students were now working. An explanation was needed of how the writing teacher was involved in more than writing issues. That is, such an explanation should depend not upon slavery metaphors, but upon a professional perspective that understands the writing classroom as one point within a larger system of social and class oppression. Without an organization which creates connections between such scholars and political organizations, however, the critical mass needed to effect such possibilities in the definition of the writing teacher could not occur.

In fact, conservative forces were circling around the SRTOL. At the 1977 CCCC business meeting, there was a direct attempt to revise the SRTOL resolution. Lou Kelly offered a resolution calling for the CCCC to endorse the NCTE version of the SRTOL (CCCC business meeting, 1 April 1977). As noted in chapter 5, the NCTE SRTOL had explicitly called for the inclusion of standard English instruction. Although the SRTOL language statement had clearly stated that students should be given the option of learning standard English, any attempt to introduce such language into the actual CCCC resolution was seen as a backing down to the Right's call for a limited definition of writing instruction. That is, any attempt to abrogate the "right to one's own language" into the more moderate language of the NCTE was seen as an attack upon the need for composition teachers to educate students concerning the intellectual respectability of all dialects. It was, after all, a founding concept in the resolution that any dialect is intellectually appropriate for any situation; it was only cultural or racial biases which did not make it so in practice. As a consequence, according to one participant in the meeting, Elisabeth McPherson and Gregory Cowan quickly mobilized forces to defeat the proposed amendments.

This act, however, would represent the beginning of the end for the forces which had created the SRTOL. Ultimately, the strongest possibility for a progressive statement on teaching practice and the SRTOL would fail to materialize; the proposed teachers' guide was never finished. At the 1978 Executive Committee meeting, Elisabeth McPherson stated that the proposed SRTOL ERIC publication "must be abandoned because of the illness of Geneva Smitherman, co-editor, and the lack of enough high quality submissions" (CCCC Secretary's Report, 22 November 1978). (Given McPherson's own attempt, it is unclear how effectively a completed teachers' guide would position the SRTOL against the corporate right in any case.) Therefore, entering the end of the 1980s, while the SRTOL resolution remained intact, there was no official statement by SRTOL advocates concerning how it should be implemented. Nor did there appear to be an active organization primarily concerned with organizing writing teachers for progressive social action within the CCCC. It is into this institutional limbo that the SRTOL spun into the 1980s. As might be expected, the New Right was waiting. From this point on, the SRTOL would fall back into the domain of conservative critics and elder scholars who had not participated, nor endorsed, the activism of the 1960s.

Coup d'Etat? 1981–1983

The years between 1974 and 1980 had seen no progress by the CCCC in articulating the meaning and import of the students' right to their own language. In fact, advocates had been placed in the position of blocking or blunting attempts to replace or amend the resolution. In 1981, William Irmscher read the institutional politics of the CCCC and decided that a serious attempt was once again underway to overturn the SRTOL. In writing to Lynn Troyka, then chair of the CCCC, Irmscher (1981) suggested a counterstrategy; rather than returning to an old statement with limited historical reach, a new one could be created without necessarily casting the SRTOL in a bad light.

> [I] would like to propose that a new study group be appointed *to consider a statement on multilingualism and multi-dialectalism* in this country, particularly with reference to priorities concerning the use of language forms different from the numerically dominant Standard English. I make this recommendation because of growing threats to take action on the floor of the business meeting either to rescind *The Students Right To Their Own Language* or to amend it. *I think those*

particular actions would be unfortunate, particularly since the statement addressed its time and served a useful purpose. It should stand as a record, despite its limitations.

It is not uncommon for organizations to refine position statements in view of a changing situation. Almost ten years have passed since the adoption of *The Students Right.* But more important than the passage of time, I think, is a growing literature on language policy and language processing that *can help us formulate a statement that will promote unity among its members at the same time that it encourages respect for diversity.*

It is possible, for instance, to declare the equality of dialects as means of expression and communication and also acknowledge a principle of functional differentiation—a principle that reflects the kind of intuitive decisions we make about language for different situations and purposes. A policy might explain some of the expectations that ordinarily define priorities in our use of language—differences of writing situations, differences of speaking situations, differences of location (home, school, courts), differences of occasion (ceremony, committee meeting), differences of social implication (intimacy, solidarity), differences of symbolic import (ethnic identity, professional identity). I have tried to suggest that it is not enough to make simple distinctions between speaking and writing. The use of language is far more complex.

Furthermore, *a new statement might try to describe an increasingly* complex situation in this country that concerns foreign languages. The chauvinistic attitude of most Americans toward other languages poses an obstacle to respect for speakers of other languages and an accommodation of their language needs to the national scene. The language problem has acquired new dimensions since 1972. CCCC should now address the new decade in an informed way. We need a statement that reflects both an idealistic and realistic assessment of the language situation in this country.

Responding to an opportunity to officially take up the issue of language politics again, the CCCC Executive Committee initiated an effort to examine whether it needed to make another statement. In particular, the Executive Committee formed the "Committee to Study the Advisability of a Language Statement for the 1980s and 1990s" (CCCC Secretary's Report, 1981). It was charged with deciding "whether recent findings and developments in multilingualism and multi-dialecticism make it *desir-*

able for CCCC to prepare a statement on language for the 1980s and 1990s." The committee was chaired by Harold Allen, and among its members were Milton Baxter, Jimmy Cato, Louie Crew, Sara Garnes (Executive Committee member), Grace Holt, Doris Ginn (Executive Committee member), Richard Rodriguez, and Constance Weaver. Notably, this new committee contained no members from Lloyd-Jones's committee, nor did it contain any members from community or junior colleges. It would later be argued that the original members and constituencies out of which the CCCC SRTOL emerged had been deliberately excluded.

Soon after the committee's formation, Allen contacted its members, specifically asking whether a new language statement should be recommended. It is unclear the extent to which Allen asked the committee members to comment upon the SRTOL. As the committee charge was written, there was no specific reference to it, yet as evidenced by the committee responses to Allen, it appears that members felt the need to discuss the future utility of the SRTOL as language policy. One committee member responded that the SRTOL must be rewritten to take into account the changing political times such as the "Back to the Basics" movement. Another member urged a revision of the SRTOL in terms of the Ann Arbor decision recognizing Black English and the emerging computer culture. Still another member suggested examining Joseph Williams's (n.d.) document on nonstandard dialects. (The status of that document, however, was uncertain. Sledd [1983] argues that the document was written for the NCTE. It was unclear, however, if the document represented the actual position of Williams or the NCTE. Once introduced into the committee's work, however, it became part of a general examination of the usefulness of the SRTOL. In that sense, it took on an official status that was perhaps not intended.) The remainder of the committee felt that a more detailed statement needed to be created which would limit the ability of the CCCC to become wrapped up in ideological wars which were of little concern to them. It appears that only Louie Crew argued that no revision of the SRTOL nor any new statement was necessary (Daniels 1983, 6). All the responses, however, indicate an attempt to position the CCCC as a supporter of language diversity. No one was arguing that CCCC should not support a student's ability to learn through the use of his or her own language. The issue appeared to be the extent to which the SRTOL could be asked to perform such political work for the CCCC in the new situation of the 1980s.[1]

The request to have the committee examine Joseph Williams's "Status of Non-Standard Dialects" (n.d.), however, created a much different image of the committee's work. As noted earlier, in examining the work of Williams, the committee was bringing in a figure who represented a different type of writing classroom and social politics than had traditionally surrounded the SRTOL. Previous conceptions of the SRTOL had limited a teacher's authority to decide what constituted the student's voice; in fact, from the Dartmouth Conference on, the protection of the student's voice had served as a lever to allow new formations of language communities (with their own consequent politics) to be envisioned in the writing classroom. While Williams's document continues to endorse students' learning to respect a variety of dialects, it does so in a paradigm that reinvigorates traditional teacher authority. As opposed to the SRTOL resolution, which allowed students their own language to understand, frame, and organize social groups, Williams's statement embeds the recognition of differing dialects within the conservative context of "legitimacy." He writes, "[W]e must demonstrate that we respect dialects different from our own in the same way we respect any other social behavior that expresses in *legitimate* ways the identity and the values of a socially cohesive, socially responsible group" (emphasis added, 2). With such phrasing, Williams is clearly limiting the terms by which dialects (and their political associations) could be understood. One might ask if the actions of the Black Panthers would represent a "socially responsible group" expressing itself in "legitimate ways"?

Having created a paradigm which would limit the types of dialects brought into the classroom as legitimate examples of social expression, Williams (n.d.) then argues that morality demands standard English instruction. That is, Williams rejects the primary claim of the SRTOL that *forcing* students to learn other dialects is "an attempt of one social group to exert its influence over another." He writes:

To argue that requiring our students to learn such a Standard is coercive, socially offensive, or psychologically damaging is to confess our inability to explain successfully the arbitrary and idiosyncratic nature of those features that distinguish prestigious and non-prestigious dialects. (2)

For the sake of being more humane to a "student's self-respect," Williams argues, such arguments "deprive our students of their freedom to choose later" (n.d., 3). It should be noted that *there is not one example* in this book which states that the teaching of standard English should not be offered; as noted in chapter 2, even Vernon (Friedrich and Kuester 1972) sought and received such instruction. But as a consequence of Williams's belief that the SRTOL represents an abandonment of such practices, he concludes,

If we include [the preceding] facts in our deliberations about language, then the claim that students have a right to their own dialect can be only half of the truth: Our students have a right not only to their dialect, but to Standard Written English and to a standard spoken dialect as well. It is, however, a right that they can exercise only after they have acquired the means to exercise it. (n.d., 4)

(The insistence on pronunciation exceeds the parameters of any previous revision of the SRTOL.)

The reframing of standard English instruction as the moral choice, coupled with an increased attention to legitimacy of certain dialects, creates a counterstatement to the origins of the SRTOL, which had argued that the moral choice was allowing students not to choose standard English. In effect, Williams repositions the teacher as a figure who should legitimate the need for standard English and enable students to overcome any cultural or psychological resistance. In addition, and perhaps most important, the teacher becomes the arbiter of what counts as a legitimate social group. In fact, based upon these arguments, Williams makes the following recommendation: "The document 'Students' Right To Their Own Language' should be set aside as representing the position of the National Council of the Teachers of English" (Williams n.d., 4; Daniels 1983, 7). Notably, the

NCTE had already distanced itself from the CCCC resolution proper.

At first, the Williams's report (n.d.) appeared to have little impact on the Allen committee. The committee continued its discussion concerning what elements needed to be addressed by any future language statement. Initially, the committee discussed the need to expand any statements' audience beyond the "new teachers from the 60's." Daniels (1983, 6) reports that the committee believed that

> [t]he teachers of ten years ago are unchanged; new ones from the 60's become very conservative once they get behind a desk. These new ones have lower ATC scores and so they are less flexible. If we want a statement to have impact, it must be constructed as to reach the targets of boards of education, publishers, school boards, and curriculum makers.

In making these comments, the committee appears to be arguing that the SRTOL had failed to create an intergenerational alliance among teachers; an examination of this cross section of teachers would, it was argued, reveal a more conservative bias than represented by the SRTOL. Furthermore, any new document must also address the wider community in which teachers exist, the aforementioned institutional domains of boards of education and so on. Finally, the meeting also concluded that the SRTOL language statement "about attitudes being largely the result of English teaching should be replaced by one that recognizes the influence of state departments of education and their mandates about course content"(Committee on the Advisability of a New Language Statement for the 1980s and 1990s, 1982). None of these statements necessarily affect the SRTOL; in fact, they might be argued as merely admitting the diverse political domains where any such statement would have to be argued. Even the SRTOL language statement had been imagined as addressing an audience outside of college instructors. (In speaking of "school boards," however, the committee was also beginning to step outside the context of "college composition." This move would come back to haunt the committee.)

Even when discussing the economic importance of respecting a student's dialect, the minutes from the committee meeting do not indicate a strong move to create a conservative document. Instead, the committee participates in a similar rhetorical strategy used by various liberal and leftist activists; the student imagined as the test case for any language rights statement is the black-dialect speaker. The committee meeting minutes record the following considerations:

> Right should be defined more specifically. E.g., does it mean the right to use Black English in a letter of application for a job? Does it mean the right to use a kind of Black English interlanguage in an English-speaking business context? Does it mean the right of a student using Black English in a theme to receive the same grade as a student using Standard English, other qualities of the theme being approximately equal? Does the right have equal relevance in public and in private communication? (Committee on the Advisability of a New Language Statement for the 1980s and 1990s, 1982)

It might be argued that the committee was distancing itself from a certain politics of Black English. For instance, unlike the language of Vernon in *It's Mine and I'll Write It That Way* (Friedrich and Kuester 1972), here Black English is evaluated by how it conforms to the traditional work and academic world. Rather than being the tool by which to push the envelope of social and political dialogue, Black English becomes the test case for conformity. Absent are even McPherson's more moderate attempts to state that the business world must change or begin to accept the responsibility for worker training in standard English. The social politics which had used Black English to rediscover an African heritage or an international economic order are displaced into questions of domestic employment and grading policies. Yet even here, it is unclear that the meeting was engaged in creating an image of a student as merely an academic cog. Instead, as with the previously mentioned discussions, the committee seems to be merely expanding the range that *any* possible new document must encompass.

I am thus intentionally reading the committee as engaged in a discussion concerning the required impact and proposed audiences that any language statement should take into account, for it seems to me that it was based upon the extent to which these new areas and domains appeared to need addressing that the committee decided that a new language statement was necessary. This decision seems to have been made regardless of the status of the SRTOL. Further, it was based upon this committee discussion that Allen concluded a decision had been made for a "new statement." The work of the committee now turned to what the new statement should look like and how to present the arguments for it. Here is where the previous introduction of the Williams "Status of Non-Standard Dialects" document (n.d.) becomes crucial, for the placement of that document into the committee's work, despite the uncertainty of that document's status, immediately placed any call for a new statement as a *complete* rejection of the SRTOL in its entirety.

It is from this conjuncture of events that problems began to arise concerning the Allen committee. From the outset, Crew had positioned himself as a strong supporter of the SRTOL. Crew would argue that much of the committee's work had set the terms of the debate against the political and social context from which the SRTOL had emerged. The committee had cast "60's teachers" as naive. It had used Black English as a way to show the vagueness or impracticality of the SRTOL. Through the introduction of Williams's document (n.d.), the committee aligned with efforts to overturn the SRTOL as NCTE policy. The decision that a new statement was necessary thus appeared to be an attempt, not to reinvigorate a debate from the left, but to moderate such debate for the New Right. In response, it appears that Crew attempted to alert and share committee documents with organizations and individuals who would oppose such actions. Crew was acting within the professional paradigms articulated by Haber (1966) at the Radical Education Project conference (see chapter 1). That is, ignoring "professional" decorum, Crew began to broadcast what he perceived as the tentative decisions of committee meetings. In response, organizations such as the Progressive Composition Caucus (PCC) and individuals such as James Sledd began to organize against the Allen committee. That is, an effort began to begin to both save the SRTOL and reframe it as a document concerning class and economic oppression; such a statement would have particular currency in a period of massive layoffs and industry shutdowns.

This emphasis is particularly evident in James Sledd's "In Defense of the Students' Right" (1983). In this article, he positioned the SRTOL as a document concerned with social and class equity. He writes that "standard American English . . . is by its origin and nature a class dialect, essentially an instrument of domination" (669). Sledd also draws Williams directly into the debate, despite Williams having no official role in the committee:

> As Joseph Williams says in his "tentative draft," "linguistically minor differences can . . . carry great social weight" in societies where a standard language has been imposed. Williams inexplicably finds that brutal fact inexplicable; but if linguistic markers of social class are to be effective as barriers and as filters, if they are to flatter the vanity of the privileged and damage the egos of the subordinate, it is necessary that they should be niggling and arbitrary, insignificant for communication among those who honestly want to communicate. If the class-markers really interfered with communication, people who want to communicate would learn them naturally, as we learn our native speech, without formal instruction. The class-markers would cease, then, to mark the classes, and new and more trifling distinctions would have to be invented. (cited in Daniels 1983)

Sledd (1983) continues by stating that the framers of the SRTOL, while confused, ultimately produced a document which spoke to the interests of those outside mainstream, that is, those students who ultimately might be unable or unwilling to learn standard English but still deserved an education. Any attempt to undercut the political concern which the document indicates, to Sledd, would repudiate this concern for the political needs of the underrepresented and oppressed of society.

Unlike other efforts to save the SRTOL, supporters were also able to draw upon a newly reorganized radical left in the CCCC: the Progressive Composition Caucus (PCC). Organized in March 1982, it represented a collective of writing teachers broadly identifying themselves with issues of class and feminism. As broadcast on their letterhead, the PCC enunciated its mission in terms very similar to the NUC:

> The Progressive Composition Caucus is composed of compo-
> sition instructors who view writing as a potentially liberating
> activity and teach from a leftist-feminist perspective. Our cur-
> riculum often emphasizes non-canonical literature, and exposes
> sexist, racist, political, and corporate manipulation of language.
>
> This Newsletter provides a forum for organizing around
> pedagogical and political issues at the national meetings of the
> CCCC and other professional organizations as well as a place
> to share writing assignments, course outlines, bibliographical
> information and any other material which contributes to a stu-
> dent-centered writing curriculum. (PCC 1983).

That is, PCC imagined its role to be the production of academics who believed a key element of their academic identity should be working to counter corporate capitalism and create broad-based social justice. Unlike the NUC, however, this organization was clearly interested in reforming writing instruction. Its primary concern seemed at the outset to be creating a network of support for like-minded writing teachers. And, in practice, its newsletters offer pragmatic tools for the radical leftist academic. Among regu-lar features of the newsletter were course syllabi designed to bring race, class, and gender awareness into the classroom, guides to what panels to attend at the CCCC, and resolutions that pulled together political activism and writing instruction. In fact, one way to imagine the newsletter would be as a progressive version of the SRTOL teacher's guide, for a continual emphasis in the early newsletters is the question of how to connect students to collective anticorporate politics. In published assignments, stu-dents were often asked to juxtapose their reality with the reality of work. This comparison was designed to give students insights into issues of racism, classism, and sexism. For instance, the first newsletter featured a CCCC proposal by Richard Collier (1982) which states the need for students to engage in studying capital-ist culture.

> What can be done is more intimately connected to altering a
> student's consciousness and helping her demystify her role in
> capitalist culture than it is with heuristics, audience analysis or
> sentence combining techniques. . . . Ultimately a successful

writing class must be in some degree revolutionary: committed writing will engage the author's tacit and acquired knowledge of language more fully than writing which is imposed and which therefore will appear to the author to be irrelevant and trivial; only writing that springs from the dissonance, the sudden awareness of incongruity between the author's implicit map of reality and her immediate experience of that reality, can create that commitment. The unreflective use of language results in unreflective acceptance of the forms of social relations; a critical use of language helps one to assess and understand these forms. Thus, the writing class should help the student reconstruct her world view. By emphasizing the analysis of experience, discovering universals, especially in work and social relations, confronting value problem, such as racism and sexism, demystifying a consumer society, and encouraging collective interaction through collaborative writing and group criticism, a progressive perspective in composition would teach that control of language produces awareness and awareness is power.

Within a broader anticorporate ideology, the PCC attempted to bring language instruction into contact with how the corporate world was reframing public debate. It asked students to work as a collective to examine how their language participated in the perpetuation of oppressive structures.

Here the role of political and academic caucuses within and around the CCCC becomes important. The original version of Sledd's (1983) article, which contained citations of Williams's (n.d.) document, was rejected by *CCC*. *College English* agreed to publish the document only if Sledd "removed 'all references' to matter not already published," that is, Williams's document and other committee correspondence (Sledd 1983, 668). At a time when Sledd was unable to find a public venue in official journals, then, he was able to spread his concerns through caucuses such as the PCC and its newsletter.[2] The caucuses were then able to publish these unedited arguments to their members, forcing a debate which might not have otherwise occurred. For instance, it was the journal of the Conference on Language Attitudes and Composition (CLAC) that, through Daniels's article, published part of Sledd's critique of Williams. It was the May 1983 *Progressive Composition Caucus Newsletter* that, after announcing Sledd's efforts on their front page, also endorsed his call for letters to be sent to Donald Stewart, now CCCC chairperson, objecting to the Allen committee's proposed actions. (The CLAC had previously decided to initiate a similar letter-writing campaign.)

I do not want to overestimate the importance of these organizations. In 1983 the PCC probably had fewer than one hundred members. But the existence of journals in which to publish articles, organize individuals, sponsor writing campaigns, and enunciate committee actions within a CCCC bureaucracy that was susceptible to internal pressure must not be underestimated. In fact, these articles, with their warnings about proposed revisions to the SRTOL, coupled with the discussion being generated by other SRTOL supporters, appear to have applied pressure on the Allen committee to back away from its conclusion that a new statement was necessary. One committee member wrote to Allen, objecting to his language regarding the "the desirability of a new *statement.*" Instead, the member argued, the committee had decided on the need for a new *document* (Committee on the Advisability of a New Language Statement for the 1980s and 1990s correspondence).

It is probably more to the point that the committee found itself in a bind. Since its charge was to decide whether a new language statement was needed, and Williams's (n.d.) document within the Allen committee had characterized "new" as against the SRTOL, the committee could not recommend a more thorough pragmatic statement that took on issues such as bilingualism or computers, for instance, without appearing to move against the SRTOL. To move against the SRTOL, however, was to validate the emerging vision of the Allen committee as a pawn in a conservative counterattack. The committee, then, was forced into a box; it had to recommend a more thorough discussion of the implication of language diversity in the 1980s without implying criticism of the SRTOL. The "new document" language appears to escape this bind. This recommendation seems most in line with the original mission of the committee, since the original mission did not discuss the SRTOL at all. Such a suggestion also appeared to maintain the integrity of the SRTOL's political and philosophical underpinnings, while allowing the CCCC to position itself in relationship to the emerging issues of bilingualism, standard usage, and conservative politics. In effect, since the new document would define the current status of the politics of the SRTOL, no new statement was needed. Perhaps this was Irmscher's intention from the outset.

At the end of June, Allen sent out a draft committee report (Committee on the Advisability of a New Language Statement for the 1980s and 1990s, 1983a). As might be expected, the report attempts to position itself as sympathetic to the SRTOL. In fact, this version calls for the CCCC to reaffirm its commitment to the SRTOL. In its rhetorical positioning of the SRTOL, however, the committee clearly attempts to turn it into a historical document with little current use. That is, reflecting the committee notes that placed the SRTOL as a statement by 1960s teachers, it argues that the SRTOL's time has passed:

> The committee has attended to various criticized weaknesses in the CCCC publication, *The Students' Right To Their Own Language*. The Committee is aware of the criticism that the statement offers problems with respect to its style, its logic, and its inadequate reliance upon insights available in the research of American dialectologists, sociolinguists, and linguistic anthropologists. It is sensitive to the oft-repeated criticism that the term *right* is never defined—that the sense intended by the authors is never made clear or even identified.
>
> The committee realizes, however, that *The Students' Right* was set forth not as a programmatic statement but rather as a philosophical (perhaps even political) statement. The basic validity of this courageously adopted philosophical position the committee is quick to affirm. Because some misunderstanding has arisen about the function of this committee, we declare positively that we have no desire for either replacement nor rescission of that statement. Indeed, to quell any doubts on this score, we suggest that, just as a married couple may choose to repeat the marriage vows on the occasion of its golden anniversary, the members of CCCC may find it satisfying to reaffirm their position by readopting the statement during the 1984 convention.
>
> But we are quick to also add that this suggestion does not mark the be-all and end-all of our concern. The initial charge to the committee implies that something more may be required, that there is a need not met by the simple statement that students have a right to their own language or even by the ex-

planatory material in the publication. We have found that there is an even greater need than the one implied by the charge. . . .

An analogy comes to mind at this point. The Declaration of Independence takes the philosophical position that all men are created equal. But that simple credal statement was not enough. Necessary specificity later had to be provided in the United States Constitution and the Bill of Rights and in certain following amendments as part of a process that the continuing drive for an equal rights amendment demonstrates is still unfinished. And particular practical applications have led to numerous federal and local legislative acts during the past two centuries.

It is then the practical programmatic implications of the CCCC credal statement that the committee found itself addressing during its initial correspondence and increasingly during the discussions in Washington and in Detroit. Members raised, for instance, the question whether the students' right to their own language does not imply as well the right to assistance in learning a dialect prestigious beyond their own community, to instruction that empowers them to choose among dialect options rather than by omission restricting them to the dialects of their nurture. (Committee on the Advisability of a Language Statement for the 1980s and 1990s, 1983a, 1–2)

By comparing the SRTOL to the Declaration of Independence, the document clearly attempts to validate it as a statement of principle while also stating that it needs further explication. Even its call for standard English instruction is moderated with a rhetoric focusing on a "right to assistance" instead of educational mandates. That is, given the time period of cutbacks and restrictions of federal initiatives, the document clearly signals a difference from the New Right. Although the brunt of this book has featured the difficulties of such alliances, the committee at this point clearly is attempting to align itself with moderate liberal forces.

Having created this moderate image, however, the committee then goes on to state the need for the SRTOL to be taken up as a statement concerning the education of elementary and secondary school teachers. These needs include increased linguistic training, an understanding of the effect of teacher attitudes on student performance, and a recognition of every student's ability to be bidialectal. While none of these goals seem particularly controversial, a conservative agenda begins to manifest in the discussion of teacher training materials:

> [M]aterials relating to *The Students' Right*'s goal in teacher-training must be both fiscally and educationally conservative if they are not to be dismissed out of hand as offering only "pie-in-the-sky" goals. If such materials demand radical curriculum changes and involve large expenditures of time and money, they will not be acceptable to the target audience that should be affected by the CCCC statement. Rather, with that distant goal in mind, writers of the materials should present a step-by-step practical outline of what can be done to move the entire field of teacher education closer to accepting the viewpoint and the position advocated by the CCCC. (Committee on the Advisability of a Language Statement for the 1980s and 1990s, 1983a, 6)

Clearly, the NUC's OUTS document is not being imagined here, nor, I would argue, are the more moderate politics of the document's opening. At this point, the document is attempting to finesse the SRTOL into a conservative era through the politics of pragmatism. Since radical politics will not attract funding, particularly at the local level, it argues, they must be held only as that "distant goal" in the future. At no point were the CCCC's SRTOL committee members viewing their document as a "distant goal." Instead, they were worried about the treatment of the student in the classroom of today. This gesture by the Allen committee has the effect of simultaneously turning the SRTOL into a piece of history and into a future utopian politics. Either way, its current impact is nullified.

Furthermore, in its focus on elementary and secondary school teachers, the Allen committee positioned itself outside the parameters of the CCCC. In fact, the committee clearly avoids an opportunity to describe what training *college* and *university* instructors need to adequately understand their students' writing and speaking patterns. Why the committee chose to take this path of argument is unclear. The effect of such an argument, however, is to create a situation where the CCCC can no longer claim scholarly or institutional control over the SRTOL.

It must now be apparent that, if the need is for materials to reach the entire English-teaching profession and relevant segments of the field of education as well as various groups with the concerned public, then that need cannot be met by a revision of the existing CCCC statement or even by a new statement produced by CCCC.

The constitution of the Conference on College Composition and Communication limits its area of concern and responsibility. Article I, Section 2, reads: "The broad object of the CCCC is to unite teachers of composition and communication in organization which can consider all matters relevant to their teaching, including teachers, subject matter, administration, methods, and students. The specific objects are (1) to provide an opportunity for discussion of college composition and communication courses, (2) to encourage studies and research in the field, and (3) to publish a bulletin containing reports of conferences and articles of interest to teachers of composition and communication."

Clearly constitutional limitations as well as the limitation imposed by CCCC's field of competence itself, i.e., the college field, demand that the torch set aflame by the CCCC statement should now be passed to those who can carry it along a wider highway.

At this point, then, your committee may seem to depart from the specific charge it received from you, but in doing so it is convinced that it acts within the spirit of the original statement by calling for full professional action on a front wider than that of CCCC.

The committee therefore recommends that the CCCC executive committee approach the executive committee of the National Council of Teachers of English with a proposal for the creation of a major task force whose members will represent not only the CCCC but also all the various areas of professional specialization in the English teaching profession, and who will work with consultants from the fields of anthropological linguistics, sociolinguistics, and psycholinguistics. The responsibility of this task force will be to explore in depth the various aspects of the problem that first led to the preparation of the CCCC statement and then to prepare a document or documents that will propose and explicate practical ways for moving toward the realization of the ideal situation stated in *The Students' Right To Their Own Language,* i.e. general respect for the dignity and worth of the students' variety of the language. (Committee on the Advisability of a Language Statement for the 1980s and 1990s, 1983a, 7–8)

This gesture confirmed many of the fears of opponents of the Allen committee. Article I, Section 2, with its narrow interpretation of what is relevant to college writing and communication instructors, had been used consistently against leftist politics within the CCCC. Or rather, when organizations such as NUC or political resolutions such as anti–Vietnam War resolutions were proposed, opponents could argue that they fell outside the CCCC's role. Citing this clause could only appear as an attempt to totally redefine and depolemicize the goals of the SRTOL. In fact, what is particularly unfortunate about this document and this gesture is that they confirmed the suspicions of SRTOL supporters that the Allen committee was designed from the outset to destroy the SRTOL.

The argument that the Allen committee was designed to gut the SRTOL had been circulating from the committee's inception. James Sledd (1984) summarized this aspect of the criticism of the Allen committee succinctly in the *Progressive Composition Caucus Newsletter:*

[S]ome facts about the creation and proceedings of the committee should not be forgotten. . . .

1. When William Irmscher as president of NCTE proposed to the chair of the College Conference that the Conference should "address the new decade" with a new "assessment of the language situation in this country" (letter of September 30, 1981), he explained that he hoped to head off more drastic action against the *Students' Right:* "I make this recommendation because of growing threats to take action on the floor of the business meeting either to rescind *The Students' Right To Their Own Language* or to amend it. *I think that those particular actions would be unfortunate, particularly since that statement addressed its time and served a useful purpose.* It should stand as a record, despite its limitations" [Irmscher's emphasis]. Irmscher later explained privately to Crew (Crew to Sledd, March 22, 1983) that "he would like to see the profession off the hook for some of the ways *The Students' Right* had set us up for attack from John Simon & Company." He asked Crew to read *Paradigms Lost,* "toxicity" (Crew said) which he would not risk until he could "jog the convention's tobacco poisoning" out of his lungs.

2. When James Hill appointed Harold Allen to chair the committee whose creation Irmscher had prompted, he appointed a man who had voted against the *Students' Right* when it was originally proposed as a 4C's resolution. . . .

3. On January 24, 1983, two months after his committee's meeting in Washington, Allen sent the committee a much more direct attack on the *Students' Right*, "a copy of the relevant tentative draft prepared some time ago for NCTE by Joseph Williams of the University of Chicago, a statement referred to during our meeting as having special value for us." . . . According to Crew (Crew to Sledd, March 22, 1983), even Irmscher had found Williams suggested policy "reactionary."

4. Not surprisingly, Williams was infuriated with Crew for "sharing committee proceedings and casual comments" which "surely," Williams said (Williams to Crew, March 28, 1983), had been "exchanged on the assumption that they would not be repeated." Williams complained that he would now "have to be on guard" with Crew about anything he might say "about anyone else" for fear that Crew would "repeat it in public." "Nothing CCCC or NCTE promulgates," Williams went on, "will have the faintest effect on anything," but by his "profoundly destructive behavior" Crew had rendered himself "useless in the future." There was "no possibility" that Williams "would ever serve on a committee" with him. (8–9)

It all "fit together too nicely," for as detailed by Sledd, from the outset there was no possibility but the overturning of the SRTOL. As he portrays the situation, a coup d'état had been the intent of Irmscher, Hill, and Allen from the outset.[3] In this situation, the introduction of Williams's (n.d.) document on nonstandard dialects appears all the more ominous. In a footnote to his "In Defense of the Students' Right" (1983), Sledd continues this attack by implying that *College English* also participated in this strategy. When told he could not publish material not "already published" (Williams's report), Sledd (1983, 667) writes: "In effect, that meant that an attack on the Students' Right, a CCCC document, could be prepared for the NCTE and officially circulated, with words of praise, to the members of an officially appointed CCCC committee, yet that members of CCCC and NCTE could not refer to that attack in an NCTE journal." In effect, Sledd argued that a conspiracy of silence was being used to gut the SRTOL.

By April, Donald Stewart, now CCCC chairperson, was forced to respond to the growing rumors that the Allen committee was acting to abrogate the SRTOL with little or no input from the CCCC general body. Addressing his memo to "CCCC officers, Executive Committee, and other interested persons," Stewart wrote:

> A number of misconceptions about the nature and scope of this committee's work seem to be circulating from one part of the country to the other. I wish to clarify the situation.

> The charge of the committee reads as follows:

>> To decide whether recent findings and developments in multilingualism and multi-dialecticism make it desirable for CCCC to prepare a statement on language for the 1980s and 1990s.

> I have discussed the wording of the charge with James Hill, Immediate Past Chair of CCCC who appointed the Committee, and with Harold Allen, the committee's chair. Both agree that the statement above represents their understanding of the committee's charge. I wish to call your attention to one fact in particular: the committee is *not* charged with drafting any statement on language. Its mission is to *advise* the CCCC Executive Committee on whether or not to create a committee to draft such a statement. (Stewart 1983a)

Stewart then outlined a set of procedures designed to ensure that members have adequate input into any future decisions concerning the SRTOL.[4] He stated that he would circulate copies of the proposal to Executive Committee members and "interested persons," plan a special meeting at the NCTE convention, and then ask the Executive Committee to "accept or reject the committee's recommendation at the Executive Committee's regular scheduled meeting" (Stewart 1983a).

Despite the overlay of conspiracy charges resulting from the actions of caucuses supporting the SRTOL, however, I would argue that the effect of letters, memoranda, and articles detailing the actions of the committee was to effectively block the possibility of the more conservative Allen report being ratified. To this extent, the caucuses within the CCCC served a productive role.

Unfortunately, the full possibilities of their actions were ultimately not realized, for at a time when the United States was experiencing massive job losses in steel, textiles, and manufacturing, Sledd's argument concerning social and class mobility could have easily been merged with the concerns about multilingualism and multidialectalism. These arguments could have been articulated within a history of the SRTOL that clearly linked it to anticorporate and anticonservative agendas. By making the SRTOL stand for a certain type of political advocacy, opponents of the Allen committee could have furthered in the public journals the reemergence of leftist organizations within the CCCC. Such work might have highlighted the ways in which political alliances between progressive forces, writing instructors, nonuniversity workers, students, teaching fellows, and professional organizations could work to stave off the threats of the New Right. In short, by returning to models of broad-based activism highlighted throughout this work, a new type of voice within the CCCC could have gained institutional currency. Also, and more important, such efforts might have supplied support to those members of the Allen committee who, while not wanting to gut the SRTOL, were concerned with reinvigorating the discussion of progressive language politics within the CCCC.

This was not to be the case. One of the few sites with any legitimate institutional status left from which to enunciate a productive and forward-looking vision of language politics within the Allen committee was the minority report. Indeed, Crew had stated as early as April that he would prepare such a report. In his report, Crew does not touch upon any ulterior or conspiratorial aspects of the committee, except to note that it was "very difficult to buy a copy" of the actual SRTOL language statement (Crew 1984, 2). Instead, he begins his report by supporting the Allen committee's call to reaffirm the SRTOL: "With the majority I wholeheartedly recommend that the members of CCCC be given an opportunity to reaffirm the *Students' Right To Their Own Language*" (1). Immediately afterward, he begins his critique of the committee's actions. He writes that the committee exceeded its charge: "A simple yea or nay would suffice" (1). In doing so, the committee improperly concluded that the NCTE is the proper site for the SRTOL. Crew states,

> Taking the matter out of the hands of CCCC and putting it into the hands of NCTE would diffuse the responsibility for a covert repudiation of the document. Meanwhile, both can claim to respect it as a moral imperative. What kind of moral imperative is involved if you no longer respect students' language enough to let the students survive academia while writing and speaking it well? (2)

Crew then warns of the import of the Allen committee revisions. He argues that currently the SRTOL endorses a teacher's right to pass students "who demonstrate competence in the subject matter." The new document, however, would allow teachers to "require prestigious dialects before teachers can grant passage to otherwise bright students" (1). Notably, the committee report does not actually endorse such requirements, but Crew believes that the ambiguity of the report's language ("the students' right to assistance") allows such a reading. Consequently, Crew argues that since both documents allow various interpretations, it is wiser to leave the SRTOL intact since its ambiguity is on the side of students. In fact, as his report continues, Crew begins to associate this defense with the social and political project earlier associated with the NUC. Invoking the need to address "state bureaucrats," he writes:

> Isn't it more important to teach students how state-supported education thus supports the state, how standard languages were developed and have been imposed as a means of mobilizing and controlling people, especially those isolated in language communities which have never been respected by the rich and powerful? Isn't the control of Standard English infinitely less important to genuinely humane purposes than the ability to read a document like the Majority report and to understand its real intent? (2)

Crew argues that teachers should not just accept the "inevitability" of language standards, but educate students in how to resist them. More important, Crew indicates the extent to which the committee's report is a conservative document. When discussing what teachers need to know to instruct a classroom containing diverse dialects, the Allen committee had stated:

> Such teachers should know the distinctive nature of American social and regional dialects in terms of their grammar, lexicon, and pronunciation. To develop respect for the integrity of a dialect or a language they should learn that a dialect or a language is not intrinsically inferior to or superior to another dialect or another language. The description of social dialects should enable them to perceive the relationship of those dialects to the power structure of society. (Committee on the Advisability of a New Language Statement for the 1980s and 1990s, 1983b, 3)

Crew argues, however, that the document never states what it would mean to understand the power relationships between language and society; nor does it offer any guidelines as to how this discussion would not reinvoke the radical image that had plagued the SRTOL. In fact, in the section on teacher training, the Allen committee document discusses the type of education teachers should have concerning dialect. Referring to Section XV of the SRTOL language statement, the Allen committee states:

> With some exceptions, Section XV is a satisfactory initial outline of desirable content for a teacher-training program. But a full-scale revision of this content should provide better language examples, as, for instance, evidence from Appalachian English. Indeed, new materials should stress the details of practical approaches to the problems rather than idealized and well-nigh unattainable goals. (6)

This moment of invoking Appalachian English is similar to the NCTE CEL "Statement on Usage" (see chapter 4). While Appalachian English might invoke images of President Kennedy discovering poverty, it did not invoke the social protests and politics associated with the New Left, nor did it address the increasingly multicultural student population. As with the CEL statement, a dialect is chosen which effectively masks the actual student populations. To the extent that the history of the SRTOL had grown out of the New Left and NUC's efforts to create a broad-based movement for social justice, the capitulation of the larger economic and moral politics surrounding the SRTOL indeed represented a gutting of the document. Crew (1984) states, "The Majority Report [of the Committee] abrogates the Students' Right and appeases so-called conservatives who are actually radical revolutionaries. The Majority Report abandons the principles of the Declaration of Independence and abets the division of this nation into dominant haves and subservient have nots" (3).

Crew's document, however, fails to articulate a vision of how the SRTOL can speak to the present. Although it contains punchy statements concerning social justice, it lacks a clear statement on what the SRTOL would mean in practice; what should the composition teacher as a member of the CCCC do to serve the have-nots? Crew's statement does not offer an alternative vision of how the United States functions and the CCCC's role within that alternative framework. Of course, with rare exceptions, no author had attempted such a vision for the SRTOL, yet at a moment when such a vision had the possibility of attaining official institutional status, Crew settles for what appears to be a condensation of 1960s rhetoric. His piece is so couched in slogans that in comparison to the Allen committee report, it reads as if the left had not articulated any vision for its actions in the 1980s. In fact, at moments, the rhetoric transcends any particular political alignment and becomes difficult to read as a serious counter-proposal. For instance, in speaking about the need for professional organizations not to succumb to social pressure, he writes:

> [P]lastic surgeons are right when they talk about the tremendous psychological need some people with love handles feel when they try to measure up to the thin standards of the culture. However, it is one thing to make available the best plastic surgery possible, but quite another for a professional organization to acquiesce in the stupid standards of weight or dialect. Rather we should critique the culture which requires them in the first place. Like the plastic surgeons, the majority allow their pocketbooks to misplace both compassion and scalpel.
>
> Let love handles and dialects flourish. Operate instead on the culture sick enough to devalue them. That's the surgery the *Students' Right To Their Own Language* effects, and that's why many fear it. (Crew 1984, 2–3)

Almost ten years after the initial passage of the SRTOL, dialects are now being compared to the fat of middle age. Surely, this is an apt metaphor for a document which was unable to prepare a rhetoric for its present or its future. What the Allen committee report creates, which Crew does not, is a rhetoric which views the SRTOL as a document with a future, albeit a conservative one. Writing in 1983, however, Crew seemed unable to articulate a similarly powerful rhetoric. It was an opportunity lost.

Endgame

The Allen and Crew reports, then, offered two alternative visions for the CCCC Executive Committee. The Allen report argued that a more moderate vision of the SRTOL should be endorsed and that the project of creating the necessary documents should be accorded to the NCTE. Crew's report argued that the SRTOL should stand untouched and that the CCCC should continue to stand for the have-nots. Within these options, accusations of secrecy and hidden agendas continued. In fact, upon receipt of both Allen's majority report and Crew's minority report, Donald Stewart (1983b) sent a letter out to the CCCC officers and Executive Committee. This letter indicates that copies of both reports will be sent to the Executive Committee. Anticipating a complaint from Sledd and Crew, he states,

> I decided not to send the report to all members of CCCC because a majority of you told me not to, some in very strong terms. The two reasons most frequently given were (1) the expense and (2) the fact that since this committee was charged to do its work by the Executive Committee, the EC should first review what has been done before considering the matter of wider distribution of the report. *No secrecy is involved.* (emphasis added)

In addition, a special public meeting of the Executive Committee was arranged on November 19 "at a site to be determined. . . . We will not do any voting." The meeting, however, which might have turned into a discussion not only of the future of the SRTOL, but of the next set of conversations that the CCCC should take up during the 1980s, turned out quite differently.

At the meeting, Stewart explained that its purpose was to solicit responses "to the draft of the Committee for a Language Statement for the 1980's and 1990's." Only individuals on the agenda would be given the opportunity to speak, after which, CCCC Executive Committee members would ask questions. According to the minutes of the meeting, events transpired as follows:

> *Elisabeth McPherson:* McPherson urged Executive Committee to take no action that would weaken or appear to weaken its resolution on the Students' Right To Their Own Language, and expressed the view that the Committee Report was ambiguous on the issue of whether it seeks to strengthen the position or shift responsibility to NCTE. In her summary, she urged the Committee to leave the Language Statement alone, and to ask NCTE to put some teeth into its 1974 Resolution.

> *Steve Zemelman:* Zemelman explained that he does not question the motive or intentions of the Committee's members, but that he thinks CCCC needs to consider how the Report may *appear* to readers. He discussed a number of passages which, regardless of their intent, seem to him to undercut the resolution on the Students' Right To Their Own Language. And he urged the Executive Committee to wait until March 1984 to vote on the Committee Report.

> *Vivian Davis:* Davis expressed concern about the "revisionism" of past statements that seems to be part of the Committee's Report. And she urged the Executive Committee to let the Resolution on the Students' Right To Their Own Language stand in its original form without such changes.

> *Discussion:* Stewart called for questions and comments from the Executive Committee members. The Committee had no specific issues to explore.

> *Adjournment.* (CCCC special officers meeting, Denver, 19 November 1983)

Without strong support from the committee's participants and with the argument of supporters of the SRTOL available to meeting participants, the Executive Committee was faced with accepting a report which SRTOL participants and former CCCC presidents felt undermined the intent of the original resolution. That is, there was no strong showing by the forces William Irmscher had warned against several years prior. Consequently, the Executive Committee appeared to feel no pressure to take the action proposed by the Allen report and had strong feelings against accepting its implications. For that reason, two days later, the Executive Committee took the following response to the work of the Allen committee:

> To accept but take no action on the report by the Committee on the Advisability of Preparing a Language Statement for the 1980s and 1990s..
> To affirm that there is no need to prepare a Language Statement for the 1980's and 1990's (CCCC Secretary's Report, 21 November 1983)

The committee also voted to reaffirm the SRTOL, yet accepting the report while simultaneously reaffirming that the SRTOL represents an ambiguous moment. One interpretation of this moment would be as a success for SRTOL advocates. McPherson, Davis, Sledd, and Crew had effectively battled the conspiratorial Allen committee and won a reaffirmation of the SRTOL. An alternative reading would be to suggest that the sheer act of the Allen committee's deliberations effectively positioned the SRTOL as representing a past history, irrelevant for today. It might even be argued that accepting the report but taking no actions on its conclusions worked to criticize the SRTOL. The Executive Committee might be seen as accepting the SRTOL as a limited document but taking no action to expand it or work for its full implementation. Here, the SRTOL becomes a vague statement about respecting students; it does not become an institutional tool against the emergent politics of the New Right. Consequently, given the material available to them, I would argue that the actions of the Executive Committee resulted in an endgame. Neither position can claim victory. That is, the Executive Committee was unable to articulate a way for the SRTOL to both speak to the conservative present and respect its leftist past. There appeared to be no ground for the CCCC to move forward on the SRTOL.

In effect, the SRTOL became history.

---

1. These conclusions are drawn from committee correspondence shared with me from various sources. Given the controversy which surrounded the committee, I have also purposely decided not to indicate the positions of various committee members as indicated in committee correspondence or committee minutes, except when absolutely necessary. In part, unlike Executive Committee members, who assume a public scrutiny of their actions, few individuals on this committee have chosen to publicly recount the aims and intentions of its work. (Louie Crew is the exception.) Few, I believe, imagined their meetings would become embroiled in such a public CCCC fight. Also, my aim is not to discuss individual committee members' positions, but to study how the work of the committee was picked up and framed by outside forces, so the particular positions of individuals do not seem relevant. Instead, I focus on their final public statement: their report to the Executive Committee.

2. Sledd (1982) had actually published the following in the first PCC newsletter:

> (A) The research machine serves mainly the researchers. (B) Research in composition is generally a flop because (i) the students feel no need to learn the kinds of writing that academics are capable of teaching and (ii) the colleges and universities refuse to support anything that doesn't serve the dominant Powers. (C)The serious comp. teacher HAS to work for social change, even when there seems little hope—or none. One place to begin is with the staffing of comp. courses—by either graduate students or a "wage section"/ "resource pool." That sort of academic peonage will ultimately reduce the humanistic departments to academic slums, with a tiny handful of docile, privileged luminaries and a vast majority of underpaid, overworked, untenured, transients.

3. In his letter submitting the final report to Donald Stewart, Allen (1983) defends himself against what he perceives to be unfair charges:

> In sending the final draft of the report to you and to the CCCC executive committee [via Donald Stewart] I find it nostalgic to realize that this is surely my last active relationship with the organization for which seven of us laid the foundation at midnight on the balcony of the former Stevens Hotel in Chicago years ago. I am indulging that nostalgia by xeroxing an ancient letterhead for this note.

I thank those of you who have attended one or both meetings of the committee, especially those who have substantially contributed to the writing and criticism of the report. It is a good report; I hope that CCCC will find it so.

I appreciate the support several of you voiced during the *sturm und drang* period last spring. That period I had not anticipated. Had I done so, I might have been tempted to reject the request to chair the committee. I really had no need to endure such a storm of abuse from people whose behavior hardly grace our profession.

Much was made by them of my earlier vote against the resolution, a vote, they said, that disqualified me as chair. As you know, I deliberately tried to be neutral during our meetings. It is odd that in taking their graceless inductive leaps my detractors either ignored or forgot my expressed reasons for the negative vote, and they chose not to ask me. In voting no, I said I was not opposed to the spirit of the resolution but was in favor of the basic concept. But I was disturbed by the lack of input from relevant linguistic disciplines and because a newspaper experience led me to believe that the form of the resolution would arouse a storm of opposition form the press and from self-appointed guardians of the language. So I wanted the resolution rewritten. No simple amending would do, so I voted to reject.

I think that what you all have helped to produce is a document that will lead to what should have been sought years ago. I hope that you may have a share in the future deliberations. As for me, I have finished.

Allen's statement that the committee's report will produce what "should have been sought years ago" in juxtaposition with his belief no "simple amending would do" seems to support Sledd and Crew's point that the committee had always intended to overturn the SRTOL. Such a reading, however, seems to demonize Allen and portray a founding member of the CCCC as unsympathetic to the needs of marginal or nontraditional students. It might be better to say that in the politically tense time of the 1980s, there was little room made for earlier efforts (and understandings) of how to publicly respect dialect difference. In such an environment, Allen was unable to gain the recognition his earlier efforts had earned.

4. In fact, in October 1980, new CCCC Chairperson Donald Stewart (1980) had actually written a defense of the resolution. In opposition to those who saw the SRTOL as "a complete abandoning of 'standards' for written discourse" or as "merely the latest in CCCC's absurd but harmless attempts to be trendy," Stewart attempted to show how the resolution could be productively used in the classroom. The article includes a student paper replete with surface grammatical errors. The paper concerns the student's arrest for stealing a pair of gloves, although the narrative makes clear that theft was not the student's intention. Arguing against a reading which would consider only surface errors, Stewart instead focused on questions that allow the student to realize the implications of the paper:

How should one respond to this paper? I would suggest by reacting directly to the substance of it. Is there anyone who would honestly argue that the surface mistakes here prevent him or her from understanding the content of this paper? I do not believe that is possible.

In terms of the grade received, Stewart writes:

No, I did not come close to flunking the paper, nor did I give it an A. I marked it C because of the questions left unanswered. The student accepted the judgment, and he understood what I meant. We'll get around to editing skills another time, and in the right context. He will be more receptive to learning them, then, anyway.

Stewart's position is an attempt at forging a middle ground (neither A nor F; neither all standard nor nonstandard). In fact, unlike other discussions surrounding the SRTOL, this short piece caused little or no discussion.

Ozymandias—Creating a Program for the SRTOL

I met a traveler from an antique land,
Who said—"two vast and trunkless legs of stone
Stand in the desert . . . Near them, on the sand,
Half sunk a shattered visage lies, whose frown,
And wrinkled lip, and sneer of cold command,
Tell that its sculptor well those passions read
Which yet survive, stamped on these lifeless things,
The hand that mocked them, and the heart that fed;
And on the pedestal, these words appear:
My name is Ozymandias, King of Kings,
Look on my Works, ye Mighty, and despair!
Nothing beside remains. Round the decay
Of that colossal Wreck, boundless and bare
The lone and level sands stretch far away.

PERCY BYSSHE SHELLEY, *"Ozymandias"*

The figure of Ozymandias has haunted the writing of this work. Initially, the SRTOL struck me as a monument sculpted by the hands of students embittered by its failed promises of collective action. When the history of the SRTOL emerged before me, its opponents and advocates assumed the singular role of the traveler, reminding me of the difficulty in any attempt to instantiate a progressive politics. As the future of progressive education came under increasing attack by conservative and reactionary forces, I began to realize how these forces stepped into the chasm between communities and universities to create urban "deserts." At the conclusion of this book, then, I find myself in the role of listener, wondering what moral should be drawn from a series of events occurring over twenty-five years ago.

The SRTOL originated during a time of remarkable growth for higher education. It was formulated by academics who could assume an expanding job market in the humanities. Further, increasing student enrollments seemed to validate the position of the university as a "knowledge factory." In fact, in almost every academic article examined throughout this work, there was a latent assumption that the university was the principal site for the production of knowledge. Within that world, composition was beginning its emergence as *the* developing sector in the humanities. As detailed in these pages, composition's unique struggle became to expand the university's legitimating function to an increasing set of dialects, communities, and knowledges. Indeed, there seemed little in the social terrain that appeared to undermine the hope that compositionists would soon assume the role of public intellectual, earlier assumed by other academics such as Lionel Trilling. Given this situation, it is no surprise that compositionists felt responsible for society's attitudes toward language or that some believed a switch in their position could change society's attitudes.

While composition has continued to grow as a discipline, even sparking debates about whether it will succeed literature, it is unclear whether the university still retains its role as the principal site of knowledge production. In fact, it could be argued that the role of the university in creating and legitimating knowledge is increasingly being taken over by corporations. For instance, Lawrence Soley (1995) has cogently argued the negative impact of business interests on scientific research. In doing so, he has demonstrated the extent to which corporations are distorting or altering the traditional goals of a university research program. Instead of community- or disciplined-based research, faculty are now signing contracts with multinational corporations and in the process signing away access to the outcome of their research for corporate dollars. Indeed, some departments are now accepting Federal Express or Goodyear chairs to bolster the ability of their programs to continue.

At the same time, it is also clear that corporations are creating their own in-house programs to educate employees. For instance, I was recently at a conference where a physics professor argued that he didn't need to teach as much content in physics since the student's company would offer workshops and classes to meet those needs. Instead, he could focus more broadly on critical thinking. Corporations, however, are also increasing the number of seminars they offer in critical thinking, as well as writing and small group dynamics. At the same conference, it was also hypothesized that as the equipment for some disciplines grows more expensive, corporations may take over the role of conferring "degree status" in some fields. Indeed, the impact of technology (both in cost and capability) on the classroom itself is only now being felt in the creation of "virtual universities," institutions where the traditional role of university faculty is so distorted as to have no relationship to any of the history described in these pages.

Institutions of higher education, however, seemed ill equipped to respond to these changes. As stated in the MLA report on professional service, many institutions indirectly limit the type of work academics can undertake. In a system where the university classroom is the primary focus for an academic's teaching and research, institutions of higher education hinder the ability of faculty to become vital figures in a community and its schools. Locked within limited possibilities, faculty and graduate students are unable to build the type of community or school connections that demonstrate the progressive, noncorporate possibilities of academic research. As important, communities are shut out from working with faculty on developing joint programs and initiatives. Such definitions of our work and our institutions give ground to the conservative and corporate forces who portray faculty as "effete intellectuals." It enables them to offer the "corrective" of a university providing research and workers to develop and create expanding economic markets. Forced to justify the existence of the humanities in a downsizing world, universities are being asked to give up a vision of the academic life as representing the work of a committed citizen.

As I considered the future of higher education, then, I began to believe that many of the social impulses that emerged in the 1960s still have political efficacy. For as I study the system in which academics must survive and work, it strikes me that the call to produce scholarship which serves pragmatic local community needs, to develop university ties to the community, and to educate students to participate as active citizens is more important than ever. The issue becomes how to position those goals in the new environment of higher education. In concluding the work of this book, I ask myself, What knowledge can be gained from the modern-day Ozymandias of the SRTOL? What actions can it suggest to return life to the "lone and level sands stretch[ing] far away"? In the final pages, then, I hope to articulate how the history of the SRTOL can serve as a guide to a new university.

Community Studies

One way to read the history of the SRTOL is that it created two mutually opposing positions. One, teachers are responsible for ensuring that students learn standard English. Two, teachers should not teach standard English. In part, this opposition grew out of the polarized politics of the 1960s. As Black Power began to articulate the structural racism faced by African Americans, standard English began to be seen as a tool in that oppression. Likewise, as the NUC developed its political mission, it began to attack the ways in which standard English represented an effort to hinder interracial working class solidarity. Teaching standard English, then, became synonymous with reactionary politics. Labeled as reactionary, proponents of teaching standard English were soon saddled with arguments that seemed only to confirm the suspicions of the left. Hendrickson's (1972) rather juvenile attempt at humor appeared to mock the home languages of students. Joseph Williams's (n.d.) argument on the status of non-standard dialects and his conclusion that faculty need to study the needs of business seemed to confirm the participation of standard English in "capitalist" oppression. There seemed to be no middle ground.

One of the goals of this work was to demonstrate that the polarization created by the SRTOL debate was historically inaccurate. No leftist or radical proponent of recognizing a student's language argued that standard English should not be taught. (In fact, James Sledd has been laboring for years to get this accusation removed from his work.) The Black Panthers, for instance, clearly argued that African American children needed to learn standard English. Likewise, not even the "conservative" critics of the SRTOL, such as the Allen committee, argued that teachers should disrespect or "annihilate" the student's home language. Nonetheless, locked within a polarized debate, each side failed to produce a sense of how these two apparently contradictory positions could coexist and how the contradiction which emerged in the SRTOL debate could be left behind.

Perhaps one place to begin resolving this contradiction is Lisa Delpit's *Other People's Children* (1995). In many ways, this book is written in response to the historical situation produced by 1960s language politics. In fact, at one point, when examining a set of popular attitudes toward language instruction, she almost directly refers to the SRTOL debate:

> Children have the right to their own language, their own culture. We must fight cultural hegemony and fight the system by insisting that children be allowed to express themselves in their own language style. It is not they, the children, who must change, but the schools. To push children to do anything else is repressive and reactionary. (37)

Delpit is clearly worried about such logic. For her, the result of this belief is that poor and minority children will leave school without the necessary skills for reading and writing, and as a consequence, these children will not have the skills to succeed in the marketplace. Delpit is uncomfortable, however, with how the current debate positions her arguments. She repeatedly states that rejecting the students' rights argument does not imply countless worksheets on grammar. Instead, Delpit attempts to appropriate the language of "power" to explain her position.

> Now you may have inferred that I believe that because there is a culture of power, everyone should learn the codes to participate in it, and that is how the world should be. Actually, nothing farther could be from the truth. I believe strongly, as do my liberal colleagues, in a diversity of styles, and I believe the world will be diminished if cultural diversity is ever obliterated. Further, I believe that each cultural group should have the right to maintain its own language style. When I speak, therefore, of

the culture of power, I don't speak of how I wish things to be but how they are. (39)

For Delpit, it appears that the "culture of power" transcends simple instruction in standard English. Instead, educating students in the culture of power demands critical instruction in the whole web of social attitudes, cultural habits, and economic supports which ensure the continued poverty of working-class and minority students. Also, in framing lessons for her students, it is apparent that Delpit does not imagine students leaving behind their culture. Instead, it appears that she wishes them to gain a critical understanding of the attributes of that culture in relationship to the culture of power. In her class, students would not so much fill in worksheets as imagine writing exercises which bring these two worlds into dialogue. Sometimes this could imply standard English (a report detailing the environmental dangers to a city council), and other times it could imply nonstandard English (a letter to community members about youth needs). Through such work, students develop a sense of how to inhabit the varied worlds in which they exist (for our students most assuredly live in the "standard English" world, even if it is as the "oppressed other"). The attractiveness of Delpit's solution is that she appears to have articulated a classroom practice which both teaches and critiques standard English. As Delpit writes, "[I]ndividuals have the ability to transform dominant discourses for liberatory purposes—to engage in what Henry Louis Gates calls 'changing the joke and slipping the yoke,' that is, using European philosophical and critical standards to challenge the tenets of European belief systems" (162).

The difficulty of such a solution, however, becomes evident when imagining a university curriculum designed to bring students into "what is" but move them into a place to create "what should be." Currently, most courses with primary concern for teaching standard English capabilities are squeezed into a one- or two-term experience. Entire segments of the university are not required to participate. If a student is fortunate enough to attend a university with a Writing Across the Curriculum program, writing instruction will occur, in theory, throughout her or his years at college. These courses, however, are framed within disciplines, often focusing on how to train students to write within a particular field. There is little space within the traditional university curriculum, then, for students to engage in an interdepartmental, coordinated program in how language, cultural, and economic politics interact. Furthermore, as universities find their commitment to humanities placed under pressure by state and federal cutbacks, the increasing need to find corporate sponsors for academic projects dilutes the possibility of developing such a curriculum. Today, faculty hires in business writing or computer science are made at the expense of cultural studies, linguistics, or rhetoric. There is little opportunity, then, for students to constantly test (and stretch) their abilities for "changing the joke and slipping the yoke."

Indeed the very notion of "slipping the yoke" implies an attempt to alter the economic and social terrain which had previously marginalized (and oppressed) the student. That is, if the classroom is imagined as dissatisfied with the way things are, it is incumbent upon any program to think through how to bring students into contact with the tools for social change. Obviously, these tools transcend any particular discipline. Indeed, if we are serious about providing such a thorough education for our students, it becomes necessary to design a curriculum in dialogue with the community activists and organizations who *have* produced results for the local neighborhoods. I am profoundly dubious that our students will believe in the possibility of producing change if the only model provided is academics talking about the need for social change. Such a program, that is, must seek support and validation beyond the university, for the academy and its language hold no patent on critical insights necessary for social change, and the education in how to "slip the yoke" cannot include only university training. Course offerings, grading, and educational goals would have to be developed in concert (as opposed to conflict) with perceived community needs.

Such engagement, however, limits the freedom of faculty members to design courses or research projects. As argued by Peck, Flower, and Higgins (1995, 219):

> Such relationships . . . can be problematic. When university faculty enter communities to "consult," they often assume their

expertise is immediately transferable. Research agendas, framed in the armchair of theory and untested in the context of real people and problems, misrepresent factors that matter. New curricula, uncritically packaged and turned over to community agencies, die an early death without the testing and revision that generates new knowledge. It is for these reasons that community literacy must take not just a serious, but a systematic interest in the problem of how university knowledge fares when it walks out into the world, by engaging in what Linda Flower has called "observation-based theory building."

Faculty participating in the program would have to agree to have their research affected by community demands, courses offerings affected by the needs of neighborhood groups, student work affected by local projects. It is for these reasons that the SRTOL demands to exist outside the confines of composition or any other particular discipline. To actively create the foundations for implementing the SRTOL thus requires the development of a multidisciplinary program linked to the community.

To this extent, I am arguing that the study of "Englishes" needs to move beyond the first year, but perhaps not within a discipline or writing-across-the-curriculum model. That is, the goal would be to produce a new core curriculum within the university where the language of the community, the college, and the country would be studied and analyzed through the integrated insights of a variety of disciplines and community organizations. For only by providing repeated and continuing study into the relationship of the "culture of power," as well as opportunities to work in multiple contexts within that culture, can it be said that such instruction actually works simultaneously to empower students and "slip the yoke." Only by integrating the mission of a variety of disciplines and community organizations can the university and its students learn to speak back to the culture of power.

Developing such a program, I believe, also respects the critical awareness of students entering the university. Speaking from my experience at Temple University, the majority of students possess a critical sensibility about the "culture of power." They are aware through the history of their families how economics, racism, and sexism affect their future possibilities. They possess an almost innate sense of the harsh system into which they are trying to enter. Equally important, however, they are also aware that they need to enter that culture. For my students, it is not an option to simply resist, since resistance implies continued economic deprivation. The difficulty faced by my students is how to simultaneously prepare for an economic future within that system while still acting upon their critical insights. A program which would build upon this dualistic insight and offer multiple places to work out that relationship, I believe, would respect the historical impulses which produced the SRTOL.

Ultimately, then, Delpit's re-vision of the SRTOL brings academics to consider their role in producing citizens. Indeed, in speaking about the possibilities of such a university–community relationship, Henri Giroux (1992) argues that the sheer act of positioning oneself within the culture of power necessarily implies a definition of the citizen:

> Questions of culture are deeply political and ethical and necessitate theoretical and pedagogical practices in which educators and cultural workers engage in continual dialogue and struggle that take up the obligations of critical citizenship and the construction of public spheres that provide 'the justification for a cultural pluralism, which seeks to address the needs and interests of a range of audiences . . . and be effective on a range of levels.'" (164–165)

Locating Giroux's insights within such an imagined program confirms that the university must be connected to the "naming in concrete terms what struggles are worth taking up, what alliances are to be formed as a result of these struggles, and how a discourse of difference can deepen the political and pedagogical struggle for justice, equality, and freedom" (165).

As articulated through the lenses of Delpit and Giroux, then, the right of students to their own language implies the development of a university focus on building the individual and the community into active and empowered political units, for as proven throughout this document, the SRTOL emerged from a struggle to link the university, the community, and the student's language. The instantiation of that legacy would be courses and programs which provide students an opportunity to engage in the difficult work of recognizing the culture of power and finding the alliances, programs, and struggles that expand who has power in that culture. Indeed, at a moment when corporations are developing an expanding role in defining and supplying "educations" to their workers, to have in place a reminder of how knowledge should serve the political empowerment of citizens seems particularly important. That is, perhaps the role of the university can serve as a reminder that education is about more than economic efficiency. To invoke Giroux once again, "radical educators, for example, criticize and indeed reject the notion that the primary purpose of public education is economic efficiency. Schools are more than company stores" (10).

I am not naive, however, about the possibilities of such a program. The work of building such courses (or such a university focus) would be difficult. Many humanities programs are facing cutbacks, faculty lines are being eliminated or combined, teaching loads are increasing. Also, as marketplace models increase their impact on departments, traditionally offered courses must demonstrate the ability to fill seats. That is, disciplines are increasingly finding themselves having to alter their mission to ensure student enrollment. In this environment, suggesting a plan of action which calls for interdepartmental cooperation could indirectly support arguments about the need to shrink programs. In an environment where teaching is being increased, the call for faculty and community activists to work together only increases the workload. Indeed, at a time when faculty control of the classroom is under attack, giving a role to community members might seem yet another example of decreasing authority. Finally, when tenure still depends so heavily on research, it is unclear that junior faculty should (or could) even engage in such work.

I mention these difficulties not to dismiss the possibility of developing a strong university–community alliance, but instead to indicate the variety of levels on which any such program would have to be implemented. It is this type of thinking, I believe, which the Allen report (Committee on the Advisability of a New Language Statement for the 1980s and 1990s, 1983b) attempted to introduce into the SRTOL debate. While I disagree with conclusions of the report on some levels, ultimately the future of the SRTOL depends upon the ability of committed faculty to do the slow work (or the "long march") through the institutions in which they work. It depends upon the ability to build alliances across programs, institutions, and communities. Our failure to produce such work in the future, however, will only ensure the continued dominance of corporate agendas, for it is not as if the historical winds are blowing our way. If we do not work to respect the students' right to become critical citizens, if we do not build the alliances that ensure a role for the university in producing socially valuable knowledge, Microsoft will.

Despite the inherent difficulties, then, I would argue that it is exactly by having the university rebuild its mission through community engagement that it can respond to the increasing call to commodify and market its knowledge. That is, at a time when the university is begin inundated with Federal Express and Goodyear grants, a return to the community can serve to reenergize the goals of education. More important, such a return to the community can ensure that the public is able to point to specific ways in which the goals of the university serve their needs. Such a model, according to Giroux (1992, 163), "provides the opportunity for educators and other cultural workers to rethink and transform how schools, teachers, and students define themselves as political subjects capable of exhibiting critical sensibilities, civic courage, and forms of solidarity rooted in a strong commitment to freedom and democracy."

New University Coalitions

The work of this book has been about more than just university curricula. Much of it was concerned with the very nature of disciplinary-based academic organizations. As was repeatedly shown, it is in the nature of these organizations to avoid the militant and progressive politics discussed throughout this book. More to the point, these organizations allow progressive caucuses to exist as subunits, but with bureaucratic structures that ensure that the caucuses have little impact. When confronted with resolutions to engage in popular struggles for social and economic justice, for instance, the NCTE and CCCC worked to distance themselves from immediate action. In part, such responses reflect the conservative nature of the general membership. Still, for academics concerned with creating nationwide links between progressive academics and activists, professional organizations seem to negate instead of propagate such actions. While such caucuses may prod the larger organizations, they do not provide an integrated network for professional academics to engage in larger social debates.

Beyond the structural nature of these organizations, the focus on building disciplinary knowledge also negates much of their efficacy. That is, as indicated by Bob Ross (1969), too often the militant activity in such organizations is limited to producing new disciplinary readings of traditional texts. While I would argue that the production of socially informed critical methodologies in the university serves a vital function for university reform, it remains the case that connecting such methodologies to community or nationwide organizations has not been the primary role of professional organizations. Additionally, implementing the community connections inherent in the SRTOL, as discussed earlier, requires the ability to move between disciplines and disciplinary organizations.

For that reason, I find myself in agreement with the Allen report (Committee on the Advisability of a New Language Statement for the 1980s and 1990s, 1983b) that the historical impulses of the SRTOL are not properly the sole domain of the CCCC. I would argue, however, that they are also not the sole property of the NCTE. Instead, it appears to me that a new organization is needed which will work to bring together progressive caucuses and community organizations committed to the expansion of critical democracy. Such an alliance would be concerned not just with the production of disciplinary knowledge (or the protection of disciplinary status), but with connecting such knowledge to practical community work. That is, the goal of such an organization would not be to collect fees to produce academic conferences, but to use membership dues to fund and join in the struggles being daily waged for a more vital democratic sphere.

Here is a central lesson learned from this book. The NUC did not fail because its members grew tired of struggling for social, racial, and economic justice. Indeed, the NUC faltered just at the time progressive-minded scholarship was gaining a foot-hold in academic circles. At this opportune moment to create a different type of professional organization, the NUC collapsed because of its inability to serve a productive role in organizing the professional lives of progressive academics. Members of the NUC were looking for more than just the steady delivery of a newsletter. They were looking for a vehicle to connect them nationally with progressive projects. They were looking for a vehicle to connect them with community politics (whether the community's political struggle was justice on a local, state, or national level). It is unclear whether the present is also an opportune moment. But at a time when the National Association of Scholars is the preeminent politically active organization for academics, such an effort seems a necessary one. That is, perhaps out of necessity, the possibility for an alliance of progressive caucuses can emerge.

Any alliance, however, would have to avoid some of the problems which faced earlier incarnations of progressive organizations. First, prior incarnations, such as the NUC or Movement for a Democratic Society, have all lacked a firm institutional home. The momentum necessary to build initial membership and lay out an organizational structure was not supported by a larger institution, whether a university, union, or nonprofit organization. Original members soon found themselves without the support to sustain momentum; personal commitment soon fell victim to burnout. Of course, it is idealistic to think that such an alliance could ever support the type of staff necessary to produce an MLA, yet it is feasible to think that through cost-sharing with an existing system, such an alliance could develop and gain strength. Finally, finding a firm institutional home would allow continuity; for the constant appearance and disappearance of national progressive academic organizations has served to weaken the concept itself; a long-term progressive organization seems an oxymoron.

A sustaining institutional home would also combat another difficulty in such alliances. Given scant resources and increasing workloads, it is difficult to imagine caucuses having the ability to sustain the long conversations necessary to turn a group of "progressive causes" into an alliance for progress. Having a site which serves as a consistent home for individual caucus meetings, institutional record keeping, and information dispersal would make such conversations possible. Having a system in place to keep the variety of caucuses in touch with the activity of alliance partners would work to form a dialogue in itself. Often, it is not so much a difference in politics that stops progress as failure to produce the means of communication. Out of this dialogue could grow grants, joint initiatives, and support networks for faculty, students, and activists. Finally, in such an alliance, when a caucus began to falter or lose initiative, its record of accomplishments could be kept waiting for a new set of people to take up its work. Instead of work being literally thrown out, new activists could see themselves as part of a tradition. And, just as important, new movements would have the institutional space to speak to experts about linking progressive academic work to political action. To some extent, being disorganized is a luxury that can no longer be afforded.

Most important, any such alliance would also have to move toward real connections with other facets of the labor market: nonuniversity professionals, labor unions, service workers, and sweatshop workers. That is, it no longer seems appropriate for academics to imagine themselves as separate or different from the general labor market. My own experience in the job market is still recent enough to recognize the general attack being perpetuated on nonmanual labor. Certainly, it no longer seems that white-collar labor is exempt from the general attack on working conditions, nor can we separate the plight of our students from what is occurring in urban and rural public schools. But beyond personal experience, it seems necessary to form a broad coalition to join other efforts against the slow decline in worker rights and consequent working conditions. It seems necessary to expand who counts as "our" students. Perhaps such a coalition will demonstrate that our definition of ourselves as "intellectuals" and "teachers" has masked other forms of intellectualism and teaching that exist just off campus. Working in concert, to use a Reaganism, perhaps "a rising tide will raise all ships."

Will such an organization move to implement the best of the politics of the SRTOL? Will an interdisciplinary community labor emphasis produce a critically democratic citizenry? It is unclear. Echoing Stuart Hall, "there are no guarantees." What is clear is that there is little coming about naturally to make the progressive impulses for an interracial movement for social justice occur. Straddling the line between naive optimism about the ability of progressive caucuses to work together and pessimism about the current state of things, an alliance seems to be the place where the next stage of this work begins.

Appendix 1: Students' Right to Their Own Language

Introduction

American schools and colleges have, in the last decade, been forced to take a stand on a basic educational question: what should the schools do about the language habits of students who come from a wide variety of social, economic, and cultural backgrounds? The question is not new. Differences in language have always existed, and the schools have always wrestled with them, but the social upheavals of the 1960s, and the insistence of submerged minorities on a greater share in American society, have posed the question more insistently and have suggested the need for a shift in emphasis in providing answers. Should the schools try to uphold language variety, or to modify it, or to eradicate it?

The emotional nature of the controversy has obscured the complexities of the problem and hidden some of the assumptions that must be examined before any kind of rational policy can be adopted. The human use of language is not a simple phenomenon: sophisticated research in linguistics and sociology has demonstrated incontrovertibly that many long held and passionately cherished notions about language are misleading at best, and often completely erroneous. On the other hand, linguistic research, advanced as much of it is, has not yet produced any absolute, easily understood, explanation of how people acquire language or how habits acquired so early in life that they defy conscious analysis can be consciously changed. Nor is the linguistic information that is available very widely disseminated. The training of most English teachers has concentrated on the appreciation and analysis of literature, rather than on an understanding of the nature of language, and many teachers are, in consequence, forced to take a position on an aspect of their discipline about which they have little real information.

And if teachers are often uninformed, or misinformed, on the subject of language, the general public is even more ignorant. Lack of reliable information, however, seldom prevents people from discussing language questions with an air of absolute authority. Historians, mathematicians, and nurses all hold decided views on just what English teachers should be requiring. And through their representatives on Boards of Education and Boards of Regents, businessmen, politicians, parents, and the students themselves insist that the values taught by the schools must reflect the prejudices held by the public. The English profession, then, faces a dilemma: until public attitudes can be changed—and it is worth remembering that the past teaching in English classes has been largely responsible for those attitudes—shall we place our emphasis on what the vocal elements of the public think it wants or on what the actual available linguistic evidence indicates we should emphasize? Shall we blame the business world by saying, "Well, we realize that human beings use language in a wide variety of ways, but employers demand a single variety"?

Before these questions can be responsibly answered, English teachers at all levels, from kindergarten through college, must uncover and examine some of the assumptions on which our teaching has rested. Many of us have taught as though there existed somewhere a single American "standard English" which could be isolated, identified, and accurately defined. We need to know whether "standard English" is or is not in some sense a myth. We have ignored, many of us, the distinction between speech and writing and have taught the language as though the *talk* in any region, even the talk of speakers with prestige and power, were identical to edited *written* English.

We have also taught, many of us, as though the "English of educated speakers," the language used by those in power in the community, had an inherent advantage over other dialects as a means of expressing thought or emotion, conveying information, or analyzing concepts. We need to discover whether our attitudes toward "educated English" are based on some inherent superiority of the dialect itself or on the social prestige of those who use it. We need to ask ourselves whether our rejection of students who do not adopt the dialect most familiar to us is based on any real merit in our dialect or whether we are actually rejecting the students themselves, rejecting them because of their racial, social, and cultural origins.

And many of us have taught as though the function of schools and colleges were to erase differences. Should we, on the one hand, urge creativity and individuality in the arts and the sciences, take pride in the diversity of our historical development, and, on the other hand, try to obliterate all the differences in the way Americans speak and write? Our major emphasis has been on uniformity, in both speech and writing; would we accomplish more, both educationally and ethically, if we shifted that emphasis to precise, effective, and appropriate communication in diverse ways, whatever the dialect?

Students are required by law to attend schools for most of their adolescent years, and are usually required by curriculum makers to take English every one of those years, often including "developmental" or "compensatory" English well into college if their native dialect varies from that of the middle class. The result is that students who come from backgrounds where the prestigious variety of English is the normal medium of communication have built-in advantages that enable them to succeed, often in spite of and not because of, their schoolroom training in "grammar." They sit at the head of the class, are accepted at "exclusive" schools, and are later rewarded with positions in the business and social world. Students whose nurture and experience give them a different dialect are usually denied these rewards. As English teachers, we are responsible for what our teaching does to the self-image and the self-esteem of our students. We must decide what elements of our discipline are really important to us, whether we want to share with our students the richness of all varieties of language, encourage linguistic virtuosity, and say with Langston Hughes:

> I play it cool and dig all jive
> That's the reason I stay alive
> My motto as I live and learn
> Is to dig and be dug in return.

It was with these concerns in mind that the Executive Committee of the Conference on College Composition and Communication, in 1972, passed the following resolution:

> We affirm the students' right to their own patterns and varieties of language—the dialects of their nurture or whatever dialects in which they find their own identity and style. Language scholars long ago denied that the myth of a standard American dialect has any validity. The claim that any one dialect is unacceptable amounts to an attempt of one social group to exert its dominance over another. Such a claim leads to false advice for speakers and writers, and immoral advice for humans. A nation proud of its diverse heritage and its cultural and racial variety will preserve its heritage of dialects. We affirm strongly that teachers must have the experiences and training that will enable them to respect diversity and uphold the right of students to their own language.

The members of the Committee realized that the resolution would create controversy and that without a clear explanation of the linguistic and social knowledge on which it rests, many people would find it incomprehensible. The members of the Executive Committee, therefore, requested a background statement which would examine some common misconceptions about language and dialect, define some key terms, and provide some suggestions for sounder, alternate approaches. What follows is not, then, an introductory course in linguistics, nor is it a teaching guide. It is, we hope, an answer to some of the questions the resolution will raise.

I. What Do We Mean by Dialect?

A dialect is a variety of a language used by some definable group. Everyone has a personal version of language, an idiolect, which is unique, and closely related groups of idiolects make up dialects. By custom, some dialects are spoken. Others are written. Some are shared by the community at large. Others are confined to small communities, neighborhoods, or social groups. Because of this, most speakers, consciously or unconsciously, use more than one dialect. The need for varying dialects may arise from a speaker's membership in different age or educational groups. Or, it may arise from membership in groups tied to physical localities. The explanation of what a dialect is becomes difficult when we recognize that dialects are developed in response to many kinds of communication needs. And further complications occur because the user of a specific dialect, as a function of habit, can choose alternate forms which seem effective for given situations.

A dialect is the variety of language used by a group whose linguistic habit patterns both reflect and are determined by shared regional, social, or cultural perspectives.. The user of a specific dialect employs the phonological (pronunciation), lexical (vocabulary), and syntactic patterns (word arrangement) and variations of the given "community." Because geographical and social isolation are among the causes of dialect differences, we can roughly speak about regional and social dialects. Regional differences in phonology may become quite evident when one hears a Bostonian say "pahk the cah" where a Midwesterner would say "parrk the car." Regional differences in vocabulary are also quite noticeable as in the words used throughout the country for a carbonated drink. Depending on where one is geographically, you can hear "soda," "soda water," "sweet soda," "soft drink," "tonic," "pop," or "cold drink." Regional differences in syntactic patterns are found in such statements as "The family is to home," and "The family is at home." Social differences can also be detected. Social differences in phonology are reflected in "goil" versus "girl." Social differences in vocabulary are reflected in the distinctions made between "restaurant" and "cafe." Syntactic phrases such as "those flowers" tend to have more prestige than "them flowers," and "their flowers" has more prestige than "they flowers."

It is not surprising to find two or more social dialects co-existing in a given region. In small towns where a clear social cleavage exists between the wealthier, more educated portion of the population and the mass of people, the difference may be reflected in their speechways. The local banker whose dialect reveals his group allegiance to the statewide financial community still is able to communicate easily with the local farmhand who may rarely cross the county line and whose linguistic habit patterns reveal different allegiances.

In many larger American cities people of the same ethnic origins tend to live in a single neighborhood and have a common culture and thus share a dialect. Through their clothing, games, and holidays they may preserve the values and customs of the "old country" or "back home." And in their restaurants, churches, schools, and homes, one may hear the linguistic values and customs of their heritage preserved. For example, a neighborhood group's cultural orientation may encourage its members to differentiate between action and intention in the immediate future and in a still-further immediate future through "I'm a-do it" and "I'm a'gonna do it." Yet, a neighborhood is not a country, so speakers of several dialects may mingle there and understand each other. Visitors with yet another heritage may render an approximation of such differentiation through "I'll do it now" and "Ill do it soon." Pride in cultural heritage and linguistic habit patterns need not lead either group to attack the other as they mingle and communicate.

II. Why and How Do Dialects Differ?

Differences in dialects derive from events in the history of the communities using the language, not from supposed differences in intelligence or physiology. Although they vary in phonology, in vocabulary, and in surface grammatical patterns, the differences between neighboring dialects are not sufficiently wide to prevent full mutual comprehension among speakers of those dialects. That is to say, when speakers of a dialect of American English claim not to understand speakers of another dialect of the same language, the impediments are likely to be attitudinal. What is really the hearer's resistance to any unfamiliar form may be interpreted as the speaker's fault. For example, an unfamiliar speech rhythm and resulting pronunciation while ignoring the content of the message. When asked to respond to the content, they may be unable to do so and may accuse the speaker of being impossible to understand. In another situation, vocabulary differences may require that the hearers concentrate more carefully on contextual cues. If the word "bad" is being used as a term of praise, the auditor may have to pay unusual attention to context. Although the usual redundancies of speech ordinarily will provide sufficient cues to permit a correct interpretation, still the auditor has to work harder until he becomes accustomed to the differences. The initial difficulties of perception can be overcome and should not be confused with those psychological barriers to communication which may be generated by racial, cultural, and social differences and attitudes.

III. How Do We Acquire Our Dialects?

The manner in which children acquire language (and hence dialect) competence is unknown in spite of some research and much speculation on the subject. Theories ranging from the purely behavioristic to the highly metaphysical have been proposed. What is demonstrable, and hence known, is that children at very early ages begin to acquire performance skills in the dialect(s) used in their environment, and that this process is amazingly rapid compared to many other types of learning.

Before going to school, children possess basic competence in their dialects. For example, children of six know how to manipulate the rules for forming plurals in their dialects. In some dialects children add an "s" to the word to be pluralized as in "book/books." In some other dialects, plurality is signaled by the use of the preceding word as in "*one* book/*two* book." But in either instance children have mastered the forms of plurality and have learned a principle of linguistic competence. It is important to remember that plurality signals for the nurture dialect reflect children's reality and will be their first choice in performance; plurality rules for another dialect may simply represent to them the rituals of someone else's linguistic reality.

IV. Why Do Some Dialects Have More Prestige Than Others?

In a specific setting, because of historical and other factors, certain dialects may be endowed with more prestige than others. Such dialects are sometimes called "standard" or "consensus" dialects. These designations of prestige are not inherent in the dialect itself, but are *externally imposed,* and the prestige of a dialect shifts as the power relationships of the speakers shift.

The English language at the beginning of its recorded history was already divided into distinct regional dialects. These enjoyed fairly equal prestige for centuries. However, the centralization of English political and commercial life at London gradually gave the dialect spoken there a preeminence over other dialects. This process was far advanced when printing was invented; consequently, the London dialect became the dialect of the printing press, and the dialect of the printing press became the so-called "standard" even though a number of oral readings of one text would reveal different pronunciations and rhythmic patterns across dialects. When the early American settlers arrived on this continent, they brought their British dialects with them. Those dialects were altered both by regional separation from England and concentration into sub-groups within this country as well as by contact with the various languages spoken by the Indians they found here and with the various languages spoken by the immigrants who followed.

At the same time, social and political attitudes formed in the old world followed to the new, so Americans sought to achieve linguistic marks of success as exemplified in what they regarded as proper, cultivated usage. Thus the dialect used by prestigious New England speakers early became the "standard" the schools attempted to teach. It remains, during our own time, the dialect that style books encourage us to represent in writing.. The diversity of our cultural heritage, however, has created a corresponding language diversity and, in the 20th century, most linguists agree that there is no single, homogeneous American "standard." They also agree that, although the amount of prestige and power possessed by a group can be recognized through its dialect, no dialect is inherently good or bad.

The need for a written dialect to serve the larger, public community has resulted in a general commitment to what may be called "edited American English," that prose which is meant to carry information about our representative problems and interests. To carry such information through aural-oral media, "broadcast English" or "network standard" has been developed and given precedence. Yet these dialects are subject to change too. Even now habit patterns from other types of dialects are being incorporated into them. Our pluralistic society requires many varieties of language to meet our multiplicity of needs.

V. How Can Concepts from Modern Linguistics Help Clarify the Question of Dialects

Several concepts from modern linguistics clarify and define problems of dialect. Recent studies verify what our own casual observation should lead us to believe—namely, that intelligence is not a factor in the child's acquisition of a basic language system. In fact, only when I.Q. is at about fifty or below does it become significant in retarding the rate and completeness with which children master their native spoken dialect. Dialect switching, however, becomes progressively more difficult as the speaker grows older. As one passes from infancy to childhood to adolescence and to maturity, language patterns become more deeply ingrained and more a part of the individuals self-concept; hence they are more difficult to alter.

Despite ingrained patterns characteristic of older people, every speaker of a language has a tremendous range of versatility, constantly making subtle changes to meet various situations. That is, speakers of a language have mastered a variety of ranges and levels of usage; no one's idiolect, however well established, is monolithic and inflexible. This ability of the individual speaker to achieve constant and subtle modulations is so pervasive that it usually goes unnoticed by the speaker and the hearers alike.

The question, then, is not whether students can make language changes, for they do so all the time, but whether they can step over the hazily defined boundaries that separate dialects. Dialect switching is complicated by many factors, not the least of which is the individual's own cultural heritage. Since dialect is not separate from culture, but an intrinsic part of it, accepting a new dialect means accepting a new culture; rejecting one's native dialect is to some extent a rejection of one's culture.

Therefore, the question of whether or not students *will* change their dialect involves their acceptance of a new—and possibly strange or hostile—set of cultural values. Although many students *do* become bidialectal, and many *do* abandon their native dialects, those who don't switch may have any of a number of reasons, some of which may be beyond the school's right to interfere.

In linguistic terms the normal teenager has *competence* in his native dialect, the ability to use all of its structural resources, but the actual *performance* of any speaker in any dialect always falls short of the totality implied by competence. No one can ever use all of the resources of a language, but one function of the English teacher is to activate the student's competence, that is, increase the range of his habitual performance.

Another insight from linguistic study is that differences among dialects in a given language are always confined to a limited range of *surface* features that have no effect on what linguists call *deep structure*, a term that might be roughly translated as "meaning." For instance, the following groups of sentences have minor surface differences, but obviously share meanings:

Herbert saw Hermione yesterday.

Herbert seen Hermione yesterday.

Mary's daddy is at home.

Mary's daddy is to home.

Mary daddy home.

Bill is going to the circus.

Bill, he's going to the circus.

Bill he going to the circus.

Preference for one form over another, then, is not based on meaning or even "exactness" of expression, but depends on social attitudes and cultural norms. The surface features are recognized as signs of social status.

VI. Does Dialect Affect the Ability to Read?

The linguistic concepts can bring a new understanding of the English teacher's function in dealing with reading and writing skills. Schools and colleges emphasize one form of language, the one we called Edited American English (EAE). It is the written language of the weekly news-magazines, of almost all newspapers, and of most books. This variety of written English can be loosely termed a dialect, and it has pre-empted a great deal of attention in English classes.

If a speaker of any dialect of a language has competence (but not necessarily the ability to perform) in any other dialect of that language, then dialect itself cannot be posited as a reason for a student's failure to be able to read EAE. That is, dialect itself is not an impediment to reading, for the process of reading involves decoding to meaning (deep structure), not decoding to an utterance. Thus, the child who reads

> Phillip's mother is in Chicago.
> out loud as
> Phillip mother in Chicago.

has read correctly, that is, has translated the surface of an EAE sentence into a meaning and has used his own dialect to give a surface form to that meaning. Reading, in short, involves the acquisition of meanings, not the ability to reproduce meanings in any given surface forms.

Reading difficulties may be a result of inadequate vocabulary, problems in perception, ignorance of contextual cues that aid in the reading process, lack of familiarity with stylistic ordering, interference from the emotional bias of the material, or combinations of these. In short, reading is so complicated a process that it provides temptations to people who want to offer easy explanations and solutions.

This larger view should make us cautious about the assumption that the students' dialect interferes with learning to read. Proceeding from such a premise, current "dialect" readers employ one of two methods. Some reading materials are written completely in the students' dialect with the understanding that later the students will be switched to materials written in the "standard" dialect. Other materials are written in companion sets of "Home" version and "School" version. Students first read through the "dialect" version, then through the *same* booklet written in "school" English. Both methods focus primarily on a limited set of surface linguistic features, as for example, the deletion of -*ed* in past tense verbs or the deletion of -*r* in final position.

To cope with our students' reading problem, then, we cannot confine ourselves to the constricting and ultimately ineffectual dialect readers designed for the "culturally deprived." We should structure and select materials geared to complex reading problems and oriented to the experience and sophistication of our students. An urban eight-year-old who has seen guns and knives in a street fight may not be much interested in reading how Jane's dog Spot dug in the neighbor's flower bed. Simply because "Johnny can't read" doesn't mean "Johnny is immature" or "Johnny can't think." He may be bored. Carefully chosen materials will certainly expose students to new horizons and should increase their awareness and heighten their perceptions of the social reality. Classroom reading materials can be employed to further our students' reading ability and, at the same time, can familiarize them with other varieties of English.

Admittedly, the kinds of materials we're advocating are, at present, difficult to find, but some publishers are beginning to move in this direction. In the meantime, we can use short, journalistic pieces, such as those found on the editorial pages of newspapers, we might rely on materials composed by our students, and we can certainly write our own materials. The important fact to remember is that speakers in any dialect encounter essentially the same difficulties in reading, and thus we should not be so much interested in changing our students' dialect as in improving their command of the reading process.

VII. Does Dialect Affect the Ability to Write?

The ability to write EAE is quite another matter, for learning to write a given dialect, like learning to speak a dialect, involves the activation of areas of competence. Further, learning to write in any dialect entails the mastery of such conventions as spelling and punctuation, surface features of the written language. Again, native speakers of *any* dialect of a language have virtually total competence in all dialects of that language, but they may not have learned (and may never learn) to punctuate or spell, and, indeed, may not even learn the mechanical skill of forming letters and sequences of letters with a writing instrument. And even if they do, they may have other problems in transferring ease and fluency in speech to skill in writing.

Even casual observation indicates that dialect as such plays little if any part in determining whether a child will ultimately acquire the ability to write EAE. In fact, if speakers of a great variety of American dialects do master EAE—from Senator Sam Ervin to Senator Edward Kennedy, from Ernest Hemingway to William Faulkner—there is no reason to assume that dialects such as urban black and Chicano impede the child's ability to learn to write EAE while countless others do not. Since the issue is not the capacity of the dialect itself, the teacher can concentrate on building up the students' confidence in their ability to write.

If we name the essential functions of writing as expressing oneself, communicating information and attitudes, and discovering meaning through both logic and metaphor, then we view variety of dialects as an advantage. In self-expression, not only one's dialect but one's idiolect is basic. In communication one may choose roles which imply certain dialects, but the decision is a social one, for the dialect itself does not limit the information which can be carried, and the attitudes may be most clearly conveyed in the dialect the writer finds most congenial. Dialects are all equally serviceable in logic and metaphor.

Perhaps the most serious difficulty facing "non-standard" dialect speakers in developing writing ability derives from their exaggerated concern for the *least* serious aspects of writing. If we can convince our students that spelling, punctuation, and usage are less important than content, we have removed a major obstacle in their developing the ability to write. Examples of student writing are useful for illustrating this point. In every composition class there are examples of writing which are clear and vigorous despite the use of non-standard forms (at least as described by the handbook)—and there are certainly many examples of limp, vapid writing in "standard dialect." Comparing the writing allows the students to see for themselves that dialect seldom obscures clear, forceful writing. EAE is important for certain kinds of students, its features are easily identified and taught, and school patrons are often satisfied when it is mastered, but that should not tempt teachers to evade the still more important features of language.

When students want to play roles in dialects other than their own, they should be encouraged to experiment, but they can acquire the fundamental skills of writing in their own dialect. Their experiments are ways of becoming more versatile. We do not condone ill-organized, imprecise, undefined, inappropriate writing in any dialect; but we are especially distressed to find sloppy writing approved so long as it appears with finicky correctness in "school standard" while vigorous and thoughtful statements in less prestigious dialects are condemned.

VIII. Does Dialect Limit the Ability to Think?

All languages are the product of the same instrument, namely, the human brain. It follows, then, that all languages and all dialects are essentially the same in their deep structure, regardless of how varied the surface structures might be. (This is equal to saying that the human brain is the human brain.) And if these hypotheses are true, then all controversies over dialect will take on a new dimension. The question will no longer turn on language *per se*, but will concern the nature of a society which places great value on given surface features of language and proscribes others, for any language or any dialect will serve any purpose that its users want it to serve.

There is no evidence, in fact, that enables us to describe any language or any dialect as incomplete or deficient apart from the conditions of its use. The limits of a particular speaker should not be interpreted as a limit of the dialect.

Just as people suppose that speakers who omit the plural inflection as in "six cow" instead of "six cows" cannot manipulate the concept of plurality, so also some believe that absence of tense markers as in "yesterday they *look* at the flood damage" indicates that the speaker has no concept of time. Yet these same people have no difficulty in understanding the difference between "now I *cut* the meat / yesterday I *cut* the meat," also without a tense marker. The alternative forms are adequate to express meaning.

And experience tells us that when speakers of any dialect need a new word for a new thing, they will invent or learn the needed word. Just as most Americans added "sputnik" to their vocabularies a decade or more ago, so speakers of other dialects can add such words as "periostitis" or "interosculate" whenever their interests demand it.

IX. What Is the Background for Teaching One "Grammar"?

Since the eighteenth century, English grammar has come to mean for most people the rules telling one how to speak and write in the best society. When social groups were clearly stratified into "haves" and "have-nots," there was no need for defensiveness about variations in language—the landlord could understand the speech of the stable boy, and neither of them worried about language differences. But when social and economic changes increased social mobility, the members of the "rising middle class," recently liberated from and therefore immediately threatened by the lower class, demanded books of rules telling them how to act in ways that would not betray their background and would solidly establish them in their newly acquired social group. Rules regulating social behavior were compiled in books of etiquette; rules regulating linguistic behavior were compiled in dictionaries and grammar books. Traditional grammar books were unapologetically designed to instill linguistic habits which, though often inconsistent with actual language practice and sometimes in violation of common sense, were intended to separate those who had "made it" from those who had not, the powerful from the poor.

Practices developed in England in the eighteenth century were transported wholesale to the New World. Linguistic snobbery was tacitly encouraged by a slavish reliance on rules "more honored in the breach than the observance," and these attitudes had consequences far beyond the realm of language. People from different language and ethnic backgrounds were denied social privileges, legal rights, and economic opportunity, and their inability to manipulate the dialect used by the privileged group was used as an excuse for this denial. Many teachers, moved by the image of the "melting pot," conscientiously tried to eliminate every vestige of behavior not sanctioned in the grammar books, and the schools rejected as failures all those children who did not conform to the linguistic prejudices of the ruling middle class. With only slight modifications, many of our "rules," much of the "grammar" we still teach, reflects that history of social climbing and homogenizing.

X. What Do We Do about Handbooks?

Many handbooks still appeal to social class etiquette and cultural stasis rather than to the dynamic and creative mechanisms which are a part of our language. They attempt to show one public dialect (EAE) which generates its own writing situations and its own restraints. By concentrating almost exclusively on EAE, such handbooks encourage a restrictive language bias. They thus ignore many situations which require other precise uses of language. We know that American English is pluralistic.. We know that our students can and do function in a growing multiplicity of language situations which require different dialects, changing interconnections of dialects, and dynamic uses of language. But many handbooks often present only the usage of EAE for both written and spoken communication. Usage choices are presented as single-standard etiquette rules rather than as options for effective expression. This restrictive attitude toward usage is intensified by the way school grammar is presented as a series of directives in which word choice, syntax, surface features of grammar, and manuscript conventions are lumped together in guides of "correctness." These restrictive handbooks, by their very nature, encourage their users toward imitation, not toward generation of original written statements. By appealing to what is labeled "proper," they encourage an elitist attitude. The main values they transmit are stasis, restriction, manners, status, and imitation.

Teachers who are required to use such handbooks must help their students understand the implied restrictions of these texts. At best they are brief descriptions of the main features of EAE, and they clearly point out the limits of their own structures. Students should be encouraged to think of the handbook simply as a very limited language resource, and to recognize that its advice usually ignores the constraints of the situation. We alter our choices to create appropriate degrees of social intimacy.. You don't talk to your kids as if they were a senate committee. A personal letter is not a technical report. Students use different forms of language in talking to their friends than they use in addressing their teachers; they use yet another style of language in communications with their parents or younger children; boys speak differently to boys when they are in the presence of girls than when the boys are alone, and so on—the list can be expanded indefinitely by altering the circumstances of time, place, and situation.

The man who says, "He had a pain in his neck, the kind you get when you've suffered a bore too long," is creating an emotional bond with his hearers. Using the handbook rule, "avoid unnecessary shifts in person," to criticize the speaker's choice denies a very important language skill, a sense of how to adjust the tone to the situation.

Furthermore, students need to recognize the difference between handbook rules and actual performance. When, after a half hour's work on pronoun reference practice, carefully changing "everyone/their" to "everyone/his," the teacher says, "Everyone can hand in their papers now," students can recognize the limits of the rule. They can compare the handbook's insistence on "the reason that" with the practice of the national newscaster who says, "the reason for the price increase is because ..." They can go on to consider what assumption underlies the claim that "he does" is always clearer than "he do."

By discussions of actual student writing both students and teachers can learn to appreciate the value of variant dialects and recognize that a deviation from the handbook rules seldom interferes with communication.. The student who writes, "The Black Brother just don't believe he's going to be treated like a man anyway," is making himself completely clear. Students and teachers can go on to discuss situations in which adherence to handbook rules might actually damage the effectiveness of the writing. Through such discussions of tone, style, and situation, students and teachers can work together to develop a better understanding of the nature of language and a greater flexibility and versatility in the choices they make. The handbook in its clearly limited role can then be serviceable within the framework of a flexible rhetoric.

XI. How Can Students Be Offered Dialect Options?

Teachers need to sensitize their students to the options they already exercise, particularly in speaking so as to help them gain confidence in communicating in a variety of situations. Classroom assignments should be structured to help students make shifts in tone, style, sentence structure and length, vocabulary, diction, and order; in short, to do what they are already doing, better. Since dialects are patterns of choice among linguistic options, assignments which require variety will also open issues of dialect.

Role playing in imaginary situations is one effective way of illustrating such options, especially if the situations are chosen to correspond with a reality familiar to the students. Materials that demonstrate the effective use of variant dialects are also useful. A novel like John 0. Killens' COTILLION, for instance, combines an exciting, coherent narrative structure with a rich, versatile range of Black speech patterns used in various social situations, and thus can be used to show both literary and linguistic artistry.

Discussions must always emphasize the effectiveness of the various options, and must avoid the simplistic and the patronizing. Tapes, drills, and other instructional materials which do nothing more than contrast surface features (the lack of -s in third person singular present tense verbs, or -ed in past tense verbs, for instance) do not offer real options. Instead, because they are based on a "difference-equals-deficit" model, they imply that the students' own dialects are inferior and somehow "wrong"' and that therefore the students' homes, the culture in which they learned their language, are also "wrong." Such simplistic approaches are not only destructive of the students' self-confidence, they fail to deal with larger and more significant options.

Linguistic versatility includes more than handbook conformity. Becoming aware of a variety of pitch patterns and rhythms in speech can reduce failures in understanding caused by unfamiliarity with the cadence another speaker uses. Listening for whole contexts can increase the ability to recognize the effect of such ponderous words as "notwithstanding" or "nevertheless" as well as pick up the meaning of unfamiliar names of things. Recognizing contradictions and failures in logic can help students concentrate on the "sense" of their communication rather than on its form. Identifying the ways language is used in politics and advertising can help students see when they are being manipulated and reduce their vulnerability to propaganda. Practice in exercising options can make students realize that vividness, precision, and accuracy can be achieved in any dialect, and can help them see that sloppiness and imprecision are irresponsible choices in any dialect—that good speech and good writing ultimately have little to do with traditional notions of surface "correctness."

By building on what students are already doing well as part of their successes in daily living, we can offer them dialect options which will increase rather than diminish their self-esteem, and by focusing on the multiple aspects of the communication process, we can be sure we are dealing with the totality of language, not merely with the superficial features of "polite usage."

XII. What Do We Do about Standardized Tests?

Standardized tests depend on verbal fluency, both in reading the directions and in giving the answers, so even slight variations in dialect may penalize students by slowing them down. Not only are almost all standardized tests written in test jargon and focused on EAE, they also incorporate social, cultural, and racial biases which cannot hold for all students. Rural Americans may not know much about street life, and urban students will know little about the habits of cows. Words like "punk," "boody," or "joog," if they appeared in tests, would favor one dialect group over others. Tests which emphasize capitalization, punctuation, and "polite usage" favor one restrictive dialect. Even literature tests which emphasize the reading lists of the traditional anthologies favor one kind of school literature. Consequently, those students fluent in test jargon and familiar with the test subject matter are excessively rewarded.

Another problem of standardized tests is that they may further restrict the students' worlds and ultimately penalize both those who do well and those who "fail." Those who succeed may become so locked into the rewarding language patterns that they restrict their modes of expression and become less tolerant of others modes. Those who do not succeed may be fluent in their own dialects but because they are unable to show their fluency, get a mistaken sense of inferiority from the scores they receive.

Some test makers have recognized these biases and are trying to correct them, but theories governing test construction and interpretation remain contradictory. At least four major theories begin with different images and assumptions about genetic and environmental forces or verbal fluency and differences. To some extent the theory of test construction controls test results. In a sense, what goes in also comes out and thus tests tend to be self-validating. Furthermore, test results are reported in terms of comparisons with the groups used for standardizing and thus unless the purpose in giving the test is properly related to the comparison group, the results will be meaningless. For instance, a test intended to measure verbal ability for purposes of predicting probable success in reading difficult textual material is improperly used if it is part of the hiring policy for electrical technicians or telephone repairmen, as is being done in one major American city.

Ideally, until standardized tests fair to all students from all backgrounds can be developed, they should not be used for admitting, placing, or labeling students. Since they are built into the system, however, those who use and interpret the test results must recognize the biases built into the tests and be aware of the theory and purpose behind the tests. Used carelessly, standardized tests lead to erroneous inferences as to students' linguistic abilities and create prejudgments in the minds of teachers, counselors, future employers, and the students themselves.

Resolutions of the Annual Meetings of NCTE in 1970 and 1971 challenged the present forms and uses of standardized tests. Because our schools and colleges continue to administer them, we must continue to deal with the effects of such testing on students and curricula. In response to the problem, we can employ caution in using and trusting test results, and seek positive ways to neutralize the negative effects. We should develop and employ alternative methods for the measurement of our students' performance. Various types of written and oral performance-in-situation testing can be done in the classroom. Various forms of in-class study of dialect can lead students to understand what is common to all dialects and what is particular to individual dialects, and can determine, through discussion, which alternatives most effectively represent the intentions of the speaker or writer.

Tests should not be focused on whether students can think, speak or write in the institutional dialect, but on whether they can think, speak, and write in their own dialects. If it is also necessary to know whether students have mastered the forms of EAE, that should be tested separately.

XIII. What Are the Implications of This Resolution for Students' Work in Courses Other Than English?

Teachers from other fields who view English as a service course, one which will save them the labor of teaching writing, often implicitly define writing as the communication of information within a limited social context. Perhaps when they (and some English teachers) fuss about spelling and usage, they are merely avoiding difficult problems of writing or, at least, avoiding talking about them. Sometimes, what they see as incompetence in writing is merely a reflection that the student doesn't understand the materials of the history or sociology course. But often they see the student's skill only in terms of limited needs. Whatever the reason for the complaint, courses which limit themselves to a narrow view of language in hopes of pleasing other departments will not offer a view of dialect adequate to encourage students to grow more competent to handle a fuller range of the language, and thus will defeat their own purpose.

What is needed in the English classroom and in all departments is a better understanding of the nature of dialect and a shift in attitudes toward it. The English teacher can involve the entire teaching staff in examining sample essays and tests from the various departments to determine whether a student's dialect in an essay examination from Mr. Jones in Geography *really* obscures clarity, whether Mary Smith's theme for Mr. Rogers is *really* worthless because of the "she don'ts" and because "receive" is spelled with an "ie." Such activities would help everyone in defining the areas which are vitally important to us.

We can also provide help for students who find themselves in courses whose teachers remain unreasonably restrictive in matters of dialect. In business and industry secretaries and technical writers rescue the executive and engineer. Science professors have been known to hire English teachers to write their articles for publication. Even a popular technical magazine, such as *QST,* the journal for ham radio operators, offers services which will "standardize" a variant dialect:

> Have you a project which would make a good *QST* story? We have a technical editing staff who can *pretty* up the words, should they need it—*ideas are more important for QST articles than a finished writing job.* (Italics added) (*QST,* April, 1971, p. 78)

We must encourage students to concentrate on crucial exactness of content, and we must persuade our colleagues to forget their own biases about dialect long enough to recognize and respect this better kind of exactness. Students—all of us—need to respect our writing enough to take care with it. Self-expression and discovery as much as communication demand care in finding the exact word and phrase, but that exactness can be found in any dialect, and the cosmetic features of polite discourse can be supplied, when needed for social reasons.

XIV. How Does Dialect Affect Employability?

English teachers should be concerned with the employability as well as the linguistic performance of their students. Students rightly want marketable skills that will facilitate their entry into the world of work. Unfortunately, many employers have narrowly conceived notions of the relationship between linguistic performance and job competence. Many employers expect a person whom they consider for employment to speak whatever variety of American English the employers speak, or believe they speak. Consequently, many speakers of divergent dialects are denied opportunities that are readily available to other applicants whose dialects more nearly approximate the speech of the employer. But a plumber who can sweat a joint can be forgiven confusion between "set" and "sat." In the same way, it is more important that a computer programmer be fluent in Fortran than in EAE. Many jobs that are normally desirable—that are viewed as ways of entering the American middle class—are undoubtedly closed to some speakers of some nonstandard dialects, while some of the same jobs are seldom closed to white speakers of non-standard dialects.

Spoken dialect makes little difference in the performance of many jobs, and the failure of employers to hire blacks, Chicanos, or other ethnic minorities is often simply racial or cultural prejudice. One of the exceptions is the broadcast industry, where most stations at least used to require that almost all newscasters and announcers speak "network standard," but ethnic stations that broadcast "soul" (black), or country, or western, or Chicano programs tend to require the appropriate dialect. A related social bias is implied by certain large companies which advertise for receptionists who speak BBC (British Broadcasting Company) dialect, even though British English is a minority dialect when it is spoken in this country. For them prestige requires the assumption that Americans are still colonials.

The situation concerning spoken dialect and employability is in a state of change; many speakers of minority dialects are now finding opportunities that five or ten years ago would have been closed to them. Specific data is understandably difficult to find, yet it would seem that certain dialects have a considerable effect on employability. Since English teachers have been in large part responsible for the narrow attitudes of today's employers, changing attitudes toward dialect variations does not seem an unreasonable goal, for today's students will be tomorrow's employers. The attitudes that they develop in the English class will often be the criteria they use for choosing their own employees. English teachers who feel they are bound to accommodate the linguistic prejudices of current employers perpetuate a system that is unfair to both students who have job skills and to the employers who need them.

Teachers should stress the difference between the spoken forms of American English and EAE because a clear understanding will enable both teachers and students to focus their attention on essential items. EAE allows much less variety than the spoken forms, and departure from what are considered established norms is less tolerated. The speaker of a minority dialect still will write EAE in formal situations. An employer may have a southern drawl and pronounce "think" like "thank," but he will write *think*. He may say "y'all" and be considered charming for his quaint southernisms, but he will write *you*. He may even in a "down home" moment ask, "Now how come th' mail orda d'partment d'nt orda fo' cases steada five?" But he'll write the question in EAE. Therefore it is necessary that we inform those students who are preparing themselves for occupations that demand formal writing that they will be expected to write EAE. But it is one thing to help a student achieve proficiency in a written dialect and another thing to punish him for using vacant expressions of that dialect.

Students who want to write EAE will have to learn the forms identified with that dialect as additional options to the forms they already control. We should begin our work in composition with them by making them feel confident that their writing, in whatever dialect, makes sense and is important to us, that we read it and are interested in the ideas and person that the writing reveals. Then students will be in a much stronger position to consider the rhetorical choices that lead to statements written in EAE.

XV. What Sort of Knowledge about Language Do English Teachers Need?

All English teachers should, as a minimum, know the principles of modern linguistics, and something about the history and nature of the English language in its social and cultural context. This knowledge can be acquired through reading, through course work, through experience, or through a combination of these. All teachers should know something about:

A. *The Nature of Language as an Oral, Symbolic System by Which Human Beings Interact and Communicate:* If teachers understand that the spoken language is always primary and the written language is a separate and secondary or derived system, they will be able to recognize that students inexperienced in the written system may still have great competence and facility in the spoken language. Because both systems are arbitrary, there is no necessary connection between the words of a language and the things those words symbolize (leche, lait, milk, etc.) nor is there any necessary connection between the sounds of the word "milk" and the alphabetic symbols we use to represent those sounds. Once a teacher understands the arbitrary nature of the oral and written forms, the pronunciation or spelling of a word becomes less important than whether it communicates what the student wants to say. In speech, *PO*lice communicates as well as po*LICE*, and in writing "pollice" is no insurmountable barrier to communication, although all three variations might momentarily distract a person unfamiliar with the variant.

B. *The History of English and How It Continually Changes in Vocabulary, in Syntax, and in Pronunciation:* Teachers should understand that although changes in syntax and pronunciation occur more slowly than lexical changes, they do take place. The language of the King James Bible shows considerable syntactic variation from modern English, and linguists have demonstrated that speakers even as recent as the eighteenth century might be nearly unintelligible to modern ears. Vocabulary changes are easier for both teachers and students to observe. As we develop new things, we add words to talk about them—jet, sputnik, television, smog. From its earliest history, English has borrowed words from the other languages with which it has come in contact—French, Latin, Spanish, Scandinavian, Yiddish, American Indian—from sources too numerous to list. Because many of these borrowings are historical, teachers recognize and respect them as essential parts of the language. Teachers should be equally as willing to recognize that English can also increase the richness of its word stock by a free exchange among its dialects. If teachers had succeeded in preventing students from using such terms as "jazz," "lariat," and "kosher," modern English would be the poorer. Such borrowings enlarge and enrich the language rather than diminish it.

C. *The Nature of Dialects:* A dialect shares similarities of pronunciation, syntax, or vocabulary that differentiates it from other dialects. These similarities within a dialect and differences between dialects are the product of geographical, social, cultural, or economic isolation. Our perception of the difference between an acceptable and unacceptable dialect depends on the power and prestige of the people who speak it. We tend to respect and admire the dialect of people who are wealthy or powerful. The planter's daughter who asks in a pronounced drawl to be "carried" home from the dance is charming; the field hand who says "That's shonuff a purty dress" becomes an object of amusement or scorn. The teacher who realizes that the difference is not in the superiority of either dialect, but in the connotation we supply, can avoid judging students' dialects in social or economic terms.

D. *Language Acquisition:* Although little hard evidence is available about how an individual acquires language, it is known that in learning a language, we must filter out those sounds that have no significance in that language and use only those that do; then we learn to put those sounds into structures that are meaningful in the language. Babies experiment with a multitude of possible sounds, but by the time they begin to talk they have discarded sound combinations that don't appear in the dialects they hear. If, later on, they learn a second language, they encounter problems in hearing and producing sounds and sound combinations that do not exist in their first language. For instance, native speakers of English who learn Spanish as adults have trouble distinguishing "pero" and "perro" because the double "r" sound does not appear in any dialect of English. Although, phonemic differences between dialects of English are not as great as differences between English and a foreign language, differences do exist and it is unreasonable for teachers to insist that students make phonemic shifts which we as adults have difficulty in making.

E. *Phonology:* Phonology deals with the sound system of a language and the variations within that system. Teachers who understand phonology will not try to impose their own sound systems upon their students. They will not make an issue of whether the student says /hwayt hwel or /wayt weyl/ (white whale), nor will they be disturbed by shairchair, warsh-wash, dat-that. They will not "correct" a student who says "merry" like "Murray" because they themselves may say "hairy" so that it is indistinguishable from "Harry." They will realize that even though a student says "ten" and "tin" exactly alike, nobody will be confused because context makes the meaning clear.

F. *Morphology:* Morphology deals with the elements of grammatic meaning in a language—tense, aspect, person, number —and the devices the language employs for indicating them. Just as context prevents homophones from confusing the listener, so context prevents morphological variations from becoming an obstacle to communication. The variations between foot and feet in "6 foot tall," "6 feet tall," or between "Mary" and "Mary's" in such phrases as "Mary hat" and "Mary's hat" make no difference in our ability to grasp the meaning. Teachers who recognize that morphological forms vary from dialect to dialect, but that within each dialect the morphology follows a system, will be less likely to challenge a student whose morphology is different on the ground that such variations represent "mistakes."

G. *Syntax:* Syntax refers to the arrangement of words within an utterance. Syntactic patterns are not the same in all languages (in English, the *red* dress; in the Chicano dialect of Spanish, el vestido *colorado*), nor are the syntactic patterns always the same in different dialects of the same language. The syntactic patterns, however, are systematic within each dialect, and seldom interfere with communication between speakers of different dialects within a language. "That girl she pretty" is just as understandable as "That girl is pretty" and "Don't nobody but God know that" is not only just as clear as "Only God knows," but in some circumstances its meaning is more emphatic.

H. *Grammar and Usage:* Teachers often think grammar is a matter of choosing between lie and lay, who and whom, everybody/his and everybody/their. Actually these are usage choices, in the same way as deciding whether to say "I done my work" or "I did my work" is a usage choice. Grammar, on the other hand, is a description of the system by which a language conveys meaning beyond the sum of the meanings of the individual words. It includes phonology, morphology, and syntax. The grammar of one American dialect may require "he is" in the third person singular present tense; the grammar of another dialect may require "he be" in that slot. The confusion between usage and grammar grows out of the prescriptive attitude taken by most school handbooks since the 18th Century. Modern linguists see grammar not as prescriptive but as descriptive, and teachers who approach the study of grammar as a fascinating analysis of an intensely important human activity, rather than as a series of do's and don'ts, can often rid their students of the fear and guilt that accompanied their earlier experiences with "grammar." Perhaps such teachers can even help their students to find the study of grammar fun.

I. *Semantics:* Teachers should know that semantics is the study of how people give meaning to words and the way many of those meanings affect us emotionally rather than rationally. Teachers well grounded in modern semantics can help their students examine their word choices, not from the standpoint of right or wrong, proper or improper, but by analyzing the impact possible choices will have on listeners or readers. In some areas, for instance, some listeners will be turned off by the word "belly," whereas other listeners will find "stomach" affected and feel more comfortable with "gut." Students can be led to see why many newspaper readers could support a "protective reaction strike" but would have been upset by a "bombing attack."

J. *Lexicography:* Knowing that many words have strong connotative meanings will help teachers regard dictionaries not as authorities but as guides. Knowing that words are only arbitrary symbols for the things they refer to, teachers will realize that dictionaries cannot supply the "real" meaning of any word. Knowing that language changes, they will realize that expressions labeled "non-standard" or "colloquial" by the dictionaries of fifty years ago may be listed without pejorative labels in an up-to-date dictionary. Knowing that pronunciations vary, they will use the pronunciation information in a dictionary as a starting point for class discussion on how most people in the students' own area pronounce that word. In short, teachers will help their students to realize that dictionaries describe practice rather than legislate performance. Dictionaries cannot give rules for using the words of a language; they can only give information about how words have been used.

K. *Experience:* Teachers need to ratify their book knowledge of language by living as minority speakers. They should be wholly immersed in a dialect group other than their own. Although such an opportunity may be difficult for some to obtain, less definitive experience may be obtained by listening to tapes and records as well as interviewing sympathetically speakers who use minority dialects. Empathy with the difficulties often faced by such speakers can be appreciated in indirect analogies with other situations which make one an outsider. But the most vivid sense of the students' problem is likely to come from direct experience.

L. *The Role of Change:* The history of language indicates that change is one of its constant conditions and, furthermore, that attempts at regulation and the slowing of change have been unsuccessful. Academies established to regulate language by scholarly authority have little effect on the dynamic processes of language. Moreover, there is little evidence that languages "evolve" in the sense that they become more expressive or more regular; that is, they simply change, but they do not, it seems, become better or worse. Dialect is merely a symptom of change. Paradoxically, past change is considered normal, but current change is viewed by some as degradation. From Chaucer to Shakespeare to Faulkner, the language assuredly changed, and yet no one speaks of the primitive language of Chaucer or the impoverished language of Shakespeare. Few complain that French and Spanish developed from camp-Latin. Literary scholars might dispute endlessly over the absolute merits of neoclassical versus romantic poetry but no one would argue that literature would be richer if one or the other did not exist In fact, there are positive esthetic reasons for arguing in favor of diversity. Such is the case with dialects just as variety in modes of poetic perception enriches literature, so variety in dialects enriches the language for those who are not unreasonably biased in favor of one dialect. Diversity of dialects will not degrade language nor hasten deleterious changes. Common sense tells us that if people want to understand one another, they will do so. Experience tells us that we can understand any dialect of English after a reasonably brief exposure to it. And humanity tells us that we should allow every man the dignity of his own way of talking.

Committee on CCCC Language Statement

Bibliography

This bibliography of 129 entries is keyed to the statements made in the fifteen sections of STUDENTS' RIGHT TO THEIR OWN LANGUAGE. It is, therefore, sociolinguistic in intent; that is, language as a vehicle of socio-cultural interaction is its concern. It is designed for the classroom teacher who deals with the uses of language variety and who teaches oral and written composing processes. Pedagogical treatments are balanced against theoretical statements so that immediate needs can be answered from two points of departure and so that further study may be undertaken as desired.

Because it is designed to appeal to a varied audience of teachers with differing interests and preparation, elementary, intermediate, and advanced considerations of the socio-linguistic problems surveyed in the statement itself are included. Items reflect problems spanning child-adult socio-linguistic concerns and the elementary-college educational spectrum. Annotations attempt to identify items for simplicity or complexity and for practical or theoretical concerns.

Though items reflect primarily those sociolinguistic concerns of the 1960's and 1970's, some earlier publications have been included to provide background and/or situational context for understanding the present controversy. Wherever decisions, directions, and concerns of pedagogy and research have not yet been resolved, variant perspectives have been included. Many essay collections have been included (1) to demonstrate the multiplicity of views available and (2) to provide easy access to source materials. Many entries are themselves distinguished by further-study bibliographies. Items known to exist unrevised in several sources are cross-referenced. Necessarily, the bibliography reflects those areas of sociolinguistic research and pedagogy in which the greatest amount of work has been conducted and published.

I. What Do We Mean by Dialect?

Fishman, Joshua A. SOCIOLINGUISTICS. Rowley: Newbury House, 1970. Definitions of idiolect, dialect, and language (see Section II) are contained within a larger sociolinguistic definition which considers such areas as linguistic change, constraints, and repertoire range.

Kochman, Thomas. "Cross-cultural Communication: Contrasting Perspectives, Conflicting Sensibilities," FLORIDA FL REPORTER, 9 (Fall/Spring, 1971), 3–16, 53–54. Types of interference and communication failure are discussed. These are shown to result from lack of understanding of the ramifications of dialect, i.e., the cultural codes which determine the value to be given to linguistic habit patterns in situational context.

Malmstrom, Jean. "Dialects—Updated," FLORIDA FL REPORTER, 7 (Spring/Summer, 1969), 47–49, 168. Also in Bentley and Crawford (1973). The nature of dialect (components and variables, socio-economic and geographical determinants) is outlined and discussed.

McDavid, Raven I., Jr. "The Dialects of American English," in Francis, W. Nelson. THE STRUCTURE OF AMERICAN ENGLISH. New York: Ronald Press, 1958. This chapter-article surveys dialect through discussion of dialect differences and causes, dialect geography, linguistic atlases, forces underlying dialect distribution, principal dialect areas (providing samples), foreign-language influences, class dialects, and literary dialect.

McDavid, Raven I., Jr. "A Theory of Dialect," in Alatis, James, ed. LINGUISTICS AND THE TEACHING OF STANDARD ENGLISH TO SPEAKERS OF OTHER LANGUAGES OR DIALECTS. Monograph Series on Languages and Linguistics, No. 22. Washington, D.C.: Georgetown University Press, 1969. This definition of dialect points up misuses of the designation and redefines the functions and limitations of the dimensions of language varieties.

II. Why and How Do Dialects Differ?

Fickett, Joan G. "Tense and Aspect in Black English," JOURNAL OF ENGLISH LINGUISTICS, 6 (March, 1972), 17–20. An identification of tense and aspect of the Black English verb system shows how they reflect cultural attitude and value.

Hymes, Dell. "Models of the Interaction of Language and Social Setting," JOURNAL OF SOCIAL ISSUES, 23 (April, 1967), 8–28. Also in Gumperz and Hymes (1972). A "guide to analysis of speech socialization" is offered as a way of categorizing social units, components, and rules in order to understand the functional codes and roles of language. Such a guide can help the perceiver to understand how dialects differ.

Labov, William. "The Logic of Non-Standard English," in Alatis, James, ed. LINGUISTICS AND THE TEACHING OF STANDARD ENGLISH TO SPEAKERS OF OTHER LANGUAGES OR DIALECTS. Monograph Series on Languages and Linguistics, No. 22. Washington, D.C.: Georgetown University Press, 1969. Also in Aarons (1969), Bailey and Robinson (1973), and Williams (1970). This carefully-illustrated article argues that nonstandard English is not an illogical variety of speech. While showing its habit-pattern organization, Labov also argues against the verbal deprivation theory.

McDavid, Raven I., Jr. "Variations in Standard American English," ELEMENTARY ENGLISH, 45 (May, 1968), 561–64, 608. This article describes historical and current variations in phonology, vocabulary, and syntax which reflect regional differences yet represent Standard American English.

Wolfram, Walt, and Nona H. Clarke, eds. BLACK-WHITE SPEECH RELATIONSHIPS. Washington, D.C.: Center for Applied Linguistics, 1971. Eight viewpoints are represented through eight articles discussing the possible social and historical influences in the development of black-white varieties of English.

III. How Do We Acquire Our Dialects?

Arthur, Bradford. "The Interaction of Dialect and Style in Urban American English," LANGUAGE LEARNING, 21 (1971), 161–174. The interaction of dialect and style is defined and illustrated, and the implications of this for teaching acquisition of more formal variants are investigated. Understanding and acceptance of informal styles are urged.

Bernstein, Basil, and Dorothy Henderson. "Social Class Differences in the Relevance of Language to Socialisation," SOCIOLOGY, 3 (January, 1969), 1–20. A discussion of a study of ways in which mothers' orientations to language help to determine children's responses to language codes and world views is presented.

John, Vera P., and Leo S. Goldstein. "The Social Context of Language Acquisition," MERRILL-PALMER QUARTERLY, 10 (July, 1964), 265–275. The acquisition of labeling and categorizing words is discussed. Rate and breadth of shift from one to the other varies with social context and availability of mature speakers and affects cognitive development in different ways.

IV. Why Do Some Dialects Have More Prestige Than Others?

Labov, William. "Hypercorrection by the Lower Middle Class as a Factor in Linguistic Change," in Bright, William, ed. SOCIOLINGUISTICS. The Hague: Mouton & Co., 1971. Hypersensitivity to prestige markers and codes is discussed. The role of hypercorrection in the propagation of linguistic change as speakers respond to pressures from above and below the level of conscious awareness is considered.

Labov, William. THE SOCIAL STRATIFICATION OF ENGLISH IN NEW YORK CITY. Washington, D.C.: Center for Applied Linguistics, 1966. This in-depth analysis of one multi-level speech community outlines the continuous social and stylistic variation of language influenced by socio-economic stratification and the transmission of prestige patterns. The nature of social control of language variety is considered.

Lieberson, Stanley, ed. EXPLORATIONS IN SOCIOLINGUISTICS. The Hague: Mouton & Co., 1967. This collection of thirteen articles represents several views of the purposes of language/dialect. Through discussions of elaborated and restricted codes, social stratification and cognitive orientations, social status and attitude, and uniformation, the collection exposes those components which contribute to prestige or nonprestige forms.

McDavid, Raven I., Jr. "Dialect Differences and Social Differences in an Urban Society," in Bright, William, ed. SOCIOLINGUISTICS. The Hague: Mouton & Co., 1971. This article discusses the class markers by which speakers are tagged by their listeners and the resulting prestige or lack of it which is attributed to the speakers and their linguistic utterances.

V. How Can Concepts from Modern Linguistics Help Clarify the Question of Dialects?

Lenneberg, Eric H. BIOLOGICAL FOUNDATIONS OF LANGUAGE. New York: John Wiley & Sons, 1967. Language as an aspect of the biological nature of human beings is studied. See especially Chapter Four for a discussion of language acquisition in the context of growth and maturation.

Lenneberg, Eric H., ed. NEW DIRECTIONS IN THE STUDY OF LANGUAGE. Cambridge: The M.I.T. Press, 1967. Eight contributors investigate language acquisition problems from the viewpoints of maturation, social anthropology, human biology, and psychology.

Lenneberg, Eric H. "On Explaining Language," SCIENCE, 164: 3880 (May, 1969), 635–643. Also in Gunderson (1970). The argument that "the development of language in children can best be understood in the context of developmental biology" is introduced. Major problems in language acquisition are pinpointed.

Troike, Rudolph C. "Receptive Competence, Productive Competence, and Performance," in Alatis, James, ed. LINGUISTICS AND THE TEACHING OF STANDARD ENGLISH TO SPEAKERS OF OTHER LANGUAGES OR DIALECTS. Monograph Series on Languages and Linguistics. No. 22. Washington, D.C.: Georgetown University Press., 1969. This discussion of repetitive competence and its importance in developing productive competence encourages greater concern for such components in the development of materials and methods for second-dialect teaching.

VI. Does Dialect Affect the Ability to Read?

Baratz, Joan C., and Roger W. Shuy, eds. TEACHING BLACK CHILDREN TO READ. Washington, D.C.: Center for Applied Linguistics, 1969. This collection of eight articles by reading specialists and dialectologists suggests that the "problem" in the learning-to-read process is generally attributable to the teacher, not the student. Discussion of reading difficulties is illustrated through problems of speakers of Black English. Especially recommended is William Labov's article. His discussion is applicable to reading classrooms at all levels.

Gunderson, Doris V., ed. LANGUAGE & READING. Washington, D.C.: Center for Applied Linguistics, 1970. A survey of reading and language theories, reading research concerns, reading disability problems, and current instructional practices is developed through the statements of seventeen contributors.

Kavanagh, James F., and Ignatius G. Mattingly, eds. LANGUAGE BY EAR AND EYE. Cambridge: The M.I.T. Press, 1972. An overview of current knowledge of similarities and differences in the processing of language by ear and by eye is developed through twenty-two contributor statements. Language vehicles (speech and writing), speech perception and reading, and learning problems are considered.

VII. Does Dialect Affect the Ability to Write?

Braddock, Richard, Richard Lloyd-Jones, and Lowell Schoer. RE-SEARCH IN WRITTEN COMPOSITION. Champaign: NCTE, 1963. This survey considers the present state of knowledge about composition and outlines the case-study method of analysis. Part IIII emphasizes the factors influencing composition and measurement.

Emig, Janet. THE COMPOSING PROCESSES OF TWELFTH GRAD-ERS. Research Report No. 13. Urbana: NCTE, 1971. This report investigates the *writing process* and attempts "to identify the student's feelings, attitudes, and self-concepts which form the invisible components of the 'composition' which the teacher sees as a product." Especially valuable are Chapter 1 which reviews the literature and Chapter 3 which outlines the mode of analysis.

Friedrich, Richard, and David Kuester. IT'S MINE AND I'LL WRITE IT THAT WAY. New York: Random House, 1972. This freshman composition text combines an understanding of the nature of language with a demonstration that almost all students, when they write naturally about things meaningful to them, can learn to write well.

Harrison, Myrna. ON OUR OWN TERMS. Encino: Dickenson, 1972. In this collection of forceful, effective student writing, many of the selections illustrate that having something to say, and saying it well, is not affected by dialect or spelling.

Macrorie, Ken. UPTAUGHT. New York: Hayden Press, 1970. This discussion considers how conventional English classes have failed and offers some suggestions for a writing approach that emphasizes respect for students and the honesty of their expression.

Smitherman, Geneva. "God Don't Never Change: Black English from a Black Perspective," COLLEGE ENGLISH, 34 (March, 1973), 828–834. This article argues for the uniqueness of Black expression which lies in the situational context from which the style of the Black Idiom develops. The argument is placed in historical context.

Wolfram, Walt, and Marcia Whiteman. "The Role of Dialect Interference in Composition," FLORIDA FL REPORTER, 9 (Spring/Fall, 1971), 34–38. Interference problems which arise in written composition due to dialectal differences in grammatical and pronunciation features are discussed and manifestations of hypercorrection illustrated. Black English is used for illustration.

VIII. Does Dialect Limit the Ability to Think?

Cohen, Rosalie A. "Conceptual Styles, Culture Conflict, and Nonverbal Tests of Intelligence," AMERICAN ANTHROPOLOGIST, 71 (October, 1969), 828–856. Conceptual styles (rule sets and constraints) which can be identified through linguistic and attitudinal behavior are investigated. It is argued that one must identify the conceptual style in order to understand interference problems. It is shown that such styles affect responses to standardized testing.

Labov, William. "Statement and Resolution on Language and Intelligence," LSA BULLETIN, 52 (March, 1972), 19–22. "On the Resolution on Language and Intelligence," LSA BULLETIN, 53 (June, 1972), 14–16. "More on the Resolution on Language and Intelligence," LSA BULLETIN, 54 (October, 1972), 24–26. These three statements reflect the most recent stances taken by socio-linguists on the "heritability of intelligence theory." They advance the argument that linguistic variables and language varieties are not being taken into consideration in attempts to measure intelligence and cognitive ability.

Quay, Lorene C. "Language Dialect, Reinforcement, and the Intelligence-test Performance of Negro Children," CHILD DEVELOPMENT, 42 (March, 1971), 5–15. The influence of motivation (with reinforcement) and communication (Standard English/Black English dialects) on responses and scores is evaluated. It is argued that the deficit/difference theories are based on speech production, not language comprehension.

Scarr-Salapatek, Sandra. "Race, Social Class, and IQ," SCIENCE, 174: 4016 (December, 1971), 1285–1295. This discussion-definition outlines the environmental disadvantages hypothesis and the genetic differences hypothesis, demonstrating their interactions, and presenting their implications for the determination of IQ.

Williams, Frederick, ed. LANGUAGE AND POVERTY: PERSPEC-
TIVES ON A THEME. Chicago: Markham Publishing Co., 1972.
The linguistic deficit-difference controversy is surveyed through eighteen overview and position papers which attempt to explain the
interrelationships of language, linguistic variety, and poverty settings.

IX. What Is the Background for Teaching One "Grammar"?

Crowell, Michael G. "American Traditions of Language Use: Their
Relevance Today," ENGLISH JOURNAL, 59 (January, 1970),
109–115. Nineteenth and twentieth century usage attitudes are considered as they relate to (1) growth and creativity in language and
(2) maintenance of the status quo and as these attitudes have been
affected by the prescriptive-descriptive discussions of usage. Crowell
stresses that the maintenance of creativity and *status quo* attitudes
encourages a healthy tension in our thinking and discussions of
language.

James, Carl. "Applied Institutional Linguistics in the Classroom," EN-
GLISH JOURNAL, 59 (November, 1970), 1096–1105. It is suggested that the classroom study of English be focused on "distinctive
features." This format considers language variety through those
permanent (dialectal) and transient (diatypic) features by which we
identify types of speakers and writers along a usage spectrum.

Kerr, Elizabeth M., and Ralph M. Aderman, eds. ASPECTS OF AMERI-
CAN ENGLISH. New York: Harcourt, Brace & World, 1963. Thirty
statements are arranged to allow the reader to consider the developing and changing attitudes toward principles and sociolinguistic
aspects of language. Historical, regional, social, and literary aspects
are considered.

Laird, Charlton, and Robert M. Gorrell, eds. ENGLISH AS LAN-
GUAGE: BACKGROUNDS, DEVELOPMENT, USAGE. New
York: Harcourt, Brace & World, 1961. A collection of sixty statements is arranged to demonstrate changing attitudes over several
centuries toward language, dialect, grammar, dictionaries, and usage.

Lederman, Marie Jean. "Hip Language and Urban College English," COLLEGE COMPOSITION AND COMMUNICATION, 20 (October, 1969), 204–214. The value of employing, investigating, and defining "hip" language in the classroom is considered and seen as a "matter of human rights" to discuss varieties of language. All views are backed by classroom teaching illustrations.

Roberts, Paul. ENGLISH SENTENCES. New York: Harcourt, Brace & World, 1962. Chapters 1 and 2 make a clear distinction between a nongrammatical English sentence (Henry some flowers his mother brought) and a grammatical English sentence (Henry brung his mother some flowers) and discusses the social imputations of dialect differences.

Wilkinson, Andrew, ed. THE CONTEXT OF LANGUAGE. (Volume 23 of EDUCATIONAL REVIEW). Birmingham: University of Birmingham, 1971. Five articles concentrate on considering language in its situational context. Language is seen as a matter of options.

Wilkinson, Andrew, ed. THE STATE OF LANGUAGE. (Volume 23 of EDUCATIONAL REVIEW). Birmingham: University of Birmingham, 1969. Nine contributor statements present recent views on the state of grammar, language models and coding, kinds and registers of English, and reading acquisition.

X. What Do We Do about Handbooks?

Burling, Robbins. "Standard Colloquial and Standard Written English: Some Implications for Teaching Literacy to Nonstandard Speakers," FLORIDA FL REPORTER, 8 (Spring/Fall, 1970), 9–15, 47. An investigation of differences between written and spoken varieties of English and of some of the ways in which they interact is balanced against the cautionary advice that teacher attitudes toward, and knowledge of, nonstandard habit patterns is the real factor in teaching literacy. Problems in teaching language usage are clarified.

Funkhouser, James L. "A Various Standard," COLLEGE ENGLISH, 34 (March, 1973), 806–827. A discussion of how nonsituational handbook rules may be superseded in the classroom by situational rules for effective communication in writing is presented. Rule consistency is illustrated through Black English writing samples.

Hall, Richard. "A Muddle of Models: The Radicalizing of American English," ENGLISH JOURNAL, 61 (May, 1972), 705–710. The proliferation of models by which to determine one's usage is considered. Such pluralism forces the teacher to consider language options, to teach about the shifts in language values which are occurring, and to aim for greater student consciousness in the making of decisions about usage.

Hartung, Charles V. "Doctrines of English Usage," ENGLISH JOURNAL, 45 (December, 1956), 517–525. Also in Laird and Gorrell (1961). The four main "propriety of language usage" doctrines (of rules, of general usage, of appropriateness, of linguistic norm) which have influenced our thought are discussed. Hartung concludes that the doctrine of the linguistic norm with its concern for "maximum expression" would seem suitable for the classroom.

Joos, Martin. THE FIVE CLOCKS. New York: Harcourt, Brace & World, 1967. This discussion of the five styles of spoken and written English encourages a tolerant view of varying linguistic habit patterns by illustrating the complexities of usage.

Lloyd, Donald. "Structure in Language," COLLEGE ENGLISH, 24 (May, 1963), 598–602. In discussing the "social structuring of usage," Lloyd reiterates that all speakers adjust language to fit specific social situations by responding to situational cues.

Sledd, James. "On Not Teaching English Usage," ENGLISH JOURNAL, 54 (November, 1965), 698–703. This argument against teaching English usage presents new views of language use which help to develop broader definitions of usage based on responsible judgment.

XI. How Can Students Be Offered Dialect Options?

Baratz, Joan C. "Should Black Children Learn White Dialect?" ASHA, 12 (September, 1970), 415–417. Also in Smith (1972). It is argued that "standard English" is not "white dialect" but the *lingua franca* of the "American mainstream" culture to which the Black student has a right. A definition is attempted.

Burling, Robbins, ENGLISH IN BLACK AND WHITE. New York: Holt, Rinehart and Winston, 1973. This systematic explanation of major facts of nonstandard English dialects is designed for teachers and nonspecialists. Each chapter answers a practical question such as "What is the problem?" or "How is it used?" and offers study-discussion topics of use in the classroom.

Cassidy, Frederick. "American Regionalisms in the Classroom," ENGLISH JOURNAL, 57 (March, 1968), 375–379. This article is a discussion of the regional variations existent in Standard English and a description of available dialect resources for classroom exploration of the language varieties which the student and the community use.

Davis, A. L., ed. CULTURE, CLASS, AND LANGUAGE VARIETY. Urbana: NCTE, 1972. Ten articles are offered as a resource-reference for teachers who must plan classroom activities in such areas as grammar, syntax, nonverbal communication. Included are transcriptions of children's speech (a tape cartridge of that speech accompanies the text).

Evertts, Eldonna L., ed. DIMENSIONS OF DIALECT. Champaign: NCTE, 1967. Various aspects of dialect-oriented problems are considered by fourteen linguists and teachers. Dialect features and their implications for the classroom are discussed. Raven McDavid's article contains a checklist of nonstandard dialect features.

Fasold, Ralph W., and Roger W. Shuy, eds. TEACHING STANDARD ENGLISH IN THE INNER CITY. Washington, D.C.: Center for Applied Linguistics, 1970. The biloquialist perspective is presented in this collection of six articles by educators attempting to deal with the problems of inner city teaching.

Holt, Grace Sims. "Changing Frames of Reference in Speech Communication Education for Black Students," FLORIDA FL REPORTER, 9 (Spring/Fall, 1971), 21–22, 52. An argument for the role *affect* has in Black communication and its importance in linguistic-cultural patterns is presented. Classroom activities for the study of affect are provided.

Imhoof, Maurice L., ed. "Social and Educational Insights into Teaching Standard English to Speakers of Other Dialects." VIEWPOINTS. Bloomington: Indiana University Press, 1971. This overview considers system and order in varietal differences, effects of cultural attitudes toward given varieties, teacher attitudes, design and system of learning activities, competencies needed by ghetto teachers.

Jacobson, Rodolpho, ed. STUDIES IN ENGLISH TO SPEAKERS OF OTHER LANGUAGES & STANDARD ENGLISH TO SPEAKERS OF A NON-STANDARD DIALECT. Monograph No. 14, New York State English Council, 1971. This collection of twenty-four articles argues against the melting-pot theory and for the linguistic-cultural pluralism theory. Many viewpoints are represented as contributors approach the problem through discussion of attitudes toward language varieties, bidialectalism, bilingualism, the "Pygmalion effect," and testing.

Kochman, Thomas. "Culture and Communication: Implications for Black English in the Classroom," FLORIDA FL REPORTER, 7 (Spring/Summer, 1969), 89–92, 172–74. Communication channels, mechanisms, and networks, audience dynamics, goals and assumptions for language programs, and speech styles are discussed.

Labov, William. THE STUDY OF NONSTANDARD ENGLISH. Champaign: NCTE, 1970. This statement surveys the theoretical and educational issues surrounding the controversy over nonstandard English. Nonstandard English is considered within the context of the nature of language, sociolinguistic principles, educational implications, and needed in-school research. Space is given to informal and formal approaches to testing for varieties of language in order to determine presence of differences, perceptual competence in varieties, grammatical competence, and speech competence.

Shuy, Roger. DISCOVERING AMERICAN DIALECTS. Champaign: NCTE, 1967. This simplified introduction to dialects discusses regional and social varieties of American dialects, how and why they differ, foreign language influence, and literary dialects.

Shuy, Roger, ed. SOCIAL DIALECTS AND LANGUAGE LEARNING. Champaign: NCTE, 1964. Twenty statements by linguists and educators provide an overview of social dialectology, field projects, teaching programs, social factors affecting learning of Standard

English and behaviorists reactions, and research implications. Many viewpoints—sometimes conflicting—are offered on such problems as acquisition of Standard English, usage problems and attitudes, dialect and multi-dialect behavior, and programs for the English classroom.

Smitherman, Geneva. "English Teacher, Why You Be Doing the Thangs You Don't Do? ENGLISH JOURNAL, 61 (January, 1972). This article, written in Black [dialect], suggests teaching technologies for inner-city English classrooms.

Wolfram, Walt. "Sociolinguistic Premises and the Nature of Non-standard Dialects," SPEECH TEACHER, 19 (September, 1970), 177–184. Also in Smith (1972). This article is a discussion of sociolinguistic considerations which affect teacher evaluation of speech behavior and teacher attitudes toward nonstandard speech behavior. Verbal options as arbitrary and established by custom, dialect adequacy as a communicative system, language as learned in community context are considered.

XII. What Do We Do about Standardized Tests?

Barth, Carl A. "Kinds of Language Knowledge Required by College Entrance Examinations," ENGLISH JOURNAL, 54 (December, 1965), 824–829. Knowledge of traditional grammar is found not necessary for success on such standardized national tests as the SAT, ACT, College Board Achievement Test. Knowledge of usage and linguistic sensitivity gained through modern language teaching are adequate preparation.

Derrick, Clarence. "Tests of Writing," ENGLISH JOURNAL, 53 (October, 1964), 496–99. This article criticizes the efficiency and reliability of national essay and objective "writing" tests designed for group testing. The essay tests are dismissed as unreliable; the objective tests are consigned to having reliability in producing information about skills related to writing. Derrick feels the answer to the problem lies in careful classroom testing and evaluating of writing samples.

Goslin, David A. "What's Wrong With Tests and Testing," COLLEGE BOARD REVIEW, Nos. 65/66 (Fall/Winter, 1967), 12–18, 33–37. These statements discuss the types and uses of tests, influences which scores exert, criticisms of validity, concern for their self-fulfilling prophecy, and the implications for group social structure, membership selection, and society.

Hackett, Herbert. "Three Against Testing," COLLEGE COMPOSITION AND COMMUNICATION, 15 (October, 1964), 158–163. This article reviews *The Brain Watchers, They Shall Not Pass,* and *The Tyranny of Testing* and finds their authors guilty of the same pretentiousness and carelessness which the authors found in the designers and users of standardized tests. The charges are specific and illustrate those authors' misconceptions by focusing on what such tests can and cannot do. It points out that validity, not reliability, is the problem area in standardized testing.

Osenburg, F. C. "Objective Testing, the New Phrenology," COLLEGE COMPOSITION AND COMMUNICATION, 12 (May, 1961), 106–111. This review of measurement problems inherent in vocabulary, multiple-choice reading, and English battery tests also touches on some of the ways in which students "learn" to answer test questions without really understanding what they're doing with language.

Schroth, Evelyn. "Some Usage Forms Die Hard—Thanks to College Entrance Exams," ENGLISH JOURNAL, 56 (January, 1967), 97–102. This article argues that College Board tests still test as substandard certain usage items which authorities on usage consider to have been accepted within the boundaries of current acceptable usage.

XIII. What Are the Implications of This Resolution for Students' Work in Courses Other Than English?

Budd, Richard W., and Brent D. Ruben, eds. APPROACHES TO HUMAN COMMUNICATION. New York: Spartan Books, 1972. The viewpoints of twenty-four contributors provide a survey of theories and attitudes toward communication in fields such as art, history, zoology. Each position statement reflects the world view within which each type of communicator conceptualizes and is, therefore, able to accept statements about his field.

Cazden, Courtney B., Vera P. John, and Dell Hymes, eds. FUNCTIONS OF LANGUAGE IN THE CLASSROOM. New York: Teachers College Press, 1972. Focusing on early education, the twenty contributors consider language problems which affect all classrooms— supplying perspectives on nonverbal communication, discussions of varieties of language and verbal repertoire, and of varieties of communicative strategies. They attempt an ethnography of communication in classrooms.

Smith, Holly. "Standard or Nonstandard: Is There an Answer?" ELEMENTARY ENGLISH, 50 (February, 1973), 225–235. This research report-survey summarizes the controversy of school attitudes toward dialect and acceptability, a controversy which must be faced before staff can react to students' needs.

Williams, Frederick, et al. "Ethnic Stereotyping and Judgments of Children's Speech," SPEECH MONOGRAPHS, 38 (August, 1971), 166–170. Working with the "Pygmalion effect" (attitudes which language characteristics may elicit in listeners), the researchers investigate biases which lead to stereotypes. Implications for teacher training are considered.

XIV. How Does Dialect Affect Employability?

Billiard, Charles, Arnold Lazarus, and Raven I. McDavid, Jr. IDENTIFICATION OF DIALECT FEATURES WHICH AFFECT BOTH SOCIAL AND ECONOMIC OPPORTUNITY AMONG THE URBAN DISADVANTAGED. Final Report. Washington, D.C.: Office of Education, 1969. (EDRS—ED 038 483). The authors undertook a study to determine (1) dialect features associated with three ethnic groups (Anglo, Black, Latin American) and four social classes which were unacceptable to a dominant, urban culture (Fort Wayne, Indiana), (2) social markers which might handicap such speakers socio-economically and culturally, and (3) the implications of this for teacher preparation and classroom teaching. The results offer specific illustrations of code markers which may affect socio-economic mobility.

O'Neil, Wayne. "The Politics of Bidialectalism," COLLEGE ENGLISH, 33 (January, 1972), 433–39. A linguist considers the underlying ideology of school language programs and argues that they are informed by economic-political requirements. Bidialectalism is viewed as "part of the social and political machinery meant to control."

Sledd, James. "Bi-Dialectalism: The Linguistics of White Supremacy," ENGLISH JOURNAL, 58 (December, 1969), 1307–1315. A linguist argues against bidialectalism as a politically-oriented move to control minorities and as an answer to economic mobility needs.

Sledd, James. "Doublespeak: Dialectology in the Service of Big Brother," COLLEGE ENGLISH, 33 (January, 1972), 439–57. Also in Smith (1972). A dialectologist discusses the racial and political implications of the controversy over minority dialects, stating that "doublespeak" is used as a political, economic weapon for control.

XV. What Sort of Knowledge about Language Do English Teachers Need?

Aarons, Alfred C., Barbara Y. Gordon, and William A. Stewart, eds. LINGUISTIC-CULTURAL DIFFERENCES AND AMERICAN EDUCATION. Special Issue. FLORIDA FL REPORTER, 7 (Spring/Summer, 1969). Multiple viewpoints, classroom projects and research results of forty-three contributors are arranged to focus on the cultural role of the school, on linguistic pluralism, on English teaching, on theory, and on curriculum development in this overview of current concerns.

Abrahams, Roger D., and Rudolph C. Troike, eds. LANGUAGE AND CULTURAL DIVERSITY IN AMERICAN EDUCATION. Englewood Cliffs: Prentice-Hall, 1972. This introductory reader organizes its thirty-five articles to consider the interactions of cultural pluralism, linguistic knowledge, socio-linguistic approaches, and educational applications to our present understandings. Several articles illustrate these considerations through responses to Black English.

Allen, Harold, ed. READINGS IN APPLIED ENGLISH LINGUISTICS. Second Edition. New York: Appleton-Century-Crofts, 1964. Sixty-two articles are organized to represent the spectrum of linguistic thought and application through 1960. Historical background, current viewpoints, linguistic geography, usage, dictionary development, and linguistics' contributions to the teaching of grammar, composition, and literature are considered.

Allen, Harold B., and Gary N. Underwood, eds. READINGS IN AMERI-CAN DIALECTOLOGY. New York: Appleton-Century-Crofts, 1971. This introductory reader presents forty-one research statements arranged for the study of regional and social dialects.

Bailey, Richard W., and Jay L. Robinson. VARIETIES OF PRESENT-DAY ENGLISH. New York: The Macmillan Company, 1973. This introductory reader investigates the causes, differences, and persistence of varieties of English and considers teaching strategies through the statements of eighteen contributors. Study problems are included.

Baugh, Albert C. A HISTORY OF THE ENGLISH LANGUAGE. Second Edition. New York: Appleton-Century-Crofts, 1957. This standard language history traces the changes that have taken place over 1500 years and relates those changes to the political and social events of English history.

Bentley, Robert H., and Samuel D. Crawford, eds. BLACK LANGUAGE READER. Glenview: Scott, Foresman and Company, 1973. This arrangement of twenty-nine statements from research, media, and classroom sources represents a self-contained introductory course for teachers in the origins, uses, and misuses of Black English.

Bolinger, Dwight. ASPECTS OF LANGUAGE. New York: Harcourt, Brace & World, 1968. This introductory text is designed to familiarize the reader with the terms and concepts of linguistics. Ways of talking about language are developed through careful definitions and question-application sequences after each chapter.

Cattell, N. R. THE NEW ENGLISH GRAMMAR: A DESCRIPTIVE INTRODUCTION. Cambridge: The M.I.T. Press, 1969. This introduction to generative transformational grammar presents a nontechnical description of the features of English grammar and the design of language.

Chase, Stuart. THE TYRANNY OF WORDS. New York: Harcourt, Brace, 1938. A discussion of how the words we select can distort our views is presented in a highly readable way.

Chomsky, Noam. ASPECTS OF THE THEORY OF SYNTAX. Cambridge: The M.I.T. Press, 1965. A study of developments in transformational generative grammar reviews, extends, and modifies earlier theory. Emphasis is on syntactic rather than phonological or semantic aspects of language.

Davis, Philip W. MODERN THEORIES OF LANGUAGE. Englewood Cliffs: Prentice-Hall, 1973. Nine twentieth century theories of language (i.e., the theories of Saussure, Hjelmslev, Bloomfield, the Post-Bloomfieldians, and the Prague School; tagmemics; Firthian linguistics; stratificational grammar; transformational generative grammar) are characterized and discussed for the linguistically knowledgeable reader.

Dillard, J. L. BLACK ENGLISH: ITS HISTORY AND USAGE IN THE UNITED STATES. New York: Random House, 1972. The ramifications of Black English, its historical development, and its cultural validity and the implications of such information for teacher training and classroom practices are explained by the author. (See Chapter VII for his discussion of the harm done Black students by failing them on the basis of dialect.)

Elgin, Suzette Haden. WHAT IS LINGUISTICS? Englewood Cliffs: Prentice-Hall, 1973. This elementary text provides an introduction to phonology, syntax, semantics, historical linguistics, psycholinguistics, sociolinguistics, stylistics, applied linguistics, field linguistics.

Falk, Julia S. LINGUISTICS AND LANGUAGE. Lexington: Xerox College Publishing, 1973. An introductory survey of basic concepts and applications of linguistics moves the reader through consideration of words, sounds and sound systems, writing, speaker control of language, grammar, dialect, language acquisition, and teaching issues.

Fishman, Joshua A., ed. READINGS IN THE SOCIOLOGY OF LANGUAGE. The Hague: Mouton & Co., 1968. This reader is designed to give a socio-linguistic perspective through forty-five articles which consider language in small-group interaction, in social strata and sectors, through socio-cultural organization, and within the scope of multilingualism, language shift, and planning.

Francis, W. Nelson. THE ENGLISH LANGUAGE. New York: Norton, 1965. An analysis of how English works is developed from the structuralists' viewpoint.

Fries, Charles C. AMERICAN ENGLISH GRAMMAR. New York: Appleton-Century-Crofts, 1940. This descriptive grammar which concentrates on uses of word form, uses of function words, and uses of word order draws its data and conclusions from contemporary social discourse (i.e., personal letters). It also considers the role of the school in grammar and language teaching.

Greenbaum, Sidney, and Randolph Quirk. ELICITATION EXPERIMENTS IN ENGLISH. (Miami Linguistics Series No. 10) Coral Gables: University of Miami Press, 1970. This report is a description of linguistic testing methods by which types of socio-linguistic acceptability may be identified and categorized. Differences between attitudes and beliefs about usage and actual usage habits are investigated through elicited items of linguistic behavior.

Grinder, John T., and Suzette Haden Elgin. GUIDE TO TRANSFORMATIONAL GRAMMAR. New York: Holt, Rinehart and Winston, 1973. This elementary text introduces the basic concepts of transformational grammar through thirteen chapters, each of which presents some aspect of the history, theory, and practice of that grammar. Teaching exercises with answers are provided.

Gumperz, John J., and Dell Hymes. DIRECTIONS IN SOCIOLINGUISTICS. New York: Holt, Rinehart and Winston, 1972. An ethnography of communication is presented through nineteen articles which explain (1) the socio-cultural shaping of ways of speaking, (2) procedures for discovering and stating rules of conversation and address, and (3) origin, persistence, and change of varieties of language.

Hayakawa, S. I. LANGUAGE IN THOUGHT AND ACTION. Third Edition. New York: Harcourt Brace Jovanovich, 1972. This discussion of semantics provides an introduction to the study of the role and uses of language in modifying behavior, transmitting information, developing social cohesion, and expressing the imagination.

Herndon, Jeanne H. A SURVEY OF MODERN GRAMMARS. New York: Holt, Rinehart and Winston, 1970. This handbook enables the reader to survey developments and concerns of modern grammars (structural and transformational-generative) and of varieties of American English. Implications of linguistics for the teaching of literature and composition are also surveyed.

Huddleston, Rodney D. THE SENTENCE IN WRITTEN ENGLISH. Cambridge: Cambridge University Press, 1971. Working within the theoretical framework of transformational grammar, this syntactic study describes the grammar of written scientific English using a limited corpus of 135,000 words. However, "common-core" English grammar concerns are investigated through that corpus.

Jacobs, Roderick A., and Peter S. Rosenbaum. ENGLISH TRANSFOR-MATIONAL GRAMMAR. Waltham: Blaisdell Publishing Company, 1968. This elementary text is based on a transformational model and moves from a description of principles of linguistic universals through discussion of constituents and features, transformations, embedding, and conjunction.

Jacobs, Roderick A., and Peter S. Rosenbaum. READINGS IN ENGLISH TRANSFORMATIONAL GRAMMAR. Waltham: Xerox College Publishing, 1970. Theoretical statements by thirteen transformational-generative linguists present current research in the concept of deep and surface structures.

Jespersen, Otto. ESSENTIALS OF ENGLISH GRAMMAR. University: University of Alabama Press, 1964. This "signal" grammar of the spoken language investigates the development of sound systems, word classes, syntax, word form, and habits in language varieties. Other-language grammatical comparisons are made wherever feasible.

Katz, Jerrold J. THE PHILOSOPHY OF LANGUAGE. New York: Harper & Row, 1966. This systematic approach to a philosophy of language provides for explanation of language from a twentieth century perspective, discussion of the current theory of language, and consideration of the implications of that theory for understanding conceptual knowledge.

Katz, Jerrold J. SEMANTIC THEORY. New York: Harper & Row, 1972. This depth study of semantic theory attempts an integrated body of definitions of meaning, sameness/difference of meaning, and multiplicity of meaning, and of the constraints at work in the development of meaning.

Kochman, Thomas, ed. RAPPIN' AND STYLIN' OUT: COMMUNICATION IN URBAN BLACK AMERICA. Champaign-Urbana: University of Illinois Press, 1972. A study of communication in the urban Black situation is presented through the views of twenty-seven contributors. The reader reviews the spectrum of Black communication from nonverbal to verbal, from expressive uses of language to expressive role behavior, and through vocabulary and culture. Visual and verbal illustrations are abundant.

Labov, William. LANGUAGE IN THE INNER CITY: STUDIES IN THE BLACK ENGLISH VERNACULAR. (Conduct and Communication No. 3.) Philadelphia: University of Pennsylvania Press, 1972. Nine essays (three previously unpublished) present a reorganization and rewriting of several earlier statements into an organized study of the structure, social setting, and uses of the Black English vernacular.

Labov, William. SOCIOLINGUISTIC PATTERNS. (Conduct and Communication No. 4) Philadelphia: University of Pennsylvania Press, 1972. Two new statements on contextual style and subjective dimensions of change are added to revisions of earlier statements on social change and motivation in language in this nine-essay collection.

Langacker, Ronald W. LANGUAGE AND ITS STRUCTURE. Second Edition. New York: Harcourt, Brace & World, 1968. This introduction to language presents modern views of the nature, structure, and components of language and language variety. Language change, language families, and linguistic systems are considered.

Lehmann, Winfred P. DESCRIPTIVE LINGUISTICS: AN INTRODUCTION. New York: Random House, 1972. This survey text presents the data of language through chapters dealing with phonetics, syntax and analysis, inflection and derivation. Also included are explanatory chapters on semantics, language theory, psycho- and sociolinguistics, and applied linguistics.

Liles, Bruce L. AN INTRODUCTORY TRANSFORMATIONAL GRAMMAR. Englewood Cliffs: Prentice-Hall, 1971. This elementary text fuses transformational theory and application throughout its treatment of phrase structure, transformations, and phonological components.

Lloyd, Donald J., and Harry R. Warfel. AMERICAN ENGLISH IN ITS CULTURAL SETTING. New York: Alfred A. Knopf, 1956. This descriptive introduction to how English works in American society treats speech and writing in terms of language learning and the role of the individual in society.

Long, Ralph B., and Dorothy R. THE SYSTEM OF ENGLISH GRAMMAR. Glenview: Scott, Foresman and Company, 1971. The structure of contemporary standard English prose is described and demonstrated in this traditional grammar. It is a "grammar of sets" which explains grammatical functions, clause types, parts of speech, and word formation and is concerned with pedagogical considerations.

Marckwardt, Albert H., and Randolph Quirk. A COMMON LANGUAGE: BRITISH AND AMERICAN ENGLISH. London: Cox and Wyman, Ltd., 1966. A discussion of the differences and similarities between British and American English is rendered through twelve dialogues. The varietal differences in each have resulted from the demands of history, politics, economics, social and cultural change. Emphasis is on positive changes in response to the needs of situational context.

McKnight, George. "Conservatism in American Speech," AMERICAN SPEECH, 1 (October, 1925), 1–17. An illustrated discussion of the history of linguistic conservatism in America to 1925 points out the various influences and groups which have not recognized the positive movements of linguistic change but have attempted to maintain a dichotomy between correctness and natural idiom.

Pooley, Robert C. THE TEACHING OF ENGLISH USAGE. Second Edition. Urbana: NCTE, 1974. Background and facts about usage are balanced against teaching procedures. Problems raised by concern for correctness and propriety are investigated. The requirements of language variety, attitude, and historical developments are considered.

Pyles, Thomas. THE ORIGINS AND DEVELOPMENT OF THE EN-GLISH LANGUAGE. Second Edition. New York: Harcourt Brace Jovanovich, 1971. This descriptive history of the language is concerned with a chronological treatment of the phonological and grammatical development of English.

Quirk, Randolph, and Sidney Greenbaum. A CONCISE GRAMMAR OF CONTEMPORARY ENGLISH. New York: Harcourt Brace Jovanovich, 1973. This transformational grammar (a shorter version of A GRAMMAR OF CONTEMPORARY ENGLISH) provides a model and data for understanding varieties of English, elements of grammar, phrasal and syntactic patterning, and kinds of prominence (i.e., focus, theme, and emotive emphasis).

Smith, Alfred G., ed. COMMUNICATION AND CULTURE. New York: Holt, Rinehart and Winston, 1966. Signals, codes, and meanings of human communication are investigated through a sequential arrangement of fifty-five contributors' statements dealing with theory, syntactics, semantics, and pragmatics.

Smith, Arthur L., ed. LANGUAGE, COMMUNICATION, AND RHETORIC IN BLACK AMERICA. New York: Harper & Row, 1972. This collection of twenty-nine essays by communications specialists and educators discusses the communication process in its totality, i.e., dialect, styles, tone, situational context, rhetorical intention. Several case studies and F. Erickson's comparison of white and Black college students in rap sessions contribute to the illustration of the theme.

Steinberg, Danny D., and Leon A. Jakobovits, eds. SEMANTICS: AN INTERDISCIPLINARY READER IN PHILOSOPHY, LINGUISTICS, AND PSYCHOLOGY. Cambridge: Cambridge University Press, 1971. This collection of thirty-three articles representing several fields of study deals with the nature, source and dimensions of linguistic meaning.

Stockwell, Robert P., Paul Schachter, and Barbara Hall Partee. THE MAJOR SYNTACTIC STRUCTURES OF ENGLISH. New York: Holt, Rinehart and Winston, 1973. This survey of transformational grammar and theory is based on Fillmore's Case Grammar framework and is comprehensive in its treatment.

Whorf, Benjamin Lee. LANGUAGE, THOUGHT AND REALITY. Ed. John B. Carroll. Cambridge: The M.I.T. Press, 1967. These selected writings present Whorf's linguistic examination of the ways in which thinking is dependent on language and the ways in which language affects one's vision of the world.

Williams, Frederick et al. SOCIOLINGUISTICS: A CROSSDISCIPLINARY PERSPECTIVE. Washington, D.C.: Center for Applied Linguistics, 1971. A survey of interactions of the five fields of speech/communication, psychology, education, sociolinguistics and linguistics/anthropology is presented through eleven contributors' statements-responses about social dialect.

Williamson, Juanita V., and Virginia M. Burke, eds. A VARIOUS LANGUAGE. New York: Holt, Rinehart and Winston, 1971. This introductory reader surveys the history and scope of dialect studies through the statements of fifty contributors.

Compiled by Jenefer M. Giannasi
with members of the Committee
on the CCCC Language Statement

Appendix 2: To the CCCC Executive Committee

The fourth and final draft of the report of the CCCC Committee on the Advisability of a Language Statement for the 1980's and 1990's

I. The Situation

Both in correspondence and in across-the-table discussion your committee has deliberated upon its charge from the CCCC executive committee:

> To decide whether recent findings and developments in multilingualism and multidialectalism make it desirable for CCCC to prepare a statement on language for the 1980's and 1990's.

The committee has attended to various criticized weaknesses in the CCCC publication, *The Students' Right to Their Own Language*. The committee is aware of the criticism that that statement offers problems with respect to its style, its logic, and its inadequate reliance upon insights available in the research of American dialectologists, sociolinguists, and linguistic anthropologists. The committee is sensitive to the oft-repeated criticism that the term *right* is not defined—that the sense intended by the authors is never made clear or even identified.

Yet the committee realizes that *The Students' Right* was set forth not as a programmatic statement but rather as a philosophical (perhaps even political) statement. The basic value of this courageously adopted philosophical position the committee is quick to affirm. Indeed, to quell any remaining doubts on that score, we suggest that, just as a married couple may choose to repeat the marriage vows on the occasion of the golden wedding anniversary, so the members of CCCC may find it rewarding to reaffirm their position by readopting the resolution during the 1984 convention.

But we are quick also to add that such an action cannot mark the be-all and the end-all of our concern. The initial charge to the committee implies that something more may be required, that there is a need not satisfied by the simple credal statement that students have a right to their own language or even by the accompanying explanatory material in the publication. We are convinced that there is an even greater need than the one implied by the charge, a need that cannot be met by any revision of the CCCC statement.

II. The Need

An analogy comes to mind at this point. The American Declaration of Independence set forth the philosophical position that all men are created equal. But that simple credal statement was not enough. Needed specificity had to be provided later in the United States Constitution and its first ten amendments as well as in certain subsequent amendments. These actions became part of a process that is still unfinished, as is demonstrated by the renewed drive for an equal rights amendment. Further practical applications have led also to numerous state and local legislative acts during the past two centuries.

Similarly, the simple credal statement of *The Students' Right to Their Own Language* is not enough. The statement is not self-executing. Indeed, it is the practical programmatic applications of that statement that the committee found itself addressing in its initial correspondence and then increasingly during the discussions in Washington and in Detroit. Members raised, for instance, the question whether students' right to their own language does not imply as well the right to assistance in learning a dialect prestigious beyond their own community, that is, the right to instruction that enables them to choose among dialect options rather than, by omission, restricting them to the dialects of their nurture.

In raising this question and related questions the committee was not able to confine its discussion to the time-span that is the declared concern of CCCC, the college years. These years are late in the life of a student. They do not even enter the life of many students for whom this basic issue is poignantly relevant. One committee member put it concisely: "*The Students' Right* is too little and too late."

The committee's attention to the potentially significant role of the CCCC statement in the lives and practices of teachers and students in the pre-college years from K through 12 was almost a foregone next step in the discussion. Attention began to focus upon three overlapping areas: pre-college education, the training of teachers for pre-college teaching, and the relevant non-professional public such as state and local boards of education, textbook publishers, parents' organizations, and the communication media including both professional and public avenues of news dissemination.

The phrase "potentially significant" in the preceding paragraph is a deliberate choice. The committee holds that as a bold but isolated philosophical position statement *The Students' Right* has had little discernible effect upon English teaching in the elementary and secondary schools. It has largely been ignored in the preparation of English and language arts teachers for those schools. Yet, if the philosophical position asserted in *The Students' Right* resolution has a moral imperative in the college field, it must have an even stronger moral imperative for positive action in the English-teaching profession as a whole, in the beginning and intermediate years as well as in the college period. And "recent findings and developments in multilingualism and multidialectalism as well as in related areas" insistently oblige the entire profession to clarify how that moral imperative can be transformed into positive action.

III. Meeting the Need—The Means

A. Elementary and Secondary Education

Language arts teachers and teachers of English in elementary and secondary schools require certain information if they are to realize for themselves and for their students the potential of *The Students' Right* statement.

> 1. Such teachers should know the distinctive nature of American social and regional dialects in terms of their grammar, lexicon, and pronunciation, To develop respect for the integrity of a dialect or a language they should learn that a dialect or a language is not intrinsically inferior to or superior to another dialect or another language. The description of social dialects should enable them to perceive the relationship of those dialects to the power structure of society.

> 2. Although it is not presumed that they should attempt the role of the professionally trained teacher of English to speakers of other

languages, they should nevertheless be acquainted with recent developments in the study of second language acquisition, particularly with respect to implications for teaching English as a second language or for teaching an English dialect as a second English dialect.

3. Again, without attempting to enact the role of the trained ESL teacher, they should know the most effective procedures for meeting the language needs of students in a classroom where a variety of language and dialect backgrounds is represented.

4. They should be familiar with recent developments in the study of the reading process and of the writing process. They should be aware, for example, of the widespread acceptance of the psycholinguistic view of reading among educators, with, again, its special relevance to students speaking a non-mainstream dialect or a language other than English. They should understand how the concept of writing as a multi-stage process facilitates the teaching of Edited American English without penalizing students for using their first dialect in initial drafts. They should learn how the incorporation of proofreading and editing stages in that process is significant to students seeking productive control of Edited American English. Not to help them develop such control, your committee believes, is to deprive thousands of students of the option of choice. But whichever option their personal aptitude and interests lead them to choose, they must have the opportunity and the freedom to choose.

5. They should know the effect of a teachers' overt or covert attitude toward students' language upon the academic achievement of those students.

6. They should understand the relative effects both of the verbal cultural background, including dialect, and of the nonverbal cultural background upon learning to read, write, and speak effectively.

7. They should be aware of the potential of their students to become bidialectal and bilingual, and they should know how to challenge their students to realize that potential.

8. They should know how to utilize the classroom study of regional and social language variation as a means of helping students to attain positive attitudes toward speech different from their own.

9. They should be familiar with bibliographical and other resources to which they can resort when seeking to meet the needs of non-

mainstream and ESL students or when teaching all students about language variation.

B. Teacher-training: Inservice and Preservice

The preparation of a document or documents containing the information identified in the previous section cannot by itself guarantee the desired result. Teachers and prospective teachers must be motivated to seek that information, preferably in an experiential situation.

True, teachers in service are likely to be already committed to an attitude and to an approach. An effort to alter their attitude and their approach to language teaching may be only partly successful. Nevertheless, the attested value of long-term inservice programs such as a summer curriculum development project or a leave of absence for further relevant graduate education is such as to warrant their utilization for the specific purpose of studying new methods and of developing new attitudes.

But it is likely that more effective and longer-lasting results can be attained if the desired information is given to candidates while they are still securing their professional training. The information can be given not only through course-work but also through attitudinal training and counseling. We recognize, of course, that merely requiring courses that offer this information does not automatically change a candidate's attitude. Some prospective teachers will need attitudinal training and controlled practice teaching that is specifically structured with reference to the goal of *The Students' Right,* that is, respect for language variation and the students' own variety.

Field experience in teacher education often tends to "socialize" the candidates through accommodation with observed field practices, practices that may or may not be in accord with the spirit of the CCCC resolution. If that field experience is negative, attitudinal training may well be required in order to counter its effect.

Consideration of teacher education, however, calls for attention to much more than the content of university courses and field experiences. State certification policies, hiring practices, the power of national and regional accreditation agencies, standardized testing policies, state and federal funding agencies, local fiscal status, schoolboard policies and politics, national and local pressure groups, the mass media, and "white papers" such as the recent report of the National Commission on Excellence in Education—all these operate as influences upon the content and methodologies of K to 12 classroom teachers. It is clearly not enough for these teachers just to receive sound information about language variation. They must also become aware of the complicated politics of curriculum development.

It is important, therefore, that any informational documents designed to help realize the ideal expressed in *The Students' Right* should address several influential audiences if it is to affect teacher education. Obviously, it must aim at administrators of schools and of teacher-training institutions. It should aim also at state accreditation agencies because of their power to determine the inclusion of dialect and language courses in the certification programs of various institutions preparing teachers. It should also aim at national accreditation agencies, in particular the National Council for the Accreditation of Teacher Education, since that organization can insist that language and dialect studies be infused throughout the curriculum, as, for instance, within that council's mandates on multicultural education and special education. It is to be observed that NCATE at present requires that teacher education curriculums reflect pertinent statements of professional subject-matter organizations, such as the teacher education guidelines prepared by the National Council of Teachers of English.

Competency tests, such as the National Teacher Examination or the Pre-Professional Test of Basic Skills, can be constructed to reflect current knowledge about dialect differentiation (and correspondingly offer the fringe benefit of de-emphasizing the presently included obscure items of usage). Teacher education faculty can be helped to perceive the need for language study in the training of teacher candidates. Information about the import of *The Students' Right* can modify such position statements of relevant professional organizations as that of the American Association of Colleges for Teacher Education entitled *Educating a Professional: Profile of a Beginning Teacher.*

At this point in this report reference to *The Students' Right* may provide examples to suggest how certain statements need to be amplified and certain kinds of materials need to be provided for the several audiences just identified. In Section III, page 4, for example, this sentence appears: "Before going to school, children attain basic competence in their dialect." Regardless of the linguistic precision or imprecision of this declaration, surely its implications for the teacher and for the local school board call for rather thorough explication of this theory of competence attainment, with study of exemplary materials.

Again, in Section VI, page 7, desirable reading materials are described as difficult to find. They are perhaps even less available today. It is most important that carefully annotated and accurate bibliography data about such resources be made readily available for teacher-training programs.

Section X assumes the teacher's ability to be flexible and the freedom to exercise that flexibility. Since most attitudes toward dialects are formed during a child's early years and hence *The Students' Right* is most powerfully applicable then, this assumption should be thoroughly and realistically discussed within the framework of the constraints often placed upon elementary teachers by the school and by the community. Teacher-education programs should prepare the future teacher to adapt teacher guidebooks and student workbooks so as to promote development and acceptance of desirable attitudes toward dialect divergence.

Section XI assumes that teachers can use whatever materials they want to use. This is not always true. Any new document or documents therefore should stress the productive use of existing materials and thus reflect actual school practice. Teacher-training programs must build on the base of current school situations if they are to gain and retain the confidence of teacher candidates.

Section XII, page 12, argues for culture-free tests. Information needs to be provided about the controversy over such tests, for as yet they have not been devised. Indeed, it may even be impossible to devise them, since language and culture intricately intertwine with knowledge. In the absence of such culture-free tests, teachers and prospective teachers need guidance in interpreting the results of existing tests.

With some exceptions, Section XV is a satisfactory initial outline of desirable content for a teacher-training program. But a full-scale revision of this content should provide better language examples, as, for instance, evidence from Appalachian English. Indeed, new materials should stress the details of practical approaches to the problems rather than idealized and wellnigh unattainable goals.

Finally, materials relating to *The Students' Right* objective in teacher-training must be both fiscally and educationally conservative if they are not to be dismissed out of hand as offering only "pie-in-the-sky" goals. If such materials demand radical curricular changes and involve large expenditures of time and money, they will not be acceptable to the target audience that should be affected by the CCCC statement. Rather, with that distant goal in mind, writers of the material should present a step-by-step practical outline of what can be done to move the entire field of teacher education closer to accepting the viewpoint and the position advocated in *The Students' Right*.

C. The Concerned Public

Your committee recognizes that the teaching of English and the language arts is an activity of concern to many groups outside the classroom. What may be done to gain acceptance of the CCCC recommended attitude toward diverse dialects and languages is liable to be misunderstood and even attacked by such groups unless they receive carefully presented persuasive elucidation. Some evidence of such misunderstanding and consequent adverse publicity can be found in the reception accorded the CCCC statement several years ago. We believe that negative reaction can be anticipated and hence prevented if these groups are adequately prepared by non-polemical and non-abrasive factual exposition of the rationale, content, and methods which the teachers will draw upon.

Concerned groups include administrators of education faculties, local and national organizations of school administrators, local and state boards of education, local and national units of the Parent-Teacher Association, writers of popular articles and books about language and usage, education editors, and educational publishers.

IV. Meeting the Need—The Instrument

It must now be apparent that, if the needed materials are to reach the entire English-teaching profession and relevant segments of the field of education as well as various groups with the concerned public, then that need cannot be met by a revision of the existing CCCC statement or even by a new statement produced by CCCC.

The constitution of the Conference on College Composition and Communication limits its area of concern and responsibility. Article I, Section 2, reads: "The broad object of the CCCC is to unite teachers of composition and communication in organization which can consider all matters relevant to their teaching, including teachers, subject matter, administration, methods, and students. The specific objects are (1) to provide an opportunity for discussion of college composition and communication courses, (2) to encourage studies and research in the field, and (3) to publish a bulletin containing reports of conferences and articles of interest to teachers of composition and communication."

Clearly constitutional limitations as well as the limitation imposed by CCCC's field of competence itself, i.e., the college field, demand that the torch set aflame by the CCCC statement should now be passed to those who can carry it along a wider highway.

At this point, then, your committee may seem to depart from the specific charge it received. But it is simply offering *in extenso* the reason why its response to that charge is negative. The committee strongly feels that it is acting within the spirit of the original statement by calling for full professional action on a front wider and deeper than that which the CCCC has provided and can provide.

Your committee therefore recommends that the CCCC executive committee approach the executive committee of the National Council of Teachers of English with a proposal for the creation of a major task force whose members will represent not only the CCCC but also all the various areas of professional specialization in the English teaching profession, and who will work with consultants from the disciplines of anthropological linguistics, sociolinguistics, and psycholinguistics. The responsibility of this task force will be to explore in depth the various aspects of the problem that first led to the preparation of the CCCC statement and then, drawing upon recent developments in language theory, educational theory, and language and educational practice, will propose and explicate practical ways to progress toward the realization of the ideal situation stipulated in *The Students' Right to Their Own Language,* namely, general respect for the dignity and worth of the students' own variety of that language or of the students' first language.

We note that NCTE has already moved in the indicated direction by publishing the following:

Position statement on issues in ESL and bilingual education.
A Handbook of Short Courses in Dialect Studies for K–12 Teachers.
Mainstreaming the Non-English-Speaking Student.
Essentials of English.
Attitudes, Language, and Change.
Non-Native and Non-Standard Dialect Students.

These publications suggest minimally what the proposed task force we hope can ultimately produce as an integrated and powerful instrument for developing in the entire profession the result first established as a goal by the CCCC.

> The Committee
> Harold B. Allen, ch.
> Milton Baxter
> Jimmy Cato
> *Louie Crew
> Sara Garnes
> Doris O. Ginn
> Grace S. Holt
> Raymond Rodrigues
> Constance Weaver

*Mr. Crew has indicated that he will submit a minority report.

BIBLIOGRAPHY

Abernathy, Ralph. 1989. *And the Walls Came Tumbling Down: An Autobiography.* New York: Harper and Row.

Allen, Harold. 1983. Correspondence to the Advisory Committee on the English Language, 24 January. NCTE Archives, Urbana, Ill.

Applebee, Arthur N. 1974. *Tradition and Reform in the Teaching of English: A History.* Urbana, Ill.: National Council of Teachers of English.

Baraka, Imamu Amiri. 1979. *Selected Poetry of Amiri Baraka/LeRoi Jones.* New York: Morrow.

Bartholomae, David. 1980. "The Study of Error." *College Composition and Communication* 31 (3): 253–269.

Bennet, John. 1908. "Gullah: A Negro Patois," *The Southern Quarterly* 7: 332–347.

Bereiter, Carl. 1968. "A Non-Psychological Approach to Early Compensatory Education." In *Social Class, Race, and Psychological Development,* ed. Martin Deutsch, Irwin Katz, and Arthur Jensen. New York: Holt, Rhinehart, and Winston.

Berlin, James. 1987. *Rhetoric and Reality: Writing Instruction in American Colleges 1900–1985.* Carbondale: Southern Illinois University Press.

———. 1988. "Rhetoric and Ideology in the Writing Class." *College English* 50 (5): 477–494.

Bird, Nancy K. 1977. "The Conference on College Composition and Communication: A Historical Study of Its Continuing Education and Professionalization Activities, 1949–1975." Ed.D. dissertation, Adult and Continuing Education, Virginia Polytechnic Institute and State University.

Birmingham, John, ed. 1970. *Our Time Is Now: Notes from the High School Underground.* New York: Bantam Books.

Bloland, Harland G., and Sue M. Bloland. 1974. *American Learned Societies in Transition.* New York: McGraw-Hill.

Bloom, Jack M. 1987. *Class, Race, and the Civil Rights Movement.* Bloomington: Indiana University Press.

Breitman, George, ed. 1965. *Malcolm X Speaks: Selected Speeches and Statements.* New York: Grove Press.

Brown, Claude. 1972. "The Language of Soul." In *Black Culture: Reading and Writing Black,* ed. Gloria M. Simmons and Helene Hutchinson. New York: Holt, Rhinehart, and Winston.

Bruner, Jerome S. 1960. *The Process of Education.* New York: Vintage Press.

Carmichael, Stokely, and Charles V. Hamilton. 1967. *Black Power: The Politics of Liberation in America.* New York: Vintage Books.

Collier, Richard. 1982. "Using Work in the Classroom." *Progressive Composition Caucus Newsletter* 1 (1): 2.

Colquit, Jesse. 1977. "The Students' Right to His Own Language: A Viable Model, or Empty Rhetoric?" *Communication Quarterly* 25: 17–20.

Committee on the Advisability of a New Language Statement for the 1980s and 1990s. Committee correspondence. NCTE Archives, Urbana, Ill.

———. 1982. Minutes, 2 November. NCTE Archives, Urbana, Ill.

———. 1983a. Draft 2, 27 June. NCTE Archives, Urbana, Ill.

———. 1983b. Final draft. NCTE Archives, Urbana, Ill.

Committee on the English Language (CEL). n.d. "Statement on Usage." NCTE Archives, Urbana, Ill.

———. 1969. "1969 Resolutions." NCTE Archives, Urbana, Ill.

"Composition as Death Attendance Sheet, 1969." 1969. NUC Archives, Wisconsin Historical Society, Madison.

Conference on College Composition and Communication (CCCC). Business meeting reports. NCTE Archives, Urbana, Ill.

———. Language committee mailing list. NCTE Archives, Urbana, Ill.

———. Officers meeting minutes. NCTE Archives, Urbana, Ill.

———. Secretary's reports. NCTE Archives, Urbana, Ill.

———. 1969. Workshop reports. *College Composition and Communication* 20 (3).

———. 1970. Secretary's Report No. 61, 26 November 1969. *College Composition and Communication* 21 (3): 299–306.

Crew, Louie. [1984]. "Minority Report of the Committee on the Advisability of a New Language Statement for the 1980s and 1990s." NCTE Archives, Urbana, Ill.

Daniels, Smokey. 1983. "The Students' Right Saga Continues." *Conference on Language Attitudes and Composition* 9 (Spring): 5–12.

Davidson, Carl. 1966. "A Student Syndicalist Movement: University Reform Revisited." *New Left Notes* (9 September): 2, 11.

Davis, Mike. 1986. *Prisoners of the American Dream: Politics and Economy in the History of the US Working Class.* London: Verso.

Delpit, Lisa. 1995. *Other People's Children: Cultural Conflicts in the Classroom.* New York: New Press.

Deutsch, Martin. 1967a. "The Disadvantaged Child and the Learning Process." In *The Disadvantaged Child: Selected Papers of Martin Deutsch and Associates.* New York: Basic Books.

———. 1967b. "The Principle Issue." In *The Disadvantaged Child: Selected Papers of Martin Deutsch and Associates.* New York: Basic Books.

———. 1967c. "Some Psychosocial Aspects of Learning in the Disadvantaged." In *The Disadvantaged Child: Selected Papers of Martin Deutsch and Associates.* New York: Basic Books.

Deutsch, Martin, and Martin Whiteman. 1968. "Social Disadvantage as Related to Intellective and Language Development." In *Social Class, Race, and Psychological Development,* ed. Martin Deutsch, Irwin Katz, and Arthur Jensen. New York: Holt, Rhinehart, and Winston.

Dhaliwal, Amarpal. 1996. "Can the Subaltern Vote." Pp. 42–61 in *Radical Democracy: Identity, Citizenship, and the State,* ed. David Trend. New York: Routledge.

Dillard, J. L. 1972. *Black English: Its History and Usage in the United States.* New York: Random House.

Dixon, John E. 1966. *Growth through English: A Report Based on the Dartmouth Seminar, 1966*. Reading, England: National Association for the Teaching of English.

Doster, William. 1969. "Response to NUC Resolutions in Chicago." *College Composition and Communication* 20: 238–241.

Draper, Hal. 1965. *Berkeley: The New Student Revolt*. New York: Grove Press.

Dwyer, Warren, Kent Baker, and Dennis McInerny. 1974. "Remarks on 'The Students Right to Their Own Language,'" 3 April. NCTE Archives, Urbana, Ill.

Ehrenreich, Barbara. 1989. *Fear of Falling: The Inner Life of the Middle Class*. New York: Pantheon Books.

"The End of SDS and the Emergence of Weatherman: Demise through Success." 1983. In *Social Movements of the Sixties and Seventies*, ed. Jo Freeman. New York: Longman.

Faigley, Lester. 1992. *Fragments of Rationality: Postmodernity and the Subject of Composition*. Pittsburgh: University of Pittsburgh Press.

Farber, Jerry. 1970. *Student as Nigger: Essays and Other Stories*. New York: Pocket Books.

———. 1990. "Learning How to Teach: A Progress Report." *College English* 52 (2): 135–141.

Flack, Richard, and Bob Ross. 1968. NUC internal document. NUC Archives, Wisconsin Historical Society, Madison.

Foner, Philip, ed. 1995. *The Black Panthers Speak*. New York: Da Capo Press.

Friedrich, Dick, and David Kuester. 1972. *It's Mine and I'll Write It That Way*. New York: Random House.

"The Future of CCCC: An Informal Discussion." 1969. *College Composition and Communication* 20 (3): 265.

Gibson, Walker. 1971. Correspondence with Raven McDavid, November. NCTE Archives, Urbana, Ill.

Gilyard, Keith. 1999. "African American Contributions to Composition Studies." *College Composition and Communication* 50 (4): 626–644.

Giroux, Henri. 1992. *Border Crossings: Cultural Workers and the Politics of Education.* New York: Routledge.

Gitlin, Todd. 1987. *The Sixties: Years of Hope, Days of Rage.* Toronto: Bantam Books.

Gonzales, Ambrose E. 1922. *The Black Border: Gullah Stories of the Carolina Coast.* Columbia, S.C.: Stak Company.

Griffin, John Howard. 1961. *Black Like Me.* New York: Signet Books.

Haber, Al. 1966. "Radical Education Project—Draft for Discussion and Comment." *New Left Notes* 1 (17): 2–3.

———. 1969. "Getting by with a Little Help from Our Friends." In *The New Left: A Collection of Essays,* ed. Priscilla Long. Boston: Extending Horizons Books.

———. 1983. "From Protest to Radicalism: An Appraisal of the Student Movement 1960." In *The New Student Left: An Anthology,* ed. Mitchell Cohen and Dennis Hale. Boston: Beacon Press.

Halliwell, Steve. 1969. "Columbia: An Explanation." In *The New Left: A Collection of Essays,* ed. Priscilla Long. Boston: Extending Horizons Books.

Harrington, Michael. 1992. *The Other America: Poverty in the United States.* New York: Penguin.

Harrison, James A. 1884. "Negro English." *Anglia* 7: 232–279.

Heath, G. Louis, ed. 1976. *Off the Pigs: The History and Literature of the Black Panther Party.* Metuchen, N.J.: Scarecrow.

Hecht, Tom. n.d. "State of the NUC: National Office Report." NUC Archives, Wisconsin Historical Society, Madison.

———. 1970. "The State of the NUC: A Critical Essay." NUC Archives, Wisconsin Historical Society, Madison.

Heineman, Kenneth J. 1993. *Campus Wars: The Peace Movement at American State Universities in the Vietnam Era.* New York: New York University Press.

Hendrickson, John R. 1972. "Response to the CCCC's Executive Committee's Resolution 'The Students Right to His Own Language.'" *College Composition and Communication* 21 (2): 191–192.

Herskovitz, Melville J. 1958. *The Myth of the Negro Past*. Boston: Beacon Press.

Hewitt, Ray "Masai." 1995. "The Black Panther Party and Revolutionary Trade Unionism." In *The Black Panthers Speak,* ed. Claybourne Carson. New York: Da Capo Press.

Hoffman, Abbie. 1968. *Revolution for the Hell of It*. New York: Dial Press.

Howe, Florence. 1970. "What Success at the MLA?" *NUC Newsletter* 2 (1): 1, 18–21.

Hughes, Langston. 1967. *The Panther and the Lash: Poems of Our Times*. New York: Knopf.

Irmscher, William. 1981. Professional correspondence to Lynn Troyka, 30 September.

Ives, Sumner. 1966. "The Relevance of Language Study." *College Composition and Communication* 20 (2): 131–137.

Johnson, Lyndon. 1964. "Special Statement for the National Education Association." *Journal of the National Education Association* 53 (1): 12.

———. 1980. "Great Society Speech." In *Presidential Rhetoric*, ed. Theodore Windt. Pittsburgh: University of Pittsburgh Press.

Judy, Stephen. 1978. "Editor's Page: 'The Students' Right to Their Own Language: A Dialogue.'" *English Journal* 67 (9): 6–9.

Kampf, Louis. 1970. "Must We Have a Cultural Revolution?" *College Composition and Communication* 21 (3): 245–249.

Kelley, Robin D. G. 1997. "Identity Politics and Class Struggle." *New Politics* 6 (2): 84–96.

Kerr, Clark. 1963. *The Uses of the University*. Cambridge: Harvard University Press.

Kimball, Roger. 1990. *Tenured Radicals: How Politics Has Corrupted Our Higher Education*. New York: Harper and Row.

King, Martin Luther, Jr. 1958. *Stride Toward Freedom: The Montgomery Story*. New York: Ballantine Books.

———. 1972. "I Have a Dream." In *Black Culture: Reading and Writing Black,* ed. Gloria M. Simmons and Helene Hutchinson. New York: Holt, Rhinehart, and Winston.

Kitzhaber, Albert R. 1967. "The Government and English Teaching: A Retrospective View." *College Composition and Communication* 8 (3): 135–145.

Kleiman, Mark. 1966. "High School Reform: Towards a Student Movement," *New Left Notes*. Reprinted in *The New Left: A Documentary History*, Massimo Teodori. Indianapolis: Bobbs-Merrill, 1969.

Knowles, Mary Tyler, Betty Resnikoff, and Jacqueline Ross. 1969. "Who(m) Does Standard English Serve? Who(m) Does Standard English Hurt?" *NUC-MLC Newsletter* 1 (5): 4–6.

Kochman, Thomas. 1972. "Language Behavior in the Black Community." In *Black Culture: Reading and Writing Black*, ed. Gloria M. Simmons and Helene Hutchinson. New York: Holt, Rhinehart, and Winston.

Krapp, George. 1924. "The English of the Negro." *American Mercury* 2: 190–195.

Krieger, Joel. 1986. *Reagan, Thatcher, and the Politics of Decline*. New York: Oxford University Press.

Kunen, James Simon. 1970. *The Strawberry Statement: Notes of a College Revolutionary*. New York: Avon Books.

Labov, William. 1969. *The Study of Non-Standard English*. Urbana, Ill.: National Council of Teachers of English.

———. 1972. "The Logic of Nonstandard English." In *Language, Socialization and Subcultures*, ed. Pier Paolo Giglioli. New York: Penguin.

Laclau, Ernesto, and Chantal Mouffe. 1993. *Hegemony and Socialist Strategy: Towards a Radical Democratic Politics*. New York: Verso Press.

Levy, Peter B. 1994. *The New Left and Labor in the 1960s*. Urbana: University of Illinois.

Lloyd-Jones, Richard. 1973. Correspondence with Elisabeth McPherson, 7 December. NCTE Archives, Urbana, Ill.

———. 1993. "Writing the Resolution: An Institutional History." Paper presented at the CCCC Convention, April 1, 1993, San Diego, Calif.

Long, Ralph B. 1973. Correspondence to Richard Lloyd-Jones, 9 March. NCTE Archives, Urbana, Ill.

Louis, Debbie. 1970. *And We Are Not Saved: A History of the Movement as People.* New York: Anchor.

Macrorie, Ken. 1970. *Uptaught.* New York: Hayden.

Mailer, Norman. 1992. "The White Negro: Superficial Reflections of the Hipster." In *Advertisements for Myself.* Cambridge: Harvard University Press.

Marable, Manning. 1984. *Race, Reform and Rebellion: The Second Reconstruction in Black America, 1945–1982.* Jackson: University of Mississippi Press.

Marback, Richard. 1996. "Corbett's Hand." *College Composition and Communication* 47 (2): 180–198.

Marckwardt, Albert. 1958. *American English.* New York: Oxford University Press.

Matthews, Donald, and James Protho. 1969. "Negro Students and the Protest Movement." In *Black Power and Student Rebellion,* ed. James McEvoy and Abraham Miller. Belmont, Calif.: Wadsworth.

McAdams, Douglass. 1982. *Political Process and the Development of Black Insurgency, 1930–1970.* Chicago: University of Chicago Press.

McDavid, Raven. 1971a. Memorandum to CEL. Madison, NCTE Archives, Urbana, Ill.

———. 1971b. "Planning the Grid." *American Speech: A Quarterly of Linguistic Usage* 46 (1–2): 9–26.

McPherson, Elisabeth. 1972a. *Annual Report to the NCTE.* NCTE Archives, Urbana, Ill.

———. 1972b. Correspondence with Melvin Butler, 8 May. NCTE Archives, Urbana, Ill.

———. 1972c. Correspondence to Richard Riel Jr., 15 November. NCTE Archives, Urbana, Ill.

———. 1972d. "Memorandum To: Members of the CCCC," 8 May. NCTE Archives, Urbana, Ill.

———. 1973. Correspondence with Richard Lloyd-Jones, 9 March. NCTE Archives, Urbana, Ill.

———. 1974. "Notes on Students' Right To Their Own Language." NCTE Archives, Urbana, Ill.

————. 1980. "Bait: The Students Right Was a Sensible Statement When It Was Adopted. We Need to Renew Our Efforts to Implement It Today." *English Journal* 69 (9): 8, 12.

Metzger, Deena. 1968. "Relevant 'Relevance.'" *College Composition and Communication* 20: 339–342.

Miller, Evelyn. 1974a. Correspondence to Richard Larson, May 28. NCTE Archives, Urbana, Ill.

————. 1974b. Memorandum to English Department at Manchester Community College, May 28. NCTE Archives, Urbana, Ill.

Miller, James. 1987. *Democracy Is in the Streets: From Port Huron to the Siege of Chicago.* New York: Simon and Schuster.

Mills, C. Wright. n.d. "The Structure of Power in American Society." In *Power, Politics, and People: The Collected Essays of C. Wright Mills,* 1st ed., ed. Irving Horowitz. New York: Baltimore Books.

————. 1960. "Letter to the New Left." *New Left Review* 5: 18–23.

Muller, Herbert J. 1967. *Uses of English: Guidelines for the Teaching of English from the Anglo-American Conference at Dartmouth College.* New York: Holt, Rhinehart, and Winston.

Murray, Donald. 1969. "Finding Your Own Voice: Teaching Composition in an Age of Dissent." *College Composition and Communication* 20 (2): 118–123.

————. 1982. "Teaching Writing as a Process not a Product." In *Learning by Teaching: Selected Articles on Writing and Teaching.* Montclair, N.J.: Boynton Cook.

"Mutiny at a Great University: Students Usurp the Seat of Power at New York's Columbia through a Six-Day Uprising." 1968. *LIFE* 64: 36–48.

National Committee of Students for a Democratic Society. 1966. "SDS Statement on SNCC." *New Left Notes* 1 (23): 5.

National Council of Teachers of English (NCTE). 1988. "Position Statements on Issues in Education from the National Council of Teachers of English." *NCTE Forum.* NCTE Archives, Urbana, Ill.

The National Interest and the Teaching of English. 1958. Champaign, Ill.: National Council of Teachers of English.

Nesemeier, Greg. 1966. "SDS or MDS." *New Left Notes* (12 August).

New University Caucus. 1969. "Response to the CCCC Resolution on Chicago." *College Composition and Communication* 20 (3): 238.

New University Conference (NUC). n.d. "A Call to Meetings by the New University Conference" (flyer). NUC Archives, Wisconsin Historical Society, Madison.

———. n.d. "Editorials." NUC Archives, Wisconsin Historical Society, Madison.

———. n.d. Policy Statement, Draft 2. NUC Archives, Wisconsin Historical Society, Madison.

———. 1968a. Statement Draft No. 1, September 9. NUC Archives, Wisconsin Historical Society, Madison.

———. 1968b. "The Student Rebellion" (flyer). NUC Archives, Wisconsin Historical Society, Madison.

———. 1968c. "The Student Rebellion" (full document). NUC Archives, Wisconsin Historical Society, Madison.

———. 1969a. NUC Constitution, June. NUC Archives, Wisconsin Historical Society, Madison.

———. 1969b. NUC Resolutions, Workshop Reports, CCCC Convention. NUC Archives, Wisconsin Historical Society, Madison.

———. 1970. NUC–Executive Committee minutes, 18 March. NUC Archives, Wisconsin Historical Society, Madison.

———. 1971. NUC Resolutions at CCCC. NUC Archives, Wisconsin Historical Society, Madison.

———. 1972. *Open Up the Schools: NUC Papers #3*. NUC Archives, Wisconsin Historical Society, Madison.

North, Stephen. 1987. *The Making of Knowledge in Composition: Portrait of an Emerging Field*. New York: Boynton/Cook.

Ohmann, Richard. 1964. "In Lieu of a New Rhetoric." *College English* 26: 17–22.

Omi, Michael, and Howard Winant. 1994. *Racial Formation in the United States: From the 1960s to the 1990s*, 2nd ed. New York: Routledge.

Open Discussion Meeting. 1971 (March 27). *College Composition and Communication* 22 (3): 300–302.

Peck, Wayne Campbell, Linda Flower, and Lorraine Higgins. 1995. "Community Literacy." *College Composition and Communication* 46 (May): 199–222.

Pines, Burton Yales. 1982. *Back to the Basics: The Traditionalist Movement That Is Sweeping Grass-Roots America.* New York: Morrow.

Pixton, William. 1972. "Response to the CCCC's Executive Committee's Resolution 'The Students Right to His Own Language.'" *College Composition and Communication* 21 (2): 192.

Prichard, Nancy. 1974. Correspondence with CCCC Officers, February. NCTE Archives, Urbana, Ill.

Progressive Composition Caucus (PCC). 1983. Mission Statement. *Progressive Composition Caucus Newsletter* 1 (6): 1.

"Regional Contacts of NUC, 1969." 1969. NUC Archives, Wisconsin Historical Society, Madison.

Resnikoff, Neal. n.d. "NUC at the CEE, Report of Activities." NUC Archives, Wisconsin Historical Society, Madison.

———. 1968a. "Report of High School Teachers' Workshop: 1968." NUC Archives, Wisconsin Historical Society, Madison.

———. 1968b. "Report of the NUC-MLA High School Teaching of Language and Literature Workshop, 1968." NUC Archives, Wisconsin Historical Society, Madison.

———. 1969a. Correspondence with Doris Gunderson, 12 November. NUC Archives, Wisconsin Historical Society, Madison.

———. 1969b. "The NUC at CCC and a Look ahead to NCTE, 1969." NUC Archives, Wisconsin Historical Society, Madison.

———. 1969c. "Progress Report." NUC Archives, Wisconsin Historical Society, Madison.

———. 1970. "Response to William C. Doster, Response to NUC Proposals." *College Composition and Communication* 21 (2): 192–193.

Ross, Andrew. 1989. *No Respect: Intellectuals and Popular Culture.* New York: Routledge.

Ross, Bob. 1969. Correspondence with Neal Resnikoff, 8 April. NUC Archives, Wisconsin Historical Society, Madison.

———. 1970. Professional correspondence, January. NUC Archives, Wisconsin Historical Society, Madison.

Rothstein, Richard. 1969a. Correspondence to Greg Calvert, 11 August. NUC Archives, Wisconsin Historical Society, Madison.

———. 1969b. Correspondence to Barbara Kessell, 30 September. NUC Archives, Wisconsin Historical Society, Madison.

———. 1969c. "Evolution of the ERAP Organizers." In *The New Left: A Collection of Essays,* ed. Priscilla Long. Boston: Extending Horizons Books.

Roxreth, Kenneth. 1960. "Students Take Over." *New Left Review* 5: 38–41.

Royster, Jacqueline Jones, and Jean C. Williams. 1999. "History in the Spaces: African American Presence and Narratives in Composition Studies." *College Composition and Communication* 50 (4): 563–584.

Sale, Kirkpatrick. 1973. *SDS.* New York: Random House.

———. 1975. *Power Shift: The Rise of the Southern Rim and Its Challenge to the Eastern Establishment.* New York: Vintage Books.

Savio, Mario. 1965. "Introduction." In *Berkeley: The New Student Revolt,* ed. Hal Draper. New York: Grove Press.

Schrecker, Ellen. 1986. *No Ivory Tower: McCarthyism and the Universities.* New York: Oxford University Press.

Seale, Bobby. 1991. *Seize the Time: The Story of the Black Panther Party and Huey P. Newton.* Baltimore: Black Classics Press.

———. 1996. Lecture, African Studies Program, Temple University, 19 March.

Shaughnessy, Mina. 1977. *Errors and Expectations: A Guide for the Teacher of Basic Writing.* New York: Oxford University Press.

Shor, Ira. 1986. *Culture Wars: School and Society in the Conservative Restoration, 1969–1984.* Boston: Routledge.

Sledd, James. 1982. "Jim Sledd on Composition." *Progressive Composition Caucus Newsletter* 1 (1): 1.

———. 1983. "In Defense of the Students' Right." *College English* 45 (7): 669.

————. 1984. "Excerpts from 'Dead Cat Drifting,' Jim Sledd's Report to CLAC on the Battle for the Students' Right." *Progressive Composition* (5): 8–9.

Smitherman, Geneva. 1972. "Black Power Is Black Language." In *Black Culture: Reading and Writing Black,* ed. Gloria M. Simmons and Helene Hutchinson. New York: Holt, Rhinehart, and Winston.

————. 1977. *Talkin and Testifyin: The Language of Black America.* Detroit: Wayne State University Press.

————. 1988. "Discriminatory Discourse on Afro-American Speech." In *Discourse and Discrimination,* ed. Geneva Smitherman-Donaldson and Teun A. van Dijk. Detroit: Wayne State University Press.

————. 1990. "The Mis-Education of Negroes." In *Not Only English: Affirming America's Multi-lingual Heritage,* ed. Harvey A. Daniels. Urbana, Ill.: National Council of Teachers of English.

————. 1999. "CCCC's Role in the Struggle for Language Rights." *College Composition and Communication* 50 (3): 349–376.

Soley, Lawrence C. 1995. *Leasing the Ivory Tower: The Corporate Takeover of Academia.* Boston: South End Press.

Stembridge, Jane. 1966. "Notes about a Class Held by Stokely Carmichael." In *The New Radicals: A Report with Documents,* ed. Saul Landau and Paul Jacobs. New York: Random House.

Stewart, Donald. 1980. "Acting on the CCCC Language Resolution and Related Matters." *College Composition and Communication* 31: 330–332.

————. 1983a. "To: CCCC Officers, Executive Committee and Other Interested Persons," memorandum, 5 April. NCTE Archives, Urbana, Ill.

————. 1983b. "To: CCCC Officers and Executive Committee," memorandum, 17 August. NCTE Archives, Urbana, Ill.

Stoper, Emily. 1983. "The Student Non-Violent Coordinating Committee: Rise and Fall of a Redemptive Organization." In *Social Movements of the Sixties and Seventies,* ed. Jo Freeman. New York: Longman.

Student Nonviolent Coordinating Committee. 1966. "The Basis of Black Power." *New York Times,* 5 August.

"Students' Right to Their Own Language" [handwritten copy]. n.d. NCTE Archives, Urbana, Ill.

"Students' Right to Their Own Language." 1974. *College Composition and Communication* 25 (3): 1–32.

"Summer Report, Newark Community Union." 1966. In *The New Radicals: A Report with Documents*, ed. Saul Landau and Paul Jacobs. New York: Random House.

Teacher Organizing Project, New University Conference. 1970. *Classes and Schools: A Radical Definition for Teachers*. NUC Archives, Wisconsin Historical Society, Madison.

Teodori, Massimo. 1969. *The New Left: A Documentary History*. Indianapolis: Bobbs-Merrill.

Thompson, C. Lamar, and Juanita V. Williamson. 1980. "Con." *English Journal* 69 (9): 9, 11, 13.

Unger, Irwin. 1985. "The 'Long March Through the Institutions': Movement for a Democratic Society and the New University Conference." In *A Master's Due: Essays in Honor of David Herbert Donald*, ed. William J. Cooper Jr., Michael F. Holt, and John McCardell. Baton Rouge: Louisiana State University Press.

United States Department of Health, Education, and Welfare, Office of Education. 1962. "Project English." *College Composition and Communication* 13 (1): 39–42.

Van Deburg, William. 1992. *New Day in Babylon: The Black Power Movement and American Culture, 1965–1975*. Chicago: University of Chicago Press.

Weaver, Constance. 1974. Correspondence with Nancy Prichard, 16 April. NCTE Archives, Urbana, Ill.

Weinberg, Jack. 1965. "The Free Speech Movement and Civil Rights." In *Berkeley: The New Student Revolt*, ed. Hal Draper. New York: Grove Press.

"Whence Cometh the Axe? An Editorial." 1969. *NUC Newsletter* 2 (1): 1, 2, 15, 21.

White, Newman. 1929. "The White Man in the Woodpile: Some Influences on Negro Secular Folk-Songs." *American Speech* 4 (3): 207–215.

Williams, Joseph. n.d. "The Status of Non-Standard Dialects, written for NCTE." NCTE Archives, Urbana, Ill.

———. 1977. "Linguistic Responsibility." *College English* 39: 8–17.

Wilson, Gordon. 1967. "CCCC in Retrospect." *College Composition and Communication* 18 (3): 127–134.

Workshop on Cultural Bias Attendance Sheet. 1969. NUC Archives, Wisconsin Historical Society, Madison.

Workshop on Oppressive Linguistics Attendance Sheet. 1969. NUC Archives, Wisconsin Historical Society, Madison.

X, Malcolm. 1965. *The Autobiography of Malcolm X*. New York: Grove Press.

Zirker, Priscila. 1968. "Toward a New University." *NUC Newsletter* 1 (1): 1, 3, 4.

INDEX

n in page locator indicates endnote; SRTOL is "The Students' Right to Their Own Language"

188–90
nationalism of, 181
politics of, 190–91
and race, 188–90
and tolerance of diversity,
183–85, 186
vote on, 203
and work of Carl Bereiter and
Martin Deutsch, 201n7
"A Student Syndicalist
Movement" (Carl Davidson),
37, 41, 44–46, 58, 66–67n28,
86
Elisabeth McPherson's views
compared with, 181
Joseph Williams's views
contrasted to, 206
Louis Kampf's views compared
with, 134
"The Study of Error" (David
Bartholomae), 3
*The Study of Non-Standard
English* (William Labov),
115–18

Talkin and Testifyin (Geneva
Smitherman), 110–12
teacher certification, 138
teacher education, 124n3, 165,
201n4, 231
Teacher Organizing Project, 131,
156n4
teachers. *See* elementary school
teachers; faculty; secondary
school teachers
"Teachers as Political Beings,"
133
Teachers for a Democratic
Culture, xviii
"Teach Writing as Process Not
Product" (Donald Murray),
80
ten-point program (of the
Black Panthers), 36, 115
Trilling, Lionel, 240

Trimbur, John, xvi
Troyka, Lynn, 210
Turner, Darwin, 159n15
Turner, Lorenzo, 104
two-year colleges. *See* junior
colleges

Unger, Irwin, 53
United Auto Workers (UAW)
and civil rights movement, 27,
32
and Students for a Democratic
Society (SDS), 40, 42
United Electrical, Radio, and
Machine Workers Union,
27–28
United Packinghouse Workers,
27
universities
and community programs,
245–49
federal funding of, 44, 70, 72,
86, 141–42, 145, 195–96,
245
role of, 240–42
university reform
and Students for a Democratic
Society (SDS), 41–42,
44–51
and white student activists,
37, 39–40
Uptaught (Ken Macrorie), 15,
68–69, 76–78
African American metaphors
used by, 82
individualism in, 86, 88, 130
John Asmead's endorsement
of, 140, 158n11
Uses of English (Herbert J.
Muller), 73

Van Deburg, William, 36,
63–64n9
Vietnam Summer, 47

Vietnam War
  Conference on College
    Composition and
    Communication's
    opposition to, 138,
    148–49, 161, 198, 226
  Modern Language
    Association's opposition to,
    126, 132
  New University Conference's
    opposition to, 1, 126, 132,
    138, 148–49
  protest movement, 43–44
  Students for a Democratic
    Society's opposition to,
    43–47, 126
Voter Rights Act, 33, 171
voting rights, 33, 62n2, 171

Watts riot, 184
Weathermen, 47
Weaver, Constance, 192, 212
Weinberg, Jack, 31
"What Success at the MLA?"
  (Florence Howe), 132
"Whence Cometh the Axe? An
  Editorial," 67n28
White, Newman, 94
Whiteman, Martin, 99
"The White Man in the Woodpile"
  (Newman White), 94
white student activists
  and African Americans,
    30–34, 60–61, 62n2, 78
  and university reform, 37,
    39–40
"Who(m) Does Standard English
  Serve? Who(m) Does Standard
  English Hurt?," 4, 86–87
  Jerry Farber's work compared
    with, 130
  and racism and classism, 114,
    183, 204
  and *The Adventures of
    Huckleberry Finn*, 68, 128

"Who Rules Columbia" (North
  American Congress on Latin
  America), 47–48
Williams, Darnel, 161
Williams, Joseph
  Committee on the Advisability
    of a New Language
    Statement for the 1980s
    and 1990s influenced by,
    206, 212–15, 217, 221,
    227
  James Sledd's critique of, 218,
    220, 227
  "Linguistic Responsibility,"
    205–6
  SRTOL opposed by, 206, 214
  "The Status of Non-Standard
    Dialects," 206, 212–15,
    217, 221, 227, 242
Williamson, Juanita, 140, 147,
  151, 154
Wilson, Rosemary, 141
Winant, Howard, 92–93, 186
Winterowd, W. Ross, 12, 161,
  191, 201n5
women in the English profession,
  149, 161
women's studies programs, 72
woofin, 110
working class
  Marxist analysis of, 14, 51
  and New Left, 38–40
  and New University
    Conference, 152–53
  political alliances of, 42–43,
    183, 252–53
"Workshop on Oppressive
  Linguistics," 133
Writing Across the Curriculum,
  244–45, 246

X, Malcolm, 109–10, 121n1

Yippie movement, 15, 77–78

AUTHOR

Steve Parks received his Ph.D. from the University of Pittsburgh. Currently, he is assistant professor of English at Temple University. He is also director of Teachers for a Democratic Culture (TDC, www. temple.edu/tdc), a national organization of progressive and liberal academic activists. As director of TDC, Parks has developed the Progressive Information Network, the Democracy Fund, and the Democracy Press. He is also an active member of the Working Class Caucus and the Labor Caucus.

At Temple University, Parks helped to found and now directs the Institute for the Study of Literature, Literacy, and Culture (www.temple.edu/isllc), an interdisciplinary organization in the College of Liberal Arts. The Institute supports a graduate certificate in cultural studies, an undergraduate service learning program, and a variety of partnerships among community, public school, and faculty organizations. Most recently, the Institute has undertaken the development of a community press, which brings together urban cultural and political organizations. Parks lives in Philadelphia with his partner, Lori, and their two children, Eliot and Sadie.

This book was typeset in Adobe Sabon by Electronic Imaging.
Typefaces used on the cover include Housebroken, Crackhouse,
and Officina.
The book was printed on 50-lb. opaque paper by Versa Press, Inc.